COSMOPOLITAN'S
HANGUP
HANDBOOK

COSMOPOLITAN'S

HANGUP HANDBOOK

edited by
Barbara Creaturo
and
Veronica Geng

COSMOPOLITAN BOOKS / NEW YORK

ACKNOWLEDGMENTS

Many writers contributed to *Cosmopolitan's Hangup Handbook*, and we are grateful to all of them. Specifically, we wish to thank the following for permission to reprint articles that appeared originally in *Cosmopolitan* magazine: Sasthi Brata, "Why Package Sex in a Love Bag?"; Myron Brenton, "Toot, Toot, Tension, Goodbye!"; Joanna Brown, "Jealousy, My God, I've Got Jealousy," Copyright © 1970 by Joanna Brown, reprinted by permission of The Sterling Lord Agency; Barbara Creaturo, "Don't Be an Uncle Tom"; "Making Men the Enemy!"; Laura Cunningham, "Let's End the Double Standard for Hangups!"; "The Losers"; Karl Easton, "Why Are You Always Late?"; Joyce Elbert, "Cosmo's Six-Week Crash Recovery Plan for a New Divorcée"; Veronica Geng, "Are You Grown-Up Yet?"; Joyce Greller, "Pow! Bam! Splat! Men Who Punch Girls"; Catherine Houck, "The Crisis at Thirty"; Nora Johnson, "Do You Think You're a Little Nothing?"; "The Secret Guilts"; "Anger—Hold It In? Let It Out?"; "Keeping Perky in a Pressure Cooker"; Carole Klein, "On Being Female"; Norma Klein, "Girls Who Have to Make It with Married Men," Copyright © 1970 by Norma Klein, reprinted by permission of Cyrilly Abels, Literary Agent; K. T. and Otis Maclay, "Living-Together Handbook"; W. H. Manville, "I Was a Sleep-Around Girl"; "What's Normal and What Isn't"; William A. McWhirter, "So Long, 'Oo' Girl"; Joyce Peterson, "Why (Sob!) Didn't He Call?" Copyright © 1970 by Joyce Peterson, reprinted by permission of The Sterling Lord Agency; Jeannie Sakol, "I'm Just a Girl Who Can Say No"; "What—Me Marry?"; "The Un-Pretty Girl"; Nora Sayre, "Pleasures of a Temporary Affair," reprinted by permission of John Cushman Associates, Inc. Copyright © 1969 by Nora Sayre; Jill Schary, "How to Get Married If You're Over Thirty"; Eugene Schoenfeld, "Plain (and Fancy) Facts About Orgasm"; Cynthia Swift, "Feminine Feminism"; Nancy Winters, "The Beautiful, Elusive Art of Self-Discipline," Copyright © 1969 by Nancy Winters, reprinted by permission of The Sterling Lord Agency; "How to Handle the Competition," Copyright © 1970 by Nancy Winters, reprinted by permission of The Sterling Lord Agency; "You Love Him More than He Loves You," Copyright © 1969 by Nancy Winters, reprinted by permission of The Sterling Lord Agency.

COSMOPOLITAN BOOKS

Editorial Director Helen Gurley Brown

Editor-in-Chief Jeanette Sarkisian Wagner
Assistant Editor Veronica Geng
Copy Editor Ellen Tabak

CONTENTS

FOREWORD I've just finished empathizing (and identifying!) my way through this little book (about problems!), and do you know, I'm feeling strangely *euphoric!* I can't help sensing that every "hung-up" girl (and I think I surely qualify!) has something special going for her. Does that sound Pollyanna-ish? Well, really it *isn't.* Listen, aren't the busiest *grapplers* with life the ones who deal with problems most often . . . and, in so dealing, don't you suppose they become a little more special than other people . . . stronger, surer, more compassionate . . . also more *able* to cope?

That's exactly the girl COSMOPOLITAN is edited for . . . the reader who, no matter how disgusting and overwhelming her problems of the moment, never takes the *easy* way out but gets in there and *fights.* That COSMO girl is alive and struggling. She craves the good life much too ambitiously to skulk around *hoping* to wake up some morning rich, famous, and beloved! She *pursues* her goals, even though in the process she may shred a warehouseful of Kleenex, and have to take emotional barometer readings every three hours! This girl is committed to getting what she wants—no matter how much effort it takes—and that means a great relationship with a super man, the independence of a career that's *all hers,* and other glorious commodities to satisfy her unique needs.

Everybody on the staff at COSMO knows (because we've *been* there!) that these goals, along with the constant self-improvement that helps us reach them, are never easy to achieve. And so, along with our own ideas, we turn to our writers for help. Here are the results: the *best* (from many thousands of words!) advice from COSMO. You might call these "emotional stories" because they examine the good and bad *feelings* that go with the exhilarating climb toward becoming *you*. The focus is mainly on conflicts in your romances, work, and self-esteem . . . but those divisions don't *begin* to suggest how much ground is covered. In *The Hangup Handbook*, at least one writer probably has hit upon *the* particular block that's tying *you* in tension knots this very minute. We hope some of this advice will be able to help you close that tantalizing gap between *where you are* and *where you want to be*. Of course, we don't have *all* the answers. But perhaps these words may help you win *more* of the big battles and tiny skirmishes that every alive girl must confront. I *know* you'll make it . . . because you are willing to *work*, and because you *care*.

Helen Gurley Brown
Editor-in-Chief, COSMOPOLITAN

HOW TO USE THIS BOOK

High, low . . . up, down . . . sunny, dreary . . . *at any given moment* life has a particular personality . . . it feels good or bad. Generally you understand *why*, too, and diligently work to profit from mistakes. But is it just *coincidence* when the same problems arise so persistently? Perhaps. Yet most people *do* find they're consistently vulnerable in certain areas, while they have very little trouble in others. To locate *your* problem sites, take the trouble-shooting quiz that precedes each section of this book. We've titled these quizzes "Barometers," believing they'll help you plot the *patterns* that make your days fair or cloudy.

On page 299 are instructions for using these Hangup Barometers so you can continue charting weekly progress in all six areas. Like most girls, you'll probably make marked advances in *some* places, lag in others. That's the *point* . . . to narrow the focus and work on those *stubborn* spots. We hope you'll eventually grow so skilled at *forecasting* troubled skies, you can ward off most bad days completely.

COSMOPOLITAN'S

HANGUP
HANDBOOK

BELIEVE IN YOU It sometimes seems that *certain* girls come into the world equipped with *all* the beautiful assets . . . flawless face, figure, intelligence, wealth, loving family. Yes, there are a *few* like that, but even *they* run into roadblocks. Only *part* of life's happiness depends on the luck of the draw. What really makes you a winner (or a loser) isn't the qualities fate parceled out, but how they're *used*.

Two examples: Sophia Loren was born poor, illegitimate, and, from the evidence of early photos, not especially pretty. Handsome, maybe, but smashing, no! With a markedly inferior start, how *did* Sophia become *numero uno* sex queen, millionairess, happy wife, and mother? Like some other quiet starters, she giftedly turned her givens (courage, charm, perseverance) to optimal advantage. Yes, *meeting* Carlo Ponti was *luck;* knowing what to *do* with him and his advice made Sophia a star.

Consider early Barbra Streisand: middle-class Brooklyn girl, built along sturdy lines, with a nose that pleaded for plastic surgery. But Barbra *felt* like a Jewish Princess (even without a nose job) and *knew* somehow she'd soar to fame. People laughed at her grandiose self-promotion, ignoring the powerful voice and chutzpah style. Quite some time ago they stopped laughing, and started believing in Barbra *too*.

1

These celebrated cases of success-against-the-odds are supervisible. But the same methods have worked for *many* girls, who (all-too-modestly endowed by nature) win, win, *win*, while others (whose natural dowry is downright *munificent*) consistently finish last. The difference? Life's victors *believe* in themselves (even with little to go on) and hang in there, while also-rans perversely seem to sabotage every chance. Winners are pretty sure they *can* succeed—if they continually make *first-class* efforts. Losers, however promising, are *lazy*, gloomily *doubt* they can ever do *anything*, perhaps even resist success . . . and fail! This section is advice to would-be champions. *Avanti!*—we know you'll like preening in the winner's circle.

BELIEVE-IN-YOU BAROMETER

Yes, self-esteem ebbs and flows . . . sometimes the world seems to conspire to reduce you to a humiliated little nobody . . . then, within days, presents you with a juicy plum that feeds your spirits for *weeks*. But think: Just *how* dependent is your self-concept on this feedback from others? Do you only think you're good if someone else says so? Can you use some advice on learning to believe in yourself *full*-time? This quiz will help you find out. During the past week:

1. *Did you pass up a good thing for a safe thing?*
2. *At that last party, did you glance away from a man who was watching you, instead of walking over to introduce yourself?*
3. *Did you worry about your age?*
4. *After buying something daring, were you too timid to wear/use it?*
5. *Did you muzzle your lone opinion in a group that disagreed?*

YOUR BAROMETRIC RATING SCALE

4–5 noes What a fine, fortunate girl—you *like* yourself. That's *basic* equipment; read how to keep it in prime condition.

3 noes *Sometimes* you feel worthwhile. For insights into those *other* times, take our refresher course.

2–0 noes Self-confidence may be the single key to *all* your hangups—and wouldn't that simplify life? *Many* girls have found *all* their troubles fanned out from something as controllable as *state-of-mind*—and a few went on to write the heaps of good advice in the following pages.

THE UNPRETTY GIRL You start to catch on early. At about four, maybe, you get the first nasty clue that your little-huggy-bear self is not quite cutting it. When you're getting ready for your cousin Mona's birthday party, you see the tension on your mother's face as she grimly brushes your hair this way and that. You are trying to cooperate, but it is clear you look rotten and are a disappointment.

"*You're* Mona's cousin?" A grown-up peers down, incredulous. "But she's such a *pretty* little girl!" And what are you, an ugly little girl?

In the following weeks of hanging out with impish, dimpled Mona, you begin to feel the gnawing invisibility of the Unpretty Girl as kids, grown-ups, boys, the ice-cream man, and your very own big brother buzz around Mona, giving her bubble gum, pushing her on the swings, and making nice-nice when she cries.

"*Me! Me! Look at me!*" you plead.

By the time you're nine, you are eavesdropping on your parents, as usual, and, as usual, they are bad-mouthing you:

"*Can't you get her to stand up straight? . . . Why does she walk around with her mouth hanging open? . . . Maybe if you took her to one of those hair stylists . . . when does she get over the awkward stage?*"

Awkward isn't the right word. Black despair is more like it. You are ugly. It's not fair. God—where were you? Why weren't you paying attention? Everybody was trying to *tell* you something!

Your early teens are when the full impact of your nongorgeousness really sinks in and becomes a cold, hard knot in your belly and a geyser of tears in your throat. All the nice things are happening to the pretty girls. You try out for the school play and get the part of the eighty-year-old man. Mona, who thinks acting means giggling, gets the lead. *Not fair.*

On your first blind date, the boy arrives and you see the look of bright expectation fade from his face. He's too inexperienced to hide his disappointment and disappears when you get to the party. You realize he was expecting his dream girl—and you are not it.

On Valentine's Day Mona gets forty-seven cards, most of them hideously insulting and thrilling. You get three, one from your Uncle Ed in Phoenix.

"Ugly, ugly, ugly," you are sobbing one night when the phone doesn't ring and the prom is next week. Your mother comes in.

"Looks aren't everything," she says. "It's what's inside that counts," she says. "What do those boys know anyway? All they can think about is a pretty face!"

Mother is right. All boys can think about *is* a pretty face. Not having one, your humiliations and miseries mount up.

The yearbook pictures: "They don't do you justice."

The gut fear of a Mixer Dance: "Fluff out your bangs a little—and for God's sake, *smile*. Look as though you're having a good time."

The nausea of having to ask, "You're sure he didn't call? He said he was going to call!"

If this sounds familiar, then you know that by the time you have grown up into full, juicy, yearning womanhood, you've got scars on your psyche and a genuine cultural problem on your hands. For a girl to enjoy all the treasures life has to offer, she must be beautiful. By some sad slipup of fate and genes, you are *not* beautiful. You are not even pretty.

To make things worse, the Unpretty Girl has been brainwashed to *accept* her dubious fate. She believes in the criteria of Beauty Worship and, instead of fighting back, gives in to the defeat of the faceless life because that's the way things are. She often ends up one of those middle-aged crones who didn't fight back and got sad and wan and cross.

But . . . Unpretty Girls don't *have* to abandon hope. The first thing they can do is take a lesson from one of the most audacious, delightful business-success stories in recent advertising history. Until a few years ago Hertz was the only car-rental firm anyone knew. They were *numero uno*. Then along came Avis, which made a virtue of being an adorable, exuberant competitor by announcing, "We try harder!"

Men loved it. They responded by renting Avis cars. Like all the exquisite front-runner Beautiful Girls, Hertz is still number one, but Avis is right in there. In second place, true, but busy and thriving.

The same approach applies to the Unpretty Girl. If you're not gorgeous, it assuredly Hertz. But there is a highway to happiness for the Rara-Avis Bird (that's you), who gets there just the same—by Trying Harder. No, you shouldn't *have* to. People should love you for *you* . . . and they *do* . . . but *not* often enough . . . or *not* with as much love as you'd *like*.

Now, the first important step is to analyze your situation with candor so you can set up defenses without being defensive.

You are not a beauty. O.K. There are certain men who will never, ever, fall in love with you. They are the Success-Status Seekers, the modern-day Soames Forsytes who drive drop-dead Bentleys and need Faye Dunaway's baby sister beside them. O.K.

When your club picks a girl to cut the ribbon or your office wants a guide for a visiting VIP it won't be you. O.K.

When the most sought-after bachelor scouts the party, his feverish eyes may rest on you in passing, but will move on to more delectable prey. O.K. That's still no reason to sulk.

True, the chances are slim that you will ever be one-half of an exquisite, enchantingly romantic couple.

I remember being in London about a year ago, walking down Bond Street, and suddenly seeing Anouk Aimée and Albert Finney, their arms entwined, their heads close together in the drizzling rain. Her hair was scraped back in an elastic, her exquisite face shiny with raindrops and love and absolutely bare of makeup. Finney was looking at her as no man has ever looked at me and I felt such a stab wound of mourning that I had to clamp on my sunglasses to hide the tears. A few months later they were married, and I felt the stab wound again, the corroding sense of loss for something the Unpretty Girl can never buy or earn or win.

Romance and brute fact clash. I cannot walk in the rain with my hair scraped back and no makeup because I would look like roll call at Auschwitz. I cannot live the reality of poetic love because poetic love is based on Grecian urns and "Behold—thou art fair" and I am not fair and it is not fair.

There are men for me, of course. They are not creeps, but deep in me is the gnawing resentment of not fulfilling the romantic vision I would like to be and, by this omission of nature, missing out on the romantic intensity inspired by Beautiful Girls.

So what does one do? One decides living is better than crying, and one tries *harder*. Being Unpretty is like a festering wound. It can go on suppurating for years, poisoning you slowly, never healing. Begin by exposing your wounds to yourself. In private.

Examine the hurt spots. Expose them to the fresh air. Try cauterizing them yourself. Yes, you wish you were dead sometimes, but, no, you prefer to live and flourish. Yes, you would like to throw acid in some pretty girl's face, but realize it wouldn't help *you*. But, oh, wouldn't it be nice, just once, only once, if only, oh God, you could look like that!

Private self-confrontation is recommended, *but*—by yourself, with a close and trusted friend, or in a professional setting of group or individual therapy. Otherwise you risk being an "Ugly Girl Bore."

Nobody loves a loser, except maybe another loser. Avis doesn't attract and beguile by reminding us of defects, but by emphasizing attributes.

Another lesson from Avis concerns knowing how to deal with the competition. It would be a big mistake to avoid the friendship of Beautiful Girls entirely.

Au contraire, Beautiful Girls are not your enemies. By having them among your friends, you become pretty-by-association. Since, as the old adage says, you are known by your companions, if your chums are knockouts, some of their moonglow will slop over on you. Unless you look like a troll, your Unprettiness is not repulsive, so that, in a bunch of perfect American beauties, the slight imperfections of one will be hard to see.

If you seek to shine by having only girl friends who are uglier than you, such an ego trip will surely backfire. When you throw a party or have to come up with another girl for a date's friend, it's guaranteed disaster not to have at least one mouth-watering friend available.

Being pretty-by-association will also give you the poise, confidence, and mannerisms of the pretty girl, little subtle bits of behavior you will acquire by proximity. Acting prettier will help make you seem prettier.

Trying harder demands physical and emotional decisions. Physically, you can double-cross nature for double-crossing you in the first place. Begin by turning a deaf ear on the wishy-washy chorus that trills, "I like you the way you are." They are the types who thought eye makeup was vulgar and fishnet tights whorish. It's your life. Forget their advice.

You think plastic surgery might make the big difference? See the best plastic surgeon in the world. Maybe a shorter, skinnier nose would be an improvement. Or a firmer jawline. Or your chin built out—or resculpted. Perhaps your ears flattened instead of flapping. A scar or mole or strawberry mark removed.

Would you look better as a blonde? And have more fun? Do it. Never mind the "natural look" fashion magazines create for already beautiful girls. Go to the best hairdresser around. Pay what you have to. A new color is worth trying; it may be *fabulous*. A radical change of hair shade requires changes in makeup as well as clothes. You may look in the mirror and find there really is a new lady there, prettier than the previous dowdy tenant.

Teeth, skin, and figure? If you don't like them, trade 'em in. We live in an age of scientific miracles. A cap job or a few months of wearing kid braces may change your entire facial contour. Dermatologists can improve your skin. Your figure, of course, is the hardest to change, but here's where the "We Try Harder" motto will give you courage. The Unpretty Girl realizes it's smarter to spend lunch hour at the gym than over a $5 martini lunch complaining about her crummy social life.

Your clothes and personal image demand major decisions.

Some Unpretty Girls play the professional kook. You know the kind—the girl with the large nose and thick lips who wears purple lipstick, paste-on moles, kinky glasses, freaky wig, and body paint. Attention-getting, sure. A kooky girl gets invited to parties and on weekends, but as the buffoon. Someone may take her home, but nobody takes her seriously. Playing the clown is hard and unrewarding. The female Pagliaccia is more pathetic than the male.

If evolving a personal image for yourself seems difficult, first find an idol to emulate. Whether she's an actress, a model, or a junior executive in the next department who sets the water cooler aflame each time she takes a sip, be sure she has something of your height, bone structure, and coloring. A tall, meaty brunette would look dumb trying to imitate a tousled, hoydenish Goldie Hawn.

Hair is your best friend. It can be your comfort, your security blanket, your best camouflage. The Unpretty Girl should always wear long or longish hair. This gives you movement, a sense of vitality, and the option of several hairstyles. Don't be conned into one of those small, sculpted heads or stark, geometric cuts. Cropped hair exposes imperfections, and when a short hairstyle gets out of hand, you look like a demented chipmunk. Wigs are wonderful, but they do tend to come off at the time you most need a mass of lovely, thick hair. Use hairpieces as a fashion accessory and not as a cover-up for a scraggy mat.

Sensory deception also aids the Unpretty Girl. Remember that there are five senses and that the visual you, the part that is seen, caters to only one. There are four more: touch, smell, sound, and taste.

Feel Appeal is easy to acquire. Smooth, creamy skin invites touching. Glossy lips. Gleamy cheeks. Clean, shimmery hair. Learn about the huggability of soft jerseys, rich velvets, slithery satins, and deep-pile furs (fake or fur-reals).

With very little effort you can have a subliminal "Touch me" tattooed across your chest. Once a man gets those two words in his message center, you can demonstrate your additional skills in knowing how to touch him.

A man's olfactory glands respond to stimuli with as much fervor as his sex glands. In fact, one thing often leads to another, as you will happily find out. Smelling good means your entire body, including hair, mouth, armpits, and other nooks and crannies. In addition, never underestimate the appeal of heady *cooking* aromas, fresh flowers, and sweet, clean sheets. Those belong in your life, too.

The range of perfumes, powders, deodorants, and other enticements is enormous. Skin-test on yourself. If you get a good reaction to one scent, stick with it. If the chemistry is right, you can't go wrong—until you want to.

"Sound" means your voice. Men's ears are very sensitive, especially on the phone. Telephone wires seem to bring out the stridency in the female voice. Learn to pitch your voice low. Purring tones are the best, and a slight breathlessness seems to turn an ordinary phone call into an urgent "Wish you were right here."

If you have a rotten laugh, get rid of it. Having a hee-haw fit at the slightest witticism will not add to your prettiness. You can be charming and responsive without cackling, snorting, or wheezing. Giggling is O.K., but use sparingly.

Besides your voice, music appeals to a man's sense of sound. Have your apartment hi-fied to create a musical background for you, especially the bedroom. Your record library should include a range of mood music from charged-up rock to soft soothers.

As for taste, you ought to know how to cook *something*. Men were raised by women who fed them and they like a cozy meal once in a while. Practice making yourself bacon and eggs so that you can at least whip those up late some night. Being a great cook will only enhance your high oral standing.

Does being great in bed help the Unpretty Girl? As sages of the past have said, it doesn't hurt.

The point to be made here is that sexual "greatness" depends on attitude as well as mechanical competence. As an Unpretty Girl, you may be tempted to dazzle a man with your exotic skills. Fine. But be careful that your attitude is not one of "See what disgusting and dirty things I'm willing to do to get you to like me!"

A man will take advantage of a pushover—but not for long. Develop your sexual skills, yes. Add delicious refinements, why not? Enjoy a man and see to it that he enjoys you. But never, never demean yourself because of your looks. You kill the whole thing if, in the cool calm after the white heat, you insist on wondering how a man as wonderful as he is could make love to a girl as grungy as you. You may think it—but keep the notion to yourself.

Yet another small comfort is the continuing great comfort of good and gratifying sex. The Unpretty Girl may worry about men trying to use her as a love object. But men try to use gorgeous girls as love objects, too. The point is not to resent a man's wanting you for just one thing. Why shouldn't he, and why should this be bad? Enjoy the just one thing. It could turn into a regular thing, and then a big thing. As the evangelists say, "You can't go under for going over."

Being sexually desired is a compliment, so don't be thin-skinned about a man's taking advantage of you. He probably is unaware of your skin being thin, his motivation being merely to fondle it.

Yes, the Unpretty Girl is touchy. She's vulnerable to a legion of ego traumas—things that make her feel ugly. Learn to anticipate ego trauma and avoid it. If you look like a boiled lobster in the sun, stay off the beach. You'll look rotten and have a rotten time. Or, carefully choose a flowing burnoose and floppy hat that look great, if slightly eccentric, and make the scene in your terms.

If you photograph like a cauliflower, develop gracious means of avoiding the camera's evil eye. Why risk having a deformed snapshot of you in the hands of someone who's been thinking you're pretty great-looking? If it's impossible to avoid, try to hold a prop in front of you. Keep your chin up. Whatever happens, don't be pressured into smiling. Even the prettiest girl can look like a crazed hippo with a wide-open mouth and squidged-up eyes.

Since cameras seem to be a growing passion with men, you can learn how to face them by doing what the movie stars do. Study your face from all angles. They can't be *all* bad. Get a friend with a Polaroid to take a few rolls of you as you keep posing in different ways. Study the instant results until you learn precisely how to tilt your chin, how to hold your mouth; in short, how to aim your face at the camera instead of letting the camera aim at you.

Another ego trauma to avoid is *people* who make you feel ugly. Think about it. Aren't there some who send out good vibrations that make you feel adorable and say neat things? And aren't there others who make you seem gross, tongue-tied, and apt to light the wrong end of the filter tip?

Avoiding bad vibes is especially vital in terms of men. Unless masochism is your thing and rejection your goal, steer clear of the man who makes you feel ugly, who deserts you at the party for the nearest cookie-cutter girl, who tells you about all the gorgeous broads he's known.

This type will make you believe you could never be the American dream girl of his fantasies. If true, why throw good loving after bad? Cut your losses and get out, because you can't possibly win.

While on the subject of fantasies, guard against your own case of media romanticism. It is equally self-destructive to get hung up on finding someone who looks like the Man from Glad.

The Unpretty Girl needs the emotional nourishment of a man who adores *her*. This does not mean settling for Sweaty Norman with the clammy palms. It does mean a sense of perspective; enjoying what's available instead of mourning what you may be missing because you're not pretty enough.

Recognize what your appeal is and what kind of men respond to it— and take your pick from them. Every girl sends out signals which attract a certain kind of man. Most girls find that, again and again, the same type of man comes sniffing around, often of the same ethnic background and frequently with similar kinds of jobs. A copywriter friend of mine always attracts lawyers. Any time a man speaks to her at a cocktail party, she knows he's going to be a lawyer. A Minnesota farm girl now working as a fashion designer continues to find herself chin-deep in swarthy Italians. They love her.

For reasons I can't figure out, I seem to be catnip for craggy Celts: Irish, Scottish, Welsh types who recite poems, drink and yell a lot, and hate to drive cars.

Instead of yearning for the hero figure who won't figure in your life, look over the lads who do yearn for you. There has to be one you will adore.

In talking to Unpretty Girls, a question that came up was this: How do you cope with an attack of "The Uglies"? Even assuming you are well along that highway to happiness, there will be moments when despair strikes, when you are reminded of too many rejections and disappointments. The tears gush. Trying harder isn't enough. A loving man and an increasingly productive life are great, but nevertheless not quite enough.

How do you handle the feeling of being gypped? . . . the black cloud that falls as you look in the mirror and weep in your heart of hearts, "It's not enough"?

As said earlier, the only way the Unpretty Girl can flourish is by being strong and self-disciplined. When you have "The Uglies," hide out and let it all hang loose. Crying is the best catharsis. You *will* feel restored.

Should you ever do your famous crying-jag scene with a man you love? Not if you can help it. However sympathetic he may be, he also will think, "If she's so ugly, why am I in love with her?"

What you *can* do is to subtly make the man who loves you the custodian of your morale. When he tells you how pretty you look, that's the perfect moment to tell him how much his approval means to you. When he volunteers compliments, that's when you hug him and say how much confidence he gives you. Part of loving is recognizing each other's needs. By gradually making him aware of the nourishment he gives you, you will encourage his responsibility for your emotional well-being.

If you must cry and chew scenery, suffer with a close friend or a member of your family. That's what friends and families are for. The friend can be a man. It might do you more good if it is a man—one who loves you but is not in love with you, perhaps a former lover who has stayed to be a friend—a man with whom you have common interests and who wishes you well, as you do him.

Each of us has at least one intimate—a girl friend, a sister, an uncle—someone who will listen with sympathy and may even have a trenchant word of advice. Your nose may be stuffed up, but your ears can be wide open for the wise words that are all around us, if only we pay attention.

As my own best example, I have lived through the visual shock of seeing myself on television over the last year. The publication of a novel and co-founding of The Pussycat League brought me invitations to do guest shots on various TV programs. After seeing myself the first time, I was overcome with such a feeling of shame and failure I could well have thrown acid in my own face. The Jeannie Sakol on my home screen was grotesque and the comments of friends and relatives did not help:

"Your eyes looked small." "It doesn't do you justice." "Why did your mouth look so big?" "I thought you had your teeth fixed." "You're much nicer looking than that." "Maybe you should dye your hair blond."

I felt exposed, demeaned, raped by default just as I have always felt the victim of cameras and my own inability to please. It was rotten. I felt rotten. Who would know that a five-eight girl had so many tears?

Finally, I got tired of splashing around. A few choked phone calls with friends and my darling sister, Mimi, and out of sympathy and affection came candor. My bangs were too long and they started too far back on my head, was one chum's comment. They made my face squatty instead of oval. O.K. My hair was too long and too straight at the sides. It covered three-quarters of my face and, between that and the bangs, my cheek-bones were lost and I looked like a sad gypsy who lost her tambourine.

The black eyelid goo that I thought was so sexy only made me look tired and, instead of opening up my warm, molten eyes, made them almost disappear in seeming dissipation.

Why hadn't somebody told me before? I had never asked. Even your best friend isn't going to break into the lunch chat with a little verbal essay on how crummy you look.

Since then I've had my bangs thinned and trimmed and they start lower down. I still hide my forehead (I really happen to *like* bangs), but the rest of my hair, still long and thick, is brushed back and hooked behind my bite-size ears. I've discovered that, if I hold my head up with pride, I *do* have a chin line, even in a three-way mirror, and that an exceedingly thin line of taupe on my eyelids nearly doubles the size of my eyes.

Seeing myself on TV has become less of a trauma and more of an education. I have an unfortunate laugh—the look of it, that is, not the sound. The mouth itself isn't bad, the smile is O.K., but the big laugh is like the end of a hee-haw. I understand Raquel Welch has trouble with her laugh, too. I have learned not to let my upper lip roll back, and, like most learned things, it is now becoming second nature.

As for the special feelings of facelessness with which the Unpretty Girl generally lives, I found out one more thing from TV exposure—I do have a face and it is recognizable, and therefore not all that bad. To my amazement, I've been stopped on the street and approached in restaurants by people who have seen me on the box. Ego food for the over-thirty was being called by a Columbia University junior to come to a party.

Of some comfort to the Unpretty Girl is that time is on your side. At eighteen, when your face is still fresh from the cookie sheet, its imperfections may be in glaring contrast to the more exquisitely molded competition. As your face grows older it reflects your personality, your character, and, even more important, your experience.

While at eighteen it is no comfort at all to know that the candy-box baby has a brain like a sieve, at twenty-eight you will begin to see that her dependence on looks alone becomes a little frantic while you are starting to relax about your appearance, to concentrate on other things. Good health, generous sexuality, and professional success go a long way toward improving a girl's looks. Just because you have never been a ribbon-covered, candy-box baby does not mean you can't be a sleek, sophisticated woman who wigwags "Winner" from every pore.

Take heart in the fact that, by the time you reach your middle thirties and can see the forties up ahead, the problem of the college girl as competition will no longer exist. Not that this is an ad for rocking chairs, but there is a life after twenty-nine, and it can be surprisingly fruitful for the Unpretty Girl Who Tries Harder.

There are big, responsible, glamorous jobs for the experienced, competent woman, and that means travel, money, and the company of exciting people.

There are the second-time-around men who married the Campus Queen and found the rah-rah just a bit wearing after fourteen years. Almost any Unpretty Girl who marries—or remarries—after thirty-five will find that her husband's first wife was prettier than she is, but never grew because number one hadn't learned to try harder.

To be born Unpretty is to learn how to live with a congenital sadness. It is a physical affliction and a very real one. Just as famous athletes have overcome polio by trying harder, so can you overcome the grief of the poorly made.

You can try harder to forget the morning regret about how wonderful it would be to wake up looking utterly gorgeous, how incredible to smile with perfect teeth gleaming from an architectural miracle of perfect jaws, exquisitely aligned and with no Bugs Bunny overlap.

You can try harder to ignore that yearning to take the sexy shower and let your hair get drowned and watch your face float away, knowing you will look sensational with a wet-look all over, hair scraped back, face naked, and the structure bare.

When you feel *any* of these longings, don't give yourself over to hopelessness; counter *immediately* with one or all of these survival tactics:

1. Do make passes at men who wear glasses. Nearsighted men see you through a nice blurry haze, especially when their glasses are off. What's nice is that when they say you look like Candy Bergen, they mean it.

2. When he cups your face in his lean, hard hand and breathes, "I never realized how beautiful you are," don't argue with him. Relax. Flutter eyelids. Enjoy.

3. Stay ruthlessly healthy. When skin, hair, eyes, and all the rest of you are busting out with glowing vitality, how bad can you look?

4. Obey the No-Knock Law. No knocking yourself. Ever. Self-deprecation may have some faint charm in the skilled hands of Phyllis Diller or Carol Burnett. You are not a stand-up comedienne. You are trying harder to be a desirable girl.

5. Be Good Value. You need not be a doormat or martyr to give generously. Your dinner party should make them hungry for more. Your little gift should be something they really and truly love. Once you learn how to give with style, you can take with style, too.

When Avis first challenged Hertz, men were amused and flattered by the cheery good spirits of the ones Trying Harder. The Gorgeous Girl still leads the race. The Unpretty Girl won't beat her time, but can run a close second as a definite front-runner. Most agree that it's better to be in the same race with the number-one girls than to retire safely to sidelines and simply watch life go by.

Like Avis, the Unpretty Girl gets there by keeping her motor humming at purr perfection. She takes extra-special care of her chassis, keeping it classy, sparkly, and tuned up in fine run-away order. Her upholstery and accessories are always gleamy good to look at and handle.

As for the ashtrays? Here's where the Unpretty Girl often fails the Avis standards. Hers are usually full to overflowing—because she's simply too busy to empty them.

2

THE CRISIS AT THIRTY

Picture a man who drives women mad—hip, funny, sexually radioactive, harem like Xerxes—only picture him married and faithful to one idiotically pleased woman. Throw in an ivy-covered cottage (in the middle of *Manhattan*), add a merry child, and sum up to The Greatest Catch Ever. Someone asked this hunk of bliss one day, playfully, if he had ever in his life been rejected, and we were stunned when he said that the last woman he had lived with had thrown him out—struggling and with his fingernails clawing the door screen. *Why,* we asked, at a loss to imagine this scene and visualizing Shakespearean complications. "It was because she turned thirty," he said. "She was bitter. She said she had been devalued, like the franc. She left me for her sugar daddy. She said he was so old he made her feel young."

"Good God," I said. "Poor thing." And then I remembered that I was thirty. I was temporarily overcome. How could anyone *possibly* feel she was a husk of a woman at thirty? Something disagreeable about *my* age? No indeed.

"I think anyone who would disintegrate for such a silly reason should be left in pieces, swept onto a dustpan, and deposited on the nearest garbage heap," I said with dignity.

But then I went home and found this conversation remained stickily in my mind. Because the truth of the matter is, who *does* go baying joyfully over that particular hill? For a girl to have a nervous breakdown seems,

19

on first thought at least, a bit much, but a certain chill in the fingers is understandable. To find oneself slightly subdued—pensive, in a word— might be *reasonable*. After all, look at the brooding that is done over adolescents. Everyone knows the nurslings of their tender psyches— finding an identity, the drug menace, what to *be*. The same for the middle-aged—countless images and words well up.

Anyone who watches television can give you an instant psychoanalytic insight on how the slightly graying but still volatile daddy is going to spend a fortune on the gorgeous opportunistic babe in order to prove he is better than ever, and meanwhile *Mrs*. Robinson is making sloshy passes at the addled delivery boy.

But when it comes to us, the thirtyish, there is mostly mystery. We are neither fish nor fowl but some sort of undocumented *amphibian*. In a peculiar way we hardly seem to exist at all. Except for a few male models like the Marlboro man, people simply refuse to *be* thirty. It is an age that is particularly subterranean among women. Everyone I know thinks of herself as being as bell-bottom-trousered and nubile as any college girl or as dignified and proper, as held together with Spray Net and crippled by high-heeled shoes, as the most carefully groomed, girdle-squeezed matron. The only widely accepted acknowledgment of our existence is as a kind of mystique—a catchword. Don't trust anyone over thirty is the cry, and of course the irony is that this has nothing whatever to do with *genuinely* being thirty. What is sneakily meant, as usual, is don't trust anyone who isn't hip. Do you dig rock music? Have you been tear-gassed? Do you smoke (and not Marlboros)? Do you have wild and interesting hair? If the answer to these questions is yes, so the mystique goes, you are under thirty even if you are over forty, and if the answer is no, you are over thirty even if you are under twenty.

This, then, only clouds the issue of what it is like to really be thirty, and nastily instills terror at the very idea. Teeny-boppers have a vague notion that they will turn to dust at thirty or, in some sort of Dorian Gray syndrome, will change from beautiful young things to death's-heads in a few hours' time. This was borne out to me cruelly on my thirtieth birthday. I was taken to a discothèque in Washington, D.C., one of those pious cities where you can't drink until you are twenty-one and IDs are checked at the door with ultraviolet flashlights and power-crazed efficiency. I had gone with an individual of twenty-two, who in his innocence hadn't an idea in the world that I was older, and I saw no reason to volunteer this information. I wanted to go dancing and *he* wanted to go dancing and that was that.

As everyone in our group produced their IDs, they were allowed one by one into the proscribed area, until *my* turn came. When I handed over the passport that has identified me without question for years in country after country and with which it is literally a federal offense to tamper, the man with the flashlight leaped up, practically out of his dark glasses, and shook my passport under my nose. "C'mon, now, you can't expect me to go for this!" Every head turned, as the music had lulled and everyone was bored anyway. Also, the man was bellowing. "You don't expect me to believe you're *thirty*!" My date was gaping in horrified disbelief *himself* and everyone else was staring with fascination. I was furious. Red and self-conscious, I went through my purse and fished out two driver's licenses with pictures, some charge cards, an employee card with picture, a bank card, a library card, and some envelopes addressed to me, all of which the official gathered up with a look of "You're a smartass, but we'll get *you*" and took to the manager's office, wherein they presumably have X-rays and God knows what sophisticated equipment to ferret out fake IDs.

By and by, after a horrible interlude during which my date and I shuffled our feet and pretended that it was all very funny and that he hadn't been shocked out of his wits, the official came back with my papers and sullenly told me he couldn't figure out how I had done it but that I could have a free beer. I glared at him with hatred and finally we were seated, my notoriety subsided, and I was able to concentrate on brooding. I had been insulted, but I didn't know why. I didn't like to look twenty when I was thirty, but *that* wasn't insulting; I didn't *really* mind being taken for a criminal; I didn't like the clumsy technique the doorman used to apprehend me, but it wasn't the *mortal* insult. No, the mortal insult lay, I decided finally, in the shock shown when it was discovered that amongst them was a thirty-year-old who looked no different than *they*, was not palsied or in a wheelchair or wearing a little hat with roses. It was the manifestation of the extent of the belief that a woman at thirty is nothing but an animated pile of *debris* that I resented.

21

As a flesh-and-blood, experienced (leer) thirty, I contend that it is the most *delightful* time of life, that admittedly there are threatening things, but that they are swamped by the happy things. Here, from firsthand experience (rather than a trip to the psychiatric barn), are some of the sensations associated with reaching thirty, and a look at the validity of each.

The First Glimpse of Failure Crisis: You feel suddenly, at thirty, that there is no more time to dawdle. Men in their thirties are still jockeying heartily for position, but by their forties they are expected to have amounted to something, and it is whispered that if he hasn't made it by now, he probably won't. The outdated but still entrenched feminine version cuts off at thirty. If she isn't married by then, she is doomed to malevolent spinsterhood and will have to sit around and tat or embroider and be called "auntie" by her sister's children. If she is married, what has she produced? Tsk, tsk, if the poor thing doesn't conceive soon, she isn't going to be able to have anything but Mongoloids.

Even if you are rational enough to know that there are always men, especially in this divorce-happy country (all the good ones, in fact, are coming around again like ducks in a shooting gallery), and to know that it is not true that you can't have children safely any time you want them, still it is easy to absorb a sense of alarm by osmosis. Even if you are a wife and mother, there are still the accusations of Women's Lib—what *else* have you done? And if you are, heaven help you, neither a wife, mother, nor executive at U.S. Steel, you feel that you had better get busy. I personally, as an abysmally lazy but ambitious writer, have picked up several telltale quirks. When I pick up a book, for instance, by another woman, I turn obsessively to the back of the jacket to see how old she is. If she is obviously of mature years, I feel relieved, but if she is younger. . . .

Dénouement: No amount of expensive analysis or skillful rationalization can ease this disquiet. There *is* one approach that works, however, and happy are those who have discovered it. Go back and *get* the master's. Write the book. Take acting lessons. Apply for the job of your dreams. One indirect delight of being thirty is that your friends are beginning to land in important places. *Use* them; people adore being important enough to be used. At thirty we have a new dignity and clout that we never had when we were tender young things. Use *them*.

The Flattened Against the Cold Flaky Wall Crisis: You become *lazier*. You no longer want to move simply to move, in a musical-chairs fashion. The grass on the other side of the hill begins to look at least as mottled as your own. It is not that you lose the urge to travel, it is more that you lose your fantasies of life being somehow better in Paris or San Francisco or whatever city it is where you aren't. (Not to mention that the sheer horror of putting things in boxes and carrying them down a lot of steps and then taking them out again is more detrimental than it was of yore.) You are willing to move *ahead*, to leave a drab job in a drab city for a better job in a livelier city, but less willing to leave a decent job in a perfectly good city for simply another job in another city. You don't abandon the idea entirely, but you become suspicious of it. You begin to lean toward the theory, hitherto scorned, that you only take your problems with you. This can be a touchy moment and often a full-fledged crisis, because it means that any problems still hanging around have to be dealt with now, after years of evasion.

You then have the classic, definitive breakdown that women of thirty are notorious for, that gives all of us the bad name. Everyone has friends who disintegrated in classic fashion. They had clung stubbornly to vile behavior patterns—irresponsibility, or surliness, or being temperamental —the whole Pandora's box, and when they got to thirty there they were, all alone, floating in an isolated eddy with no husband, no lover, no friends, but usually with children whom they claim they live for but whom they really feel keep them from living. They go to pieces. Their parents (usually despised) or a kindly ex-husband (equally despised) has to come and get them from whatever strange city they have run to like cornered rabbits and bring them home, where they usually do a great deal of brooding, reading, meditating of philosophy, seeing analysts, sleeping twelve hours at a stretch, watching daytime TV in darkened rooms, and all the other things people do when they are exhausted wrecks.

Dénouement: Almost everyone comes out of this kind of breakdown cured rather than killed, battered but healthier. They have come to terms with themselves. They are freed from the cobwebby fetters of self-absorption and often looking at the world for the first time. Second marriages are said to be happier than first marriages; this can't be mere luck. It is because the people themselves are *older* and have solved their problems.

The Eleanor Rigby Crisis: Probably the most hostile element at thirty is one's reflection in the mirror. In this country youth is glorified *ad nauseam*. The models of the mass media are without exception members of the Pepsi Generation. Trendy clothes are shamelessly designed for the young, and the slender ones at that. It is no consolation that there is a sound commercial reason for this, the reason being that whatever else American businessmen may be, they are not fools. The swollen generation of war babies has hit the market and it happens that there are more of them than there are of us, and they have *money*. We, therefore, with the advent of the first wrinkle, see ourselves as bypassed like a truck stop that the highway no longer runs by. *Scorned*, like the old gray mare. Our telephones will atrophy on their cords. We are doomed!

Dénouement: What this particular crunch amounts to is one of laziness and sloth. The hard fact is that women in their thirties can easily be *more* alluring than women in their twenties. I for one looked ghastly in my twenties. I had very short hair and wore too much lipstick and eye makeup. I looked like a tubercular brain-surgery patient. I had no individuality, too much baby fat, and was disgustingly cute. I do not know why anyone would want to look cute-eighteen any longer than they have to. The logic seems basic enough: Any man who has developed his brain is going to want an appreciative audience for it, which excludes eighteen-year-olds. If you look eighteen, this excludes, therefore, *you*.

I had a very satisfying experience along these lines. Ten years ago I spent a year in Italy. My first night I met, naturally enough, an Italian, an amorous Italian, who bought me dinner and then tried to seduce me. I made excuses, many excuses. After every possible avenue of approach had been blocked and he had ascertained the cruel fact of his rejection, which he didn't take personally but in the sense of gamesmanship in which it was intended, which was worse, he studied me thoughtfully while his mind darted about for a way to slay me. A bad sport, this Italian. I smiled at him uneasily from the hotel door, sensing that he was gathering together a vile insult, and soon indeed it arrived. He smiled sadly in a phony way—heavy-lidded weariness carrying a Red Cross evacuation warning of total annihilation—and said, "You are *girl*, not woman," and he didn't even say good night, just walked away. I felt very indignant. So that was the worst he could do. A *girl*! People were always remarking on how young I looked and I never liked it. I always suspected they meant that I was lacking in character rather than that I was in any way delightful, but no one as yet had coldly and deliberately rolled it out as their worst insult! Little did I know that before I left Italy a hundred more Italians were going to say the same thing, some of them, furthermore, before they were rejected. I became very touchy about it.

Recently, I met an elegant Italian here, who invited me to dinner. He also invited me, later, to his apartment for cognac and *l'amour*. I declined, whereupon he gave me exactly the same thoughtful look as those Italians ten years ago. I cringed with *déjà vu*. He spoke. "You are *woman*, not girl, and I am sorry you do not come!"

After I recovered from the shock, I gave him such a warm, glowing smile that he was totally confused. As for me, I felt gloriously smug. I felt, as I taxied homeward, that I had been given something I had *worked* for, that I had *earned!* Who wants to be a Sandra Dee if they can be a Jeanne Moreau?

The point is that when you reach thirty you have gained more than you have lost. You can still be lovely and have developed, as well, what Shakespeare liked to refer to as "variety"—"Age cannot wither her, nor custom stale her infinite variety." There are many, of course, who have *not* developed variety. They are the proverbial bumps on the log. They remain fond all their lives of whatever the look was when they graduated from high school. The Eisenhowerian leftovers, for instance, are easy to spot—short little bubble hairdos, chalky lipstick; skirt lengths are just now getting back to where theirs were all along. They haven't *moved*. They are afraid to. Their character is equally stagnant. After all, what is in your head at thirty is unescapably a matter of what you have *put* into it—what you read, the height of abstraction your thoughts reached, what people you knew who were smarter than you. If all you did was sit around and watch television or gossip with equally placid girl friends, the chances are the old noodle is as hollow as a bongo drum.

And it is not only the intellectual habits you have developed that are important now. *Today's Health* says that in terms of circulatory systems most Americans become middle-aged at twenty-five. They don't like to move, in other words. As one San Francisco parking-lot attendant put it, Americans would drive to the bathroom if they could. Anyone who spends her days in a sedentary heap can hardly expect to be thin and youthful. On the other hand, happily, if you have been conscientious about your exercise and diet, you probably have the same figure you had ten years ago and feel perfectly at home in the boutique section of the department store. You know that being hip to style has no age boundaries, that just as you aren't thrilled to see a gray, pedestrian man, they aren't overwhelmed by a gray, drab woman, a mud hen.

So here we are—looks intact, plenty of savvy, and style, too! *What* was it you were complaining about?

The Men Fade Away Like Geese in Winter Crisis: There is a theory that as a woman gets older and older she gets choosier and choosier and men get fewer and fewer until, by the age of thirty-one maybe, they evaporate altogether.

Dénouement: This is a very twisted thought. Do you *really* know any womanly knockout of thirty whose love life isn't flourishing or waning exactly as it *always* did? This theory implies that there is some glorious time in every woman's life when the air is thick with men clamoring for her hand—fat ones, thin ones, twits, Greek gods, poor ones, rich ones (it doesn't matter, they *all* look good). Maybe I was deprived, but I was never the cause of such flurries, even in junior high. This idea seems more relevant to terms of perception than to numbers of men. Our judgment *does* change—and for the better. After all, what is the good of marrying someone only to discover that you want to get a Ph.D. in psychology while all he wants is to stay home and run his father's dry-goods store? If you paraphrased this part of the theory, it could read "as you get older, your judgment improves, and you are able to save yourself a lot of trouble." In other words, what you have lost here was really only excess baggage *anyway*.

And meanwhile, as you become more efficient about your requirements for lovers, you become more charitable toward people in *general*. When I was an impressionable college freshman (hooked on Ayn Rand) I got it in my head that I was a very superior type and should only associate with equally superior types. There is the merest grain of truth to this—as in playing tennis you tend to be only as good as whomever you are playing with—but I overlooked the fact that it is possible to be superior in many different ways, and mine, whatever it was, was only one little one. In those days I was too insecure to like anyone until they proved themselves worthy. Now I like everyone until they prove themselves *unworthy*. This sounds like a small change, but it makes a *big* difference. Since I like more people, more people like *me*, and I have a much greater variety of friends. I know *more* men, not less. Most importantly, since *I* am more interesting, so are *they*. And this, perhaps, is the greatest reward of *all*.

One last thought-provoker that might seem at first to have more to do with being fifty than thirty but actually transcends both: "At fifty," George Orwell said, "everyone has the face he deserves."

3

HOW TO GET MARRIED IF YOU'RE OVER THIRTY

You (sob!) just *know* (gulp!) that you'll n-n-never get married. I mean, well, here you are—thirty-five next month—and nobody has even asked you since Antiperspirant-Dan finally gave up. God, maybe you should have become Mrs. Dan . . . that, at least, would be better than *nothing!*

Reconcile those schizophrenic thoughts and calmly consider these important facts: (1) Other girls, even nubile twenty-two-year-old ones, are not being proposed to every day. An offer of marriage is a very profound compliment, and men do not make such offers with any frequency. (2) There are, according to those old devil statistics, some five *million* more unmarried ladies than men in the United States today. Feel free to curse whatever gods there be, but don't wonder that you're not surrounded by eager, eligible bachelors. (3) Simone de Beauvoir says *every* girl feels a horrible, deep-down conviction that it (marriage) will never happen to her. . . . This worry is part of the built-in insecurity of being female in a (so far) man-dominated world.

Whether or not you get married is, essentially, Up To You . . . fate has absolutely nothing to do with it! First, you must sincerely *want* a husband, and that doesn't mean just coveting the security and social status of being a Married Woman. You must actively want to *live* with a man. Some girls, despite protestations to the contrary, do *not* want this; often they marry anyway and turn into punishing shrews. If you are this kind

29

of girl (and you've had thirty-odd years to find out), don't expect marriage to magically change you, though a psychiatrist might. Either look for professional help or be bravely unconventional and *accept* that marriage isn't your life-style. You might be temperamentally geared for a formidable career of exciting love affairs. If your true self really doesn't want to be married, it may be best to stay single. Forcing yourself into a mold that doesn't fit will merely make you (and some hapless man) miserable!

Now if you *do* really want the warmth and loving security of living with a man . . . fine, there is *work* to do. You must be willing to translate all those yearnings and longings into resolute, determined action. Here's some advice . . . bits of it old, much of it new . . . that's sane and sound and eminently *workable*.

Where do you live? Should you think about living somewhere *else*?

• You're *not* still bunking at home, are you? Dear girl, that is the most effective man-repellent you can name. Maybe that sense of "responsibility" you feel for dear ol' mom is really clever camouflage, hiding a fear of being out on your own and, yes, a lingering dependence on parental support. Don't allow ailing or lonely parents to play on your guilts either . . . see that they're happy as possible and *separately domiciled*.

• Out of that ladies' hotel or that nice building with all those pleasant oldsters who make you feel just like a daughter! You've lived there long enough to find out there are no eligible sons or younger brothers around. Move.

• No roommates. Three is still a crowd, at least where getting married is concerned. Don't argue that apartment-sharing shows you *can* live with someone—cohabiting with a man is an entire something else. Think about it, my friend, why are you leery about living alone?

• Have you settled down in a place so long it feels like you're sinking right *in*? Move! The accumulated baggage (and habits) of years need periodic uprootings. The change will be good . . . a new girl in town just *naturally* interests a man.

• If you live in a small town, subscribe to newspapers from cities (foreign ones included) that interest you. Think seriously about taking off for someplace remote and different . . . like Sydney or Juneau. The ratio of men to women in these two cities is *much* more promising than in New York or San Francisco.

• If you are truly in love with your job and your city, then at least explore some other neighborhoods; a city that's *worthy* of you must have alternatives. If you're a South Chicago girl, try the Near North Side. In and near Los Angeles there are some marvelous singles buildings in new oceanside developments. The social opportunities here might even be worth a cross-country trek!

• Consider a move to the suburbs . . . amazingly, girls *do* get married there. In fact, implausible as this may sound, it's often easier to find a mate outside the city . . . competition is less stiff, and the pace of life *encourages* men to settle down. (Urban bachelors are often having too good a *time* to consider marriage seriously.)

$\mathbf{D}$o your surroundings make a man feel like staying for breakfast—forever? They *can*!

• Furniture: a few samples of Late Groove, circa seventies, are fine and fun, but your apartment does not need to look like a discothèque to prove you are Young in Spirit. Have one really livable leather chair, maybe with a footstool and a good reading light, that looks like it's just waiting for a man. A mad, mod apartment could mean you're trying too hard!

• Neither should your place look like Sleeping Beauty's virginal bower, where anything more than a good-night kiss will make him feel like a rapist in muddy boots. Send your eleven-year-old niece that pink tulle skirt from your vanity table and those ruffled lamps.

• Stop hoarding family treasures (the fragile lace antimacassars, those maple sewing boxes). It's dangerous to generalize about men, but they usually *hate* clutter. Also, a houseful of mementos (not antiques but *mementos*) is frankly old-maidish, suggesting a life full of loneliness. Besides, if you crowd an apartment with too much of your stuff, a man thinks you don't have room for his tennis trophies.

• Trade in your single bed for a big inviting king-size one (you'll like it!). Have big thick towels *not* covered with flowers; bright colors and geometrical patterns are less maidenly. Keep salami and cheeses in your icebox, some wines in a cool, shady alcove. Yours should be a place where a man is welcome—where men have been.

• Don't talk a lot about your furniture, how you *adore* your mahogany credenza or how the couch needs recovering. Men like comfort, but *not* being trapped by possessions.

• Have fresh flowers (or bouquets of lemon leaves) in your apartment. Not pink roses . . . maidenly again. Daisies, yes, or big, outdoorsy mums. If you can, keep a garden, even if it's just a window box outside your fourth-floor walk-up. Grow plants on the kitchen windowsill (maybe herbs that you put in salad or fresh mint for late-night tea). You're a warm, giving woman who likes herself enough to spend a little time (or money) on delightful nonnecessities.

• Your stereo (or second set) is in the bedroom, can be played from bed. You know what relaxation is all about, and you *must* be a permanently sensual being with those plug-in earphones. There's been some love in this place; you're not waiting desperately for just any man, only holding out for the *right* one.

Can you keep a pet and *not* let the beastie wreck your love life?

• Your pets do *not* have monogrammed coats or cage covers. If you must have a bird (a maiden-lady pet), try to restrain yourself from talking to it! In fact, don't chat with *any* of your animals when a man visits.

• Avoid little darling (and nervous) animals. A big, big dog is better; treat him like a dog, not a person, when company comes. (What you two say to each other *alone* is something else.)

• Animals are good company, but if one is becoming a substitute for *human* friends, maybe you'd better figure out what to do about it.

How do you look?

• Get rid of that neat little watch with its businesslike black band (unless it's from Cartier); it makes you seem too serious about time! If you don't have a really chic wristwatch (which you rarely consult), don't wear one at all.

• Can you possibly still be wearing a girdle and a hard-line bra? Out! If your figure isn't good enough to get by in minimum underwear, you aren't serious about getting a husband. Diet, jog, join a gym or dance class. You simply *must* not be pudgy. Yes, some slobs do get married (and they wear girdles), but most men like a free-looking, uncorseted body that moves in an easy, natural way.

• Don't buy heaps of "little nothing" dresses and separates. You still need some really *good* clothes. A husband-hunter can't afford *not* to look successful (your career hasn't left you *time* to get married!).

• Use lots of blusher . . . it takes away that pinched, pale, pathetic look that sometimes comes from loneliness. You're a healthy, vital woman . . . in your prime!

• Makeup for you should never look hard. You've heard that before, but it's a real danger for a girl past thirty. Stop using black eyeliner (except just the subtlest bit) or black-black eyebrow pencil. Cut out *any* heavily drawn lines under the eyes. You want to look appealing, a trifle vulnerable, *not* chorus-girl seductive.

• When you entertain a man at home (often!), wear something not only sexy but cozy . . . panne velvet, rather than satin or lamé. Clinging knits and crochets are perfect. In the morning put on a *cuddly* bathrobe to look fleecy and rather dear! Sleep with blusher on; he'll like having given you a glow! Do *all* cosmetic fix-ups when he's not around—yes, it still has to be that way.

• Walk tall; wear shoulder bags and long breezy scarves for graceful, girl-in-motion appeal. Move your legs from the hips; think Lauren Bacall, Melina Mercouri. And don't clench your bottom when you walk; your intentions may be serious, but that doesn't mean you aren't fun. In fact, you have to be *more* fun.

• Learn the difference between sexy and cutsie. Rule out little ruffles and bows, but keep the deep-plunge neckline, unbuttoned top buttons, and cinched-in waists. Elegant (good) versus prim (bad) is a more difficult distinction to catch. Out go the ladylike graduated pearls (put them away for your daughter someday) and little circle pins; away with those prissy jacketed dresses and matching brocade coat-and-dress sets. No white cotton gloves (they really *are* finished), and hats should only be informal smashers. Never pin anything for dear life to the top of your head: if the marriage you're interested in is your *own*, you can't go out on dates looking like an afternoon wedding.

• White underwear, even in silk, is a bit surgical. Buy panties and bras in *yummy* shades you'd want someone to see. (Hopefully, someone will!)

• Elegance (see above) could also be described as class. For this, think Dina Merrill walking through an autumn landscape with great golden retrievers. Wear camel colors, off-white woolens, sage or heather tweeds (sometimes known as the Deep Country look). Suedes and leathers—but not the hippie or motorcycle variety—in tawny shades are for "now" girls. Skip the molten-pink hot pants; they tend to look entirely *classless* on anyone over nineteen!

• No matter what anyone has told you about how flattering they are to you, scratch magenta, lime green, and turquoise . . . hard orange, too . . . especially in "bold" prints. These colors tend to make a girl appear *nervous* and to drown out her face. You're more apt to radiate *calm* with more muted colors, sexy assurance with black, white, or beige. Red? Well, most men love it, and it does bespeak frankness and confidence.
• Wear what you please, but do so with verve and assurance. (I've found *my* look, and I like it!)

Now the *interior* you . . . and how do you break those little big bad habits? O.K., you're a teeny bit neurotic . . . what girl *isn't* . . . and being alone doesn't make you any more serene. Yes, analysis (or group therapy) may help, but even before you start therapy, or while treatment is in progress, it's not a bad idea to *hide* your more obvious neurotic symptoms! Be gracious even when you're almost bored to screaming; *try* not to bad-mouth ten people in one conversation; check the impulse to let your problems tumble out in conversation . . . nobody *wants* to know your sad stories! Pretending sanity is a good, healthy kind of deceit and constitutes a kind of therapy in itself. If you act as *if* you were a normal (whatever *that* means), happy woman, pretending may even help make it so.

Here are some of the more typical and unattractive tics that invade the psyches of unmarried girls . . . see if any below apply to you . . . guard against them:
• Restless, anxious hand and body movements. Do you habitually massage your upper lip, cross and uncross your legs, finger-drum? You may think these little squirms are out of your control, but they're not. Ridding yourself of nervous mannerisms takes total self-discipline, but no more so than stopping smoking or nail-biting.
• If you talk nonstop, for heaven's sake quiet down! Obsessional monologuists are terrified that if they pause for breath, their audience will go away! They live in constant fear of being ignored . . . and wind *up* that way.
• Don't be a professional Funny Girl or Good Sport. Lots of older single girls, humiliated and embarrassed by their plight, take refuge in humor, particularly the self-denigrating kind. Very bad. Of course, this is different from the ability to laugh genuinely from the gut: that is both sensual and attractive.

• *The* most common and fateful hazard for an overaged single girl is compulsive rigidity (and that's what we've been talking about all along). Do your temples throb with rage when somebody drops an open container of coffee into your nice, neat wastepaper basket or when they use *your* towel instead of the neatsie guest ones? Men are terrified, and rightfully so, of a lady with compulsive habits. If you have more than half a dozen punctilious ones, start breaking them! Eat red caviar on toast for breakfast . . . throw out your pajamas and sleep in nothing but a topaz necklace . . . stay up all night.

How do you meet a man?

General advice: be flexible and exploratory! Try as many "avenues" as possible, several at the same time. Here are some—most you've heard before, but are you *doing* them?

• Go out at least once with any man who asks. Beasts may have beautiful friends.

• Join a therapy group. There are many different kinds to choose from, and it's a great way to get close to people. Matchmaking is only incidental to the group's purpose, but the record of marriages through friendships made in these is phenomenal.

• Stop with the neighborhood bar! The habitués all know you; you're the lady who drinks too much because she's lonely. Sure, you've made some real pals, but none of them is going to marry you. You're spending too much time perched on a bar stool for too little potential.

• Take a course in Russian, German, or Japanese. Businessmen and scientists study these languages for their work. Forget romance-language courses for the time being . . . they're full of ladies getting ready for European tours.

• Join a political club. Even a women's group can prove helpful if you chum with married ladies. Be so marvelous they invite you home for dinner (where you'll meet husbands and husband-friends!). Keep eyes open for bitchy ladies who may be divorce candidates (this is *war*!). Clue: they act a lot like you used to before you got all free and calm!

• Take courses in computing, stock brokering, applied economics, law . . . any area that attracts more men than women. Many of the "possibles" will be younger than you, but they're very possibly for *you*, baby! (Ashley Montagu says a woman should be at least ten years older than her man for ideal sexual compatibility!) While studying, you may get so handy with the IBM 360 or commodity-trading that a new job will result in a field *abounding* with men.

• If you're a good saleswoman (you know whether you are), sell *cars*; men usually buy them. Or work for a real estate firm that handles office leasing, stores, restaurants.

• If your present job is in a department store, beauty shop, or some place catering mostly to women, take a secretarial course at night, and change over to office work where the *men* are. (What you want is a *whack* at some of them, and you've got to be near them to do that.)

• Join a country club or tennis and turf club. Buy a small sailboat (what are you saving for, a drizzly day? It's raining *now*, isn't it?), and join a boating group. Learn to play bridge or chess. Chess clubs are full of good intellectual men, but they're also good at the *game*. So must *you* be if you expect to win anything!

• Divorced fathers in your city probably take their children to parks and playgrounds on weekend afternoons. Find out where "dads' corner" is, and *be* there, preferably with a great romping dog who loves children. If you draw, sketching equipment gives an excuse for lingering and also interests children.

• Organizations that attract middle-class, settled suburban ladies, like women's auxiliaries and sisterhoods, *sound* like death but actually are full up with eager matchmakers. Join one!

• Oh, go ahead and register with any or all computer dating services. You can spare a few evenings out of your life (even possibly awful ones) for a good cause.

Here he is . . . what special ways say "This would be a great wife"?

• You genuinely dig sex; making love is not naughty, not an obligation. Be as fascinated by his body as he is by yours. Suggest wicked new things to do in bed; wander around the house in pretty dishabille. If you're feeling mysteriously unsexy, read pornography before seeing him . . . *Fanny Hill* or *My Secret Life* are two wildly healthy heterosexbooks that should put the naughtiness back into your eyes.

• Minimize your problems, but be genuinely caring about his. Never cry that you're flat-out broke (if you haven't learned to handle money by now, he'll wonder how you'll manage with his). Don't whimper about chapped hands or chills and fever every second time you see him. You care about *his* health though; worry about his cough, feed him vitamins. Men love (they always did and still do) the nurse instinct in women. (Yes, dear, it's *still* double standard all the way at *this* stage of the game ... he is a valuable prize, and "equality" in problem-discussing may have to come *after* you're married.)

• If you're awful in the mornings and he's a lark, *force* yourself to seem cheerful. Conversely, respect his misery if he's a late-night person who loathes waking up. Have bacon sputtering and pancakes flipping in the morning ... especially important if he's already been married and has grown *used* to homey breakfasts. (If his wife neglected him, he'll love you and your sunshiny breakfasts all the more.)

• Be busy sometimes, and don't say, "Well, Monday is my night for Yoga"; a little mystery can't hurt. Don't go into a funk if he is occasionally busy when you ask him somewhere. One of man's worst marriage or re-marriage fears is that he'll be taxed with twenty-four-hour husband duty. Let him know you dig some private times—his and yours!

• Surprise him and be giving. Send thoughtful, inexpensive presents (his favorite Hungarian sausage). Homemade is nice, but don't *suffocate* him with brownie batches, especially if his mother did or does.

• Never complain about the heat or cold; you're the girl who adores walking in the rain, frisking in the snow. Accept wrecked shoes and other mishaps (stained dresses and broken china cups) with gracious equanimity, especially if *he* did the damage.

• Suggest outings that are ridiculously romantic—a fried-chicken picnic or drive-in movie. Take corned-beef sandwiches, potato chips, and beer to the movie, and neck. Plan to stay home from work together one day and go to a ball game.

• Let him see you occasionally with children; you are calm and friendly. Do *not* go into rapturous transports of motherliness ... everyone (including the child) will be revolted.

• Don't agitate to meet *his* children by a former marriage ... you are interested, though, and listen sympathetically when he talks about them.

• Ask him to do little favors for you ... total self-sufficiency puts him off. You need him to advise on your job, open a can, scrub your back, or decide which scarf or purse to wear. Don't *constantly* badger him for advice and help, though ... in fact, don't act *any* one way all the time! You're not *always* ready when he comes to pick you up, not always *not* ready. Try to be thoughtful, not slavish.

- Learn how to give a really fine massage or great shampoo . . . there's a touch of the geisha about you.
- Don't be afraid to let him see you cry every two or three months, then be easily comforted, quick to cheer up. Cry for only *good* reasons . . . absolutely no poor-little-me tears allowed.
- Don't rearrange furniture at his place or bustle about tidying and fixing up. Spasms of hygienic housewifery are more motherly than girl-friend-like. Yes, do dishes and make the bed, but in a casual, noninterfering way. Oh, yes, you really *must* wait for an invitation before filling his closets with your clothes.

Finally, believe you will marry because you are special and when you marry, you will marry better.
- You've been a self-responsible, independent girl for years, and being married won't change that. You will never be the clingy wife who tries to take options on a man's *soul*.
- Years on your own have trained you to handle money, entertain smoothly, run an efficient house. Face it—incompetence is rarely charming, or cute, or "feminine."
- A load of career problems has been your way, so you understand his job miseries and give intelligent, sympathetic advice. Being older than some brides means you are also more *adult,* more graciously givingly female . . . you don't expect the world and the zodiac, all garnished and plattered, from a man. You're not emotionally self-centered, can live with the trifling tiffs of any intimate relationship. Sexually, you are grown-up, which means not only that your responsiveness is peaking, but that you're over the sipping-and-tasting, am-I-missing-anything stage and are content to have erotic adventures with just one man.
- Because you've waited a bit longer than most for marriage, your husband is especially precious to you. You will work hard to keep him happy.
- Your optimism about marriage is spirited, but your expectations are *realistic*; you have the emotional wherewithal to make your life with him, not only better, but the *best!*

4

DO YOU THINK YOU'RE A LITTLE NOTHING? How do you see yourself? Are you a swinger, an intellectual, an Earth Mother? Do you strive to be dashing and sporty? Liltingly feminine? Or is the whole subject of image a blur and one you would rather not think about, preferring to fade into the upholstery instead and let other people stand out? Even if you don't go in for dressing up in costumes from the thrift shop, do you hope to make a definite impression on the people you meet because you *feel* definite? Or do you think of yourself as a girl who prefers not to make *any* impression at all?

Take this special little-nothing quiz right now:

1. Your wardrobe is nearly all black, beige, navy, brown, and gray with scarcely any bright colors.

2. You almost never complain about your table in a restaurant or send back your order because it's inedible.

3. You *hate* anybody to be mad at you *ever*.

4. Everybody (even the least prepossessing people) has something you envy (her end table; his lack of jealousy).

5. You get along better with animals than people.

6. Lavish compliments, even sincere ones, make you nervous.

7. Having your photograph taken is trauma-time, although you *do* spend a great deal of time looking at pictures of yourself.

8. Any apartment or house you visit seems prettier than yours.

9. Criticism hurts but usually you think "Maybe they're right."

10. You're always a follower (never saying "Let's try that new Chinese restaurant for lunch" or "I'd rather see the new Truffaut").

11. You're convinced that nobody has less poise than you.

12. After three martinis you still wouldn't start a conversation with the best-looking man at a party.

13. It's terribly hard for you to venture an opinion even when you *know* what to say.

14. If people are especially nice to you, you suspect ulterior motives.

15. When a decision you've made is questioned you become filled with doubts or go into long explanations.

16. You privately believe that people pay too much attention to the smart or pretty girls, ignoring the simply nice ones.

17. You give yourself secret treats. Long hot bubble baths, extra Cokes, jelly doughnuts.

18. You're always afraid of looking ridiculous (if you buy a gaucho hat, you haven't the courage to wear it).

19. You may sleep around a little too unselectively.

20. You fantasize a lot. The Cinderella story is one of your favorites.

If you've answered with ten or more yeses, you *do* feel like a little nothing. Five to nine yeses and you need to work on your self-image a bit. Less than five and you're practically perfect. All noes? You cheated. (For your own sake, *why* did you?)

Now let's find out why some of us grow up thinking we're little nothings; where it all began and what we can do to transform ourselves into Somethings.

What kind of impression we create for the world and whether we even *want* to be noticed at all is the result of the longest, most complex psychological processes we go through in our entire lives. The making of a self-image starts in our very beginnings—a baby, dimly looking around him, staring at his hand, laughing at his foot, is engaged in the very important process of trying to figure out where *he* ends and everything else begins (is that hand him, or something else?). The first object that is clearly something else is his mama. As he gets older, he learns his capabilities—how he can affect the world—and that vitally important fact, whether he's (she's) a boy or a girl and what he or she thinks of being a boy or girl.

Hopefully, the little girl (with whom we are concerned here) will grow up thinking it's grand to be a girl because Mommy is so nice and loves Daddy, and she wants to grow up and love a daddy, too, and so forth. The daughter will evolve an image of what she wants to be, based on what she admires in her mommy, how she *feels* about her mommy. Ideally, she will want to be a splendid, *unforgettable* person (how she means to achieve this impression is her own unique combination), someone who will linger in the brain of everyone who meets her.

But, as with any intricate process, any number of things can go wrong in this careful construction of an identity. Schizophrenics have an identity disorder (some psychoanalysts feel) going back to infancy—they never completed this process of discovering beyond a doubt where they ended and everything else began, and they *still* don't know; they can't distinguish between themselves and their environment. One theory about schizophrenia blames a rejecting mother who never supplied herself as a foil against which the baby could constantly test himself. This rejection would be the ultimate lack of maternal identification (most mothers *do* cuddle their babies, fortunately), but less drastic forms of rejection can take place later, with less crippling but still serious results for the child.

For instance, a little girl will have poor maternal identification, as the psychiatrists say, if she has an *over*-solicitous, all-powerful mother. Some mothers can't let their children alone—they are all over them like a sheet. Janie is drawing a picture—Mommy is right there, telling her where to put the tree. Janie does her hair a new way—Mommy is full of suggestions about how it could be done more attractively. Janie, in other words, is never allowed to do anything *herself,* so after a while she doesn't even bother to try—everything withers in her hands, and she feels ineffectual. Or else Mommy, because of her own insecurity, must one-up her daughter all the time. Susie puts on a new dress and hair ribbon for lunch in town—Mommy is staggering in her Chanel suit and Italian shoes. Susie makes slice-and-bake cookies—Mommy turns out petits fours. Mommy is perpetually saying, "See, I'm better"; her daughter soon believes it and concludes that she *is* a little nothing. Or else, conversely, Mama just isn't interested. She is never around; she doesn't bother to taste the cookies or even notice that her daughter has made them; she doesn't offer herself as a foil, a critic or admirer, a judge or companion, or *anything*, as a matter of fact, because she just doesn't care.

An admiring daddy can counteract an uncaring or too concerned mother, but if the little girl's father is scarce, preoccupied by work, or disinterested himself, she'll soon reason that since she can't make any impression on him either, what's the use of trying? The father also could want to keep her a little girl who will sit on his knee and admire him forever, unlike witchy, critical (of him, too) old Mommy, or Godlike, all-powerful Mommy, who is so accomplished she makes them *both* feel like little nothings. If Mommy is first in importance in the building of a girl's identity, Daddy is a close second (no matter what we may think of the idea, it is *still* more important for girls to learn to get along with men when they grow up than vice versa). Daddy is her first admirer and, if he does his job right, he will aim to graduate her from her early attachment to him (with no more than a little grumbling) into bigger, better, and more womanly relationships—ones that (unlike Daddy's) she can complete . . . emotionally *and* physically.

When, as frequently happens, however, the mother or father (or both) play the parental role *improperly,* the result is a child with a poor self-image. As she matures, the manifestations of this identity problem may be obvious or subtle, more discernible from *what* she does than the way she appears. But whatever, she feels inferior to everyone else: fatter, thinner, poorer, dumber, or less educated, that her life is duller, her romances fewer and fainter. In general she feels that she is less competent, less capable of getting what she wants. The notion that everyone else's life is much better than hers preys on her mind to the point of obsession, and there are few fixations that have such a paralyzing effect— if everyone else has a better life, what's the point in trying? She feels hopeless and jinxed, as though the cards are stacked against her (which, in a way, they are). None of those convictions has much to do with *fact*— there is *always* somebody fatter, thinner, poorer, etc., than you are. And we can *always* make something out of what we have; the ability to do this is, of course, far more important than our given attributes.

Look at Eleanor, a somewhat baffling little nothing because she's basically a beautiful girl. This fact comes as a surprise to everyone who knows her; all of her friends at some point have suddenly said to themselves or each other, "Why, Eleanor's *beautiful!*" with an air of utter amazement. She never acts like a beautiful girl. She is slightly fretful, rather distracted, and somewhat depressed; she pushes back her loose strands of hair with a nervous, apologetic gesture, and then flashes you the most dazzling smile. She walks with a slight stoop, as though the burdens of the world were on her frail shoulders, and with a hesitating tread, too—you're never sure if Eleanor is really going to take that next step or not. Her clothes are forgettable—they might be all right in the closet, but they aren't for *her*, and there is usually a sagging hem or a button missing. What Eleanor says is somehow forgettable, too; not because she isn't intelligent, but because she never just comes flat out and says what she *thinks*. Each viewpoint is qualified, rephrased, undermined; anything that seems like an opinion is followed by "But, on the other hand, maybe you should look at it *this* way."

Sam, Eleanor's husband, is rather spectacular—good-looking, a brilliant lawyer, overflowing with charm, with the result that people are always wondering what he sees in her. Isn't she a drag? Doesn't she hold him back? He loves her, but seems a little cross with her, a little impatient. She isn't in the old-fashioned sense a submissive wife—Eleanor doesn't necessarily agree with Sam all the time; it's a more self-centered thing, as though she is groping around inside herself to find out what she *really* believes. Her abstraction, the privacy of her struggle is what makes Sam angry. He is a little like her father, though not as aggressive. Eleanor's father was a sharp-witted, opinionated, domineering man who was always *daring* his family to disagree with him, to put up a good argument and earn his respect. (Of course, he was furious if they were wrong!) Eleanor's mother merely agreed with him all the time to avoid arguments, and retreated into her own little world; Eleanor's brother fought a bloody battle with his father and got out early. That left Eleanor caught in the middle—and she never grew out of the indecisiveness developed to avoid being wrong. Her defense to herself is that she is too intelligent to embrace any opinion whole-heartedly; the world is too complicated for that. The truth is that she thinks so little of herself she is afraid to make a decisive move for fear people (Daddy, really) won't love her if she's wrong. She hasn't realized yet that it isn't so bad to be wrong, even *most* of the time. Better to be wrong and be *somebody*, with some point of view. At least you'll attract people who *share* your viewpoint!

Fay, on the other hand, had a different kind of family imbalance; she had an all-powerful, all-successful mother who intimidated her husband and daughter both, and Fay's nice, rather passive father adored Fay and considered her His Girl—His Little Girl, which she still is. Fay's taste runs to hair ribbons and Mary Janes (all slightly frayed); with women she is timid and with men she has all the childish mannerisms of a silent-screen star—rolling eyes, batting lashes, and little *moues*, all interspersed with a stream of apparently brainless chatter. She drops things, loses things, is always getting lost *herself*, as though the big world out there were simply too much for her.

Fay is intelligent, though she does her best to hide it, and she is pretty enough to attract a certain avuncular kind of man, one of whom she married. Roger, being older and divorced from a quite different, more sophisticated woman, thinks she is wonderful—or did for a while, until she had the baby. She didn't mean to get pregnant but tried to be optimistic about it—Roger wanted the baby so much, having had none in his first marriage. The pregnancy itself was all right—it was such fun fussing over the layette—but after her daughter was born Fay went into a classic postpartum depression. She had had black moods before, but nothing like this—she talked of killing herself, of killing the child, and she ended up on the psychiatric floor of the hospital with the baby going home in the care of a nurse. Here, possibly for the first time in her life, she started to grow up. The problem was so simple and so hopeless—how could a child take care of a baby? What would Fay do with another little girl, not only to be responsible for but to have as competition?

Fay had no faith in her own capabilities—she didn't even think of herself as an adult, really. She felt absolutely furious at being pushed against her will into adulthood. Slowly she arrived at a point where she could cope and went home from the hospital, but she leads a lonely life. Roger is nervous about her, the baby makes her cross, and she is *lonely*—she never got along with women and doesn't have many friends. She now consciously thinks of herself as a little nothing, realizes that she has become quite helpless. When Roger is around everything is much better, but during the day, without him, she can't function. Her own family was close to the point of claustrophobia, and Fay never learned that hard lesson, how to fill the hours of the day—somebody was always doing it for her. She also realizes that if her marriage is going to work, she will have to make some enormous changes and so will Roger.

Margot, at fifteen, *really* felt like a little nothing—or big nothing, to put it more accurately. She weighed two hundred pounds. What drove her to the refrigerator, in tears, was her attractive, weak, alcoholic father, who after a few drinks would tell Margot what a slob she was, what a failure compared to her brother, sister, girl friends, and everybody else. Margot's mother was strong but remote. During these scenes the mother would sit in tense silence, her lip twitching, but she wouldn't really step in and take a role.

Finally, either psychotherapy, college, or simply time helped, and Margot dramatically lost seventy-five pounds by dedicated starvation and exercise. Like most ex-fat girls, she tried to make up for lost time and now embraced the cult of the body. She was so concerned with how she looked and so absorbed in keeping herself attractive, however, that she dropped (or flunked, as we used to say) out of college. That wasn't too serious in itself; everyone was so glad she'd lost all the weight they weren't going to fuss about a little thing like intellectual performance. Margot went to New York and got a job as a receptionist. She was now quite attractive and fought to keep herself that way—every day it was little Baggies of raw carrots, pieces of lettuce, a can of diet cola, and almost too much time in the ladies' room with makeup, hair spray, and Wash 'n Dries.

Unfortunately, she did the same thing on dates, being far more interested in her image than the men she went out with—she was, like her mother, remote. Margot didn't know how to relax, and she never *really* seemed to have any fun. Everything was mannered—even her laugh had been practiced in front of the mirror. The good men eventually gave up on her, and the bad ones moved in; Margot fell into a series of what we may politely call unrewarding relationships. Why, her friends wondered, did she go around with such zombies and why did she let them treat her so rottenly? How could fastidious Margot get involved with the hood who moved into her apartment, ate her food and drank her liquor, and then left with half her jewelry? The friends who wondered this had never seen Margot at fifteen, for Margot still thought of herself as a fat girl, the failure, the permanent wallflower. To the world, she was rather a smashing girl—to herself she was . . . a little nothing. Privately, Margot still suffered with the belief that every other girl was better off than she was. They went to more parties, had more marvelous love affairs, while she, Margot, had been dealt the bad cards. Her obsession with the past prevented her from recognizing her *present* self.

Connie, on the other hand, comes on as a surly, rather *shabby* little nothing, who might possibly be pretty if she ever smiled, which she rarely does. Her shoulders hunch, the corners of her mouth sag, she shuffles along as though the world were in a conspiracy against her. There is something musty about Connie, something vaguely repellent. Her clothes in fact *are* old and many times made-over and occasionally even mildewed; her purse is like the back closet of a junk shop—a jumble of old, strange little totems she can't bring herself to throw out. The only reason Connie gets by at all is that she's bright and good at what she does (she works for a bizarre research outfit) and because she arrived on the scene during the do-your-own-thing generation, when eccentricity is looked upon fondly; ten years ago she would have been a disaster.

Now, Connie is what might be called a professional pauper—on what she is paid, she is poorer than anyone else could possibly be. What does she do with her adequate, if not impressive, salary? True, she sends a little home, and we all know living in New York can blast a budget, but does she have to wear that dirty poncho year after year? Connie, who was orphaned when she was young, was raised in upstate New York by grandparents whose main faults were simply being too old to bring her up and not having enough money to do the job. They were kind but undemonstrative—not because they didn't love Connie, but just because that was the way they were—and penurious. Connie grew up on noodle casseroles, little squares of Jell-O, and dresses handed down from her better-off cousins. Thriftiness was in the air she breathed.

Even though Connie now has her own money to spend as she likes, she can't break the pattern. (Like other members of the permanently poor, Connie would be broke on $50,000 a year.) If a little extra money begins to pile up—which it inevitably does, since she spends hardly anything— she manages to get rid of the excess, not by putting it in the bank, where the money would still lurk under her name, but by investing in something that is doomed to failure or by giving it away to some eccentric charity. These are always secret gestures; she not only is guilty about *having* the money, but wants to get rid of it quickly so nobody can ever accuse her of being well-off.

There is a certain belligerence about Connie, a rage at the materialistic world she lives in. She goes around with a group of people who have the same sour-grapes view of life. Within the group, Connie and her friends have their affairs, but they rarely relate deeply to each other. This keeping-love-at-arm's-length is what Connie feels most comfortable with. She grew up with undemonstrative people and doesn't really know how to show her feelings. Behind the poncho and the antimaterialistic theories lie the distortions in Connie's feelings about herself. She feels poor and *old* . . . like a little nothing. She doesn't think she *deserves* to be attractive, hasn't enough confidence in herself to go out and *buy* a smashing dress and wonders vaguely what the point would be, anyway. Life is short, so why bother, which is the way Grandma felt, but at seventy-five it's more understandable. Thinking why bother at twenty-four is something else again.

The flawed self-image of each of these girls is a subtle thing—only Eleanor, the lawyer's wife, and mildew-clothed Connie are obvious mice, while the other two, baby Fay and Margot, the former fat girl, might well be standouts in a crowd. But each girl feels constantly put down by the people around her; each feels somehow left out and unlucky. Connie blames society for her miseries, and Fay (before her breakdown) would have said that most of the time she felt just grand, as long as she had a man around. But though they differ in *why* they feel like little nothings and how they show it, they carry a common burden. Each is living someone *else's* idea of them—of how they are—what a parent or grandparent *wanted* them to be, sometimes despite what the parent actually *said*, for children are uncannily acute at sensing the real designated role behind the apparent one. Eleanor's father didn't really want her, or anybody else, to stand up to him—he was far too dominating. Margot's father, by telling her she was a fat slob all the time, was describing the way she would be least threatening to him (a self-respecting little girl would have criticized his drinking). Connie's grandparents said, without saying the words, "Be like us—be old, be frugal, cautious; don't show your feelings, don't waste your time on frivolity."

The girl who grows up relatively free of these ghosts of the past probably had parents secure enough in themselves to accept their child as she *was* without attempting to change her, either consciously or unconsciously. The mother did not feel threatened by her beautiful daughter, the father did not feel angered by the youngster whose interests were so different from his own, nor was the parent so infantile he attempted to force his offspring into premature adulthood by a too early, too heavy load of responsibility so the parent himself could remain immature. All these attitudes distort a child's self-image and make for an unhappy and self-doubting adult—like the girl with the penchant for looking at her less-than-perfect face in the mirror, sighing, and saying, "Oh, what's the use? I just haven't got it." The fact is, nobody has got it, in that sense, or there's always somebody who's got more. The only thing a girl will stand or fall on, come Judgment Day, is what she *does* with hers.

If you feel like a little nothing—and only *you* really know—here are some notes, tips, and probing questions from a veteran of the Nothing battle:

1. You can't get rid of your fears just like *that,* but you can ask yourself what you're afraid of and why. Are you wary of standing out in a crowd? Or fearful of reaching to be something and missing the mark? Do you have awful visions of appearing somewhere in your new identity and being laughed at? Like, you *finally* wear a pair of hot pants and everyone whispers, "I never realized Mary Jane had fat knees!" or you lower your dated minis to fashionable new lengths and they say, "Would you have believed Mary Jane had such a dumpy figure?" Suppose you hold forth on ecological balances at a party and make all sorts of mistakes and everybody gossips, "I never knew Mary Jane was so stupid!" Or, even if you *are* as hip as you can be and apparently your friends like and listen to you, do you still hear voices in the night saying, "Mary Jane is a fraud through and through—she doesn't know anything!" There isn't anything unique about these fantasies, believe it or not (and you probably won't); everyone has these fears—and I mean everyone! They are part of the dreck of life, like blackheads—and they behave like blackheads. You think you've gotten rid of those self-doubts, and back they come. Since you can't really eradicate them, the thing to do is try to erect something *positive* in your mind that will at least give your paranoid little notions some stiff competition.

2. Don't attack this problem by comparing your pluses and minuses with those of anybody else you know, because with your defeatist attitude, she'll always win. (Actually, you can assume she has plenty of things wrong in her life that you don't know about. Those apparently perfect

girls are the ones who surprise you by having nervous breakdowns.) Besides, in your little-nothing frame of mind you're probably a poor judge of your own pluses and minuses anyway.

3. The only thing that matters, or even *works*, is conviction about yourself. That's what the Something girls have, and that's *all*. They've decided they *are* something (they might not even know what) and that's the way they're going to come off and to hell with the rest. And so they stand up straight, have nice hearty laughs, and are willing to be friendly. They probably make more mistakes and social gaffes than you do, because they give out more, but since they aren't always worrying about whether they please other people, they usually do.

4. And while we're on the subject, is it such a *great* loss not to please somebody? Do *you* remember with absolute *loathing* people who have somewhat displeased you? Of course not! If you speak openly but without hostility, who could hate you?

5. The point is, people are attracted by *conviction*. Becoming a Something is rather like becoming an Expert. A lot of experts never worked and toiled to become experts—they just followed an interest and, rather to their astonishment, people began considering them authorities. Probably a Something girl just goes along following an interest in herself—a belief in herself—and this is like nectar to the bees.

6. If you're so far gone you can't find *anything* about yourself that you like, try this; be authoritative about *everything*. Not obnoxiously dogmatic, just definite. Firmly tell people you hate grand opera and wouldn't sit through one; that wearing glasses weakens your eyes; that your apartment is half-furnished because *you* like it with one chair. You may seem a little off-beat, but certainly not forgettable.

7. Time is with you—take comfort in that. The older you are, the less you care what anybody else thinks of you, and when that happens, you're more than halfway to Go.

THE LOSERS— WHY DO THEY WANT TO FAIL?

Case No. 1: "I've been making love with this one man for five years. I've had to really hang in there. Ken's handsome, sexy, successful—and married. But I really want him, so I've really gone all out—even rented a little apartment near his office. I'm always there when he misses the 4:54 to Greenwich. Of course, all along I've been hoping my efforts will pay off and Ken will divorce the 4:54 to Greenwich and marry me! Well, last night— it happened! My dream came true! Ken walked in the door, told me he's leaving his wife and moving in with me . . . I should have been ecstatic, but I wasn't. I felt suddenly let down, then a cold anger welled up inside me. I screamed, 'It took you five years to make up your mind! You must think I'm stupid or something. . . . What happened? Did your wife kick you out? I know you're not doing it for me. You never loved me! You never wanted us to get married. All you think about is sex!' Ken slammed out. I'm so depressed now, I could die. *I almost had him,* I keep thinking, *I almost won. . . .*"

Case No. 2: "I'm still shaking from the fight last night. Gordon slept all the way on the other side of the bed. He's never done that before in the two years we've been married. I guess it's just been piling up. We had another awful blowout only two nights ago. Gordon said I sulked at a cocktail party. I said, 'I wouldn't sulk if you wouldn't drool down the

51

cleavage of every girl in the room.' Gordon says it's all in my head—that he loves only me, that he's never slept with another woman. Sometimes I believe him. Then we make up—in bed. We say all the right things: 'I love you, honey.' 'We can work it out.' 'I'll never pick a fight again.' But then something else happens. . . . He came home from work two hours late last night. Oh, I didn't have any proof, but I couldn't help imagining him making love to his secretary . . . then coming home and eating the dinner I cooked! I won't be made a fool of like that! I threw the dinner in his face. Still so furious I can't speak—actually can't speak. I march around the apartment silently, doing all my cleaning chores—but noisily. I let the door-slams, the foot-stampings, the dish-clatterings speak for me. . . . And to think, just last night, I thought we were going to work things out, have a baby and be like other married couples. . . . Well, I'm not going to make any big plans now. . . . Damn . . . Why does everything have to get so loused up?"

Case No. 3: "I'm a Scorpio. Ambitious. Talented. Determined to be famous. With my blond hair and my good bod, everybody says I can be the next Marilyn Monroe. . . . There hasn't been a really great sex symbol since MM . . . I work hard, too . . . acting classes, exercise, diet. . . . Last week I had a fantastic break—a big Hollywood producer wanted to see me! And wouldn't you know it? I get into this taxi with the dumbest cabbie in New York. He takes me to the goddamned wrong address, and when I get there, the producer's secretary says, 'I'm sorry, but you missed the appointment. He won't have time for you now. He's flying back to the West Coast.' The bastard! And that secretary—'We're so sorry. . . .' The bitch. I'll bet they're sorry. *What about me?*"

These three girls are all in the process of "blowing it." Each of them *should* be happy. But they are all snatching defeat right out of the jaws of victory. The single girl is throwing away five years of building to get her man. The wife is creating imaginary unhappiness. The starlet is snuffing out her chance for stardom.

You can call their behavior by the popular term, "blowing it," or you can call it by a psychiatric phrase: Sigmund Freud's "moral masochism," Theodor Reik's "social masochism," Edrita Fried's "self-induced failure" . . . they are synonymous.

Whatever the psychological name, "blowing it" is damaging . . . the hurt you inflict on yourself. And it's common. Psychiatrist Edmund Bergler, who wrote a book on the subject, *Curable and Incurable Neurotics*, calls this kind of self-destructive behavior "the scourge of humanity."

Self-destructive behavior is so common *you* may be about to hurt yourself right now. This particular form of masochism is much more subtle and insidious than the physical ("Hit me! Slap me! Call me a whore!") type. Freud defines "moral masochism" as expressions of masochistic feelings which no longer show any relationship to sexuality. We all know the familiar *sexual* masochist—someone who wishes to be beaten and degraded by his or her bed partner. Interestingly, this kind of sexual pervert can never be a *moral* masochist! Freud says the person who finds the punishment he craves in bed is likely to be a success in other areas of life. The physical masochist has to have punishment and gets it in the most direct way. His needs satisfied, he can go on with his work. Freud says such people can even be *happy!*

The nonphysical masochist is *never* happy. If you are this kind of emotional deviate, you wouldn't dream of letting anyone touch a hair on your precious little head, but you are hurting yourself in other ways as surely as if you let yourself be beaten. The villain: your own subconscious. Part of your mind is plotting against you—making sure you will louse up your love affair or ruin your career. This subconscious urge to destroy can negate every marvelous talent you have, ruin every opportunity that comes your way. You can end up a lump of human garbage— your life wasted! And the scariest part? The whole time you're committing this emotional suicide, *you don't even know it!*

Theodor Reik, the late psychiatric expert and author, emphasized that in all cases of social masochism "the evil *seems* to come from without. Actually it is coming from *within* . . . even if ill will and adverse incidents can be proved. With unconscious skill, these are utilized in a masochistic sense."

The self-destructive impulses are an unsuspected time bomb in your head. Life will be going great for you—then bam! This bomb in your brain *that you know nothing about* goes off, and you louse everything up. You blow it! And you don't even realize that *you're* the enemy. Someone else gets blamed: your lover, your boss, or just plain old "bad luck." But all the time it was *you*. Think about it—about a girl like you or me who is crying and moaning "He made me pregnant, the rat!" Yes, it's all his fault, to hear most unwed mothers tell their version. Innocent victims they are—victims who, in these 1970s, never heard of the Pill, the foam, the diaphragm . . . etc. Unequivocally, these women are much more to blame for their unhappiness than the man who impregnated them. But don't tell them that or any girl who is busy accusing other people of ruining her life . . . the girl who *needs* to fail will never believe you. Reality is too painful to confront.

Recognition is the first precaution against "blowing it," but most failure addicts *can't* recognize what they've done to themselves. Their neurosis forces them to stick to the pattern of self-destruction and deception. This pattern, defined by Theodor Reik, is one most experts on the subject of self-induced failure concur with. Are you operating on a guaranteed-to-lose pattern? Operation Failure works like this:

Step One: Fantasize. Indulge in super daydreams. You have looks, money, power, mass adoration, freedom to go anywhere or do anything you like. Any kind of success fantasy will do—the starlet's Marilyn Monroe image is an example.

Step Two: Keep up the suspense. Will or won't you make it? Failure addicts choose difficult, sometimes nearly impossible, goals, then strive very hard toward them. You may go to extraordinary expense and effort—like the single girl who rented an apartment just to be near her man. You constantly anticipate and yearn for your goal—*will* he marry you or won't he? *Will* the new magazine editor see you've lost thirty pounds and turn you into a high-fashion model?

Step Three: Provoke rejection. You've almost won. He's mouthing the words "I love you—will you marry me?" Or the boss has noticed you never have to use Ko-rec-type or even an eraser and is ready to say, "Would you consider becoming my personal assistant instead of staying in the steno pool?" Or your husband is offering to "kiss and make up." Now what do you do (if you're a failure addict)? You *provoke*. Reik states that the most common provocations used range from obstinate silence to insolent tirades. You may lash out at the man you wanted (usually on an irrelevant topic). Or you can freeze him with silence. Your brain co-operates by inventing a "reason" for you to yell or sulk. The wife can imagine her husband has been unfaithful—a good excuse for her to be nasty. The single girl can rant, "You don't really love me." On a job, you can hand in sloppy work just in time to keep yourself from getting that promotion. If you're a failure addict, you'll find just the right word or action to make people reject you.

Step Four: Next come emotional fireworks. The job of "blowing it" is never complete without telling *everyone* how unfairly you've been treated. You need to weep and wander around, a red-eyed sniffling mess. Inconceivable to keep the failure to yourself. You broadcast to everyone who will listen, "Paul has left me!" "They gave Susan the job—with *my* seniority." You must also emphasize your exceptional misfortune: "This could only happen to *me*." Real failure addicts love to recount a long list of disasters. This is a typical moaning monologue:

"First there was Bob. I was a virgin, young and naïve. I didn't even know we'd done it, until he told me. Then he left for the Bahamas. After him, there was Lester. He needed me so badly. I set Lester up in his own photo studio—bought him cameras and everything. He married his model. Then George . . . I was just healing, and I thought, What a fine, sensitive man. Older, more mature. We were going to get married, then he made a pass at my brother. . . ."

Don't feel sorry for the girl who wails, "I get nothing but losers." *She's picking them!* And if *you* have been considering yourself a love martyr, stop! The easiest way to blow it is to choose men who will (a) disappoint you, (b) hurt you, (c) dump you. Of course, every girl suffers through a few unhappy relationships with losers, but the real failure addicts usually have a string of five or more "bastards." When you first meet a man, you can usually tell whether or not he's a loser. If you're self-destructive, you'll feel a magnetic pull toward the "wrong" man. But you'll kid yourself that there's nothing wrong with him and never admit the relationship was doomed from the start. . . .

Expert failure junkies don't even have to *look* for mean or psychotic men; they can bring out the beast in *good* men! I introduced a girl friend of mine to an old and dear male friend. Julian had an almost spotless record for making girls happy. It took Sheila only six weeks to turn this nice man into King Kong. The last time I saw her, she gave me a black look (surrounded by blue and black tissue) and said, "How *could* you introduce me to that rat? He broke all the furniture in my apartment, hit me with a left hook, and asked my roommate for a date!"

Puzzled, I called my old, dear male friend (fiend?) and asked if he had really behaved so badly. "Yes," he admitted in an ashamed tone. "I feel awful about it now . . . I know it sounds like a cop-out, but she really drove me to it!" He went on to describe Sheila's behavior. "At first, she was great—a dazzling girl. I was half in love with her before the trouble started, the whining. She doubted every word I said. I'd tell her I really cared for her, and she kept insisting I was lying, that I was cheating with other girls. On our last date I arrived—on time—to take her out, and she was making love with the maintenance man on the living-room rug. It was a setup—she *wanted* me to catch her. I walked out, of course, completely disgusted, but she showed up at my place later, in the middle of the night, crying . . . claimed she only wanted to hurt me the way I'd hurt her . . . to show me how *she* felt. That's when I hit her. . . ." My friend shuddered into the telephone. "I never hit a girl before. . . ."

And he probably never will again. My friend Sheila unconsciously manipulated this man into uncharacteristic, brutal behavior. We can see how Sheila organized her own hurt and humiliation. Unless she changes her pattern she'll *never* have a happy relationship with a man. But the big question is *why*? Why would any girl sabotage her own love affairs?

To understand the motivation of failure addicts, psychiatrists and psychologists have probed the darkest realms of the unconscious, for it is the "secret" brain that arranges for self-caused heartbreak.

Dr. Edrita Fried, a professor of psychiatry at New York Medical College, says that such self-induced defeat is the result of a mental defense mechanism that isn't working in a healthy way. In a good, healthy, unneurotic brain (are there any of those left?), a system of defense works for your self-preservation. This unconscious defense system knows you and protects you all the time: Don't forget your keys! Take your birth-control pill! Don't eat that fattening candy bar! And so on . . . Your unconscious brain is your guardian angel, telling you what you should do and what you shouldn't.

Sometimes self-protection can even come out in a positive, healthy *decision* to "blow it." Let's say you are a secretary bucking for a promotion to public-relations assistant. You love your old job, but people have urged you to take on more responsibility. Your unconscious "secret" brain *knows* that if you get the promotion, you will be unhappy. So your guardian angel constructs a failure for you. On the first big lunch with a client, you eat *boeuf bourguignon* with your fingers, belch uncontrollably, and call the client by the wrong name. Presto! You're speedily demoted back to your comfy niche where you can type, visit with office friends, and sip coffee from paper cups happily-ever-after. There's nothing wrong with that self-inflicted fizzle *if* you are sincerely contented with being the secretary. If so, resign yourself to refusing promotions that don't interest you. But are you sure you're not concealing a fear?

Well-adjusted people "blow" things all the time. But their defense system is eliminating the possible options that would hurt, not please, them. If you're not self-destructive, you *too* have probably "blown" relationships with men, but for good reason: he borrowed your money, liquor, clothes so you dumped him fast, screaming, "Get out of my life!" The difference between the two kinds of "blowing it" is that the healthy kind of failure leaves you happier, or at least more comfortable, in the end while the sick kind sends you zooming down into a deep well of depression. The neurotic girl would never cut short a bad relationship at the start (she *lets* him borrow all her money, liquor, clothes . . . hangs on for six months after that, waits until he kicks her teeth out before running home to mother). Healthy souls roll with the punches and move reasonably quickly on to better things.

The girl who engineers her own depressions and failures is suffering from a breakdown in her protective defense mechanism. Dr. Fried calls the problem a "pathological phenomenon." Instead of protecting the girl, her unconscious brain is short-circuiting her chances for fulfillment and, more than that, *helping* her find failure. In mild forms, the neurosis seems to evolve from a guilt complex. The motivation behind blowing it is "I've done something bad—I have to be punished for it." The girl who is having an affair with a married man may be harboring unconscious guilt feelings. On the outside, she is a cheerful, liberated, seventies girl. Deep inside, she is an inhibited prude. She can function as a mistress only on a superficial and temporary basis. The minute the man announces he's leaving his wife for her, her guilt feelings win out. She can't "live with herself" if she succeeds in stealing another woman's husband, so she manages to fail, usually by manipulating the kind of scene that makes her lose the man.

Psychiatrists believe that this guilt has its roots in early childhood. Failure addicts are diagnosed as deeply confused about their feelings toward their mothers and fathers. Sometimes the conflict is a result of leftover Oedipal fixation. The Oedipal urge, as you probably know, is the desire and need a child feels for his opposite-sex parent—"I want you to love only me, Mommy," "Can I marry you when I grow up, Daddy?" Every youngster goes through this stage. But some children are unable to deal with it normally.

Here is a typical conflicted development, cited by Dr. Fried: The young man was handsome, charming, persuasive, but he had never succeeded in getting a girl into bed. His pattern was this: he would woo someone to the point where she appeared seducible, then, at that crucial moment, turn sarcastic and vicious. The girl would invariably be turned off and reject him.

The first stage of his analysis revealed that the boy's mother had died when he was only three years old. At that young age, he was deeply dependent on her and wanted her complete love and attention. The need and desire were there, but at a primitive, almost savage level. The little boy was too young to have developed the tender feeling that we call "love." What he wanted was to suck his mother's breast, to dominate her completely. The child was shocked and hurt by his mother's death. When his care was taken over by a stepmother and sister, he developed a sarcastic, nasty attitude. Later this same sarcasm was used as his failure device on dates with girls. The young man's analyst perceived that his patient had been hurt at a vulnerable stage in forming relationships with women. He felt "rejected" by his mother and was too young to understand that she could not help dying and leaving him. His two desires as a child were: Get his mother back. Punish her for leaving him.

As an adult, the young man was still seeing his mother in every female he met, and this prevented him from making love to the girls; they were unconsciously linked to Mother. The young patient agreed with the analyst and tried to start sexual relationships with a *new* series of girls. Surprisingly, he repeated the same old pattern. Just as the girl seemed about to say yes, the young man insulted her. Then she would turn him down. He'd manufactured a cop-out.

Back to the analyst's couch for a *deeper* probing of this young man's unconscious brain. The doctor found he'd been on the right track, but there were even more serious (though still related) hangups. The patient confessed that in recurring fantasies and dreams he was always about to eat a hen's wing. Suddenly the wing turned into a girl's hand. The psychiatrist's interpretation: the young man had hidden oral, aggressive, sadistic drives. Because he was thwarted as a baby boy in obtaining his mother (and her breasts), he wanted to rip her apart, devour her flesh.

You see, the flip side of masochism is sadism. The young man really wanted to hurt girls, but he feared the results. He wouldn't let himself have sex with a girl, subconsciously afraid of hurting her (and eventually himself). So he drove women away from him before he got a chance to unleash his sadism. He chose to hurt himself instead of others. The sarcasm always worked; he was invariably rejected. The analyst used the analysis of nightmares and fantasies to guide his patient to conscious awareness of those deep urges and fears; and after many sessions the young man was able to face his hidden sadistic drives. Since he *wasn't* a psychotic, he was then able to work through his aggression in analysis. Remember, "blowing it" is the problem of neurotics. The psychotic, like the Boston Strangler or any compulsive killer, does not "blow it." He satisfies his sadistic urges in direct brutality. The neurotic is not dangerous to society because all the aggression is directed inward. The result: a man or a woman who can function in society at a reasonable level—someone who hurts only himself.

For a girl, the same neurosis can result from a poor relationship with her father. A harsh or absent father can do real harm to his daughter during the stage when every little girl wants to be "Daddy's darling." Children who are mistreated during this sensitive period of learning to relate well to adult men and women often grow up unable to form happy sexual relationships. Sometimes, as in the case of the young man, they can't establish any sex life at all. The girl who shuns all dates is "blowing it" as surely as the one who picks a string of losers. You must have known girls of this type. You may even *be* one. Take this quiz to see:

1. You have vestigial acne—and eat a chocolate bar every day.
2. Thirty pounds overweight, you've never found a diet that works for you . . . though you've tried three this week!

3. You forget to take the Pill sometimes, even though it wouldn't be exactly great to have a baby right now.

4. Every boss you've worked for has been mean, stupid, or held you back.

5. The men you meet always turn out to be bad for you.

6. You have a habit of oversleeping on big days—first day on the new job, your wedding day—or other calamities befall you.

7. Your dresses never last very long—you accidentally rip or strain them quite a bit.

8. The people you live with are hostile.

9. Sometimes you imagine you are Jackie Onassis.

10. If anyone points out that one of your disasters was your own fault, you're outraged.

If you've checked more than one of the above, you may need help. But *how* can you be kept from wrecking things for yourself? Analysis seems to be the answer, yet psychiatrists have to be careful in dealing with neurotics of this kind. Remember, self-induced failure is still a *protective* device, as we explained. *Without* the device of making himself fail, the neurotic could turn his aggressive urges outward and satisfy them by destroying *other people!* Edmund Bergler and other authorities insist that the analyst be careful not to halt treatment too soon. The doctor can't leave the patient *stranded* with her hatred and urge to destroy. At the crucial point in analysis, the patient will be open to her sadistic urges. The trick is to guide the neurotic *past* these primitive, destructive feelings, without letting her hide behind failures anymore. This means the doctor has to work through his patient's darkest, most savage desires *to hurt, tear, ravish, devour*. When the patient consciously recognizes these urges (as the young man did when he finally understood his cannibal dream), the analyst can lessen their intensity. Eventually, the patient can progress past the primitive drives into the realm of tender, mature love—for herself and for others. The guilt and fear that "I will do something terrible if I get my way—someone must stop me" will fade and free the patient to love and succeed.

HANDLE EVERY AFFAIR CRISIS . . . BEAUTIFULLY!

Finding a man, and *staying* with him, *ought* to be simple and natural. Yet, being happily mated—even for a time—is shatteringly difficult, and the long, hard road to successful togetherness is pitted with psychological potholes. Pairing in the seventies is even *more* complicated than for previous generations, because all of us are experiencing *heavy* social changes as male-female roles alter rapidly.

You are a *contemporary* girl, and must learn to thread your way through the maze of *new* man-woman relationships. It helps enormously to know you're not the *only* girl to face (and, alas, sometimes fail to overcome) the barriers that can block enjoyable coupling. We're *all* shooting the same emotional rapids (men, too!), and there isn't one of us who hasn't felt fear and panic trying to avoid the rocks along the way. Sometimes we blunder badly in an important liaison.

To help you steer a smoother course, here's savvy advice on dealing with nearly *every* affair crisis. If romantic misery is plaguing you now, or *ever* has knocked you flat, pack up these shrewd hints and press on. Pleasure-giving experience lies dead ahead.

AFFAIR BAROMETER

Every affair is problematic sometimes . . . but the turmoil should be *incidental* to the joy. Of course, *no* girl can make each exciting encounter an affair, or each affair *unremitting* pleasure. Still, by *pinpointing* problems, you can improve chances for success. Was your last affair, or is your current one, a source of more pain than pleasure? Take this quiz and see:

1. *Do you often wish it were as lovely as it was in the beginning?*
2. *Are you afraid he's going to leave you?*
3. *Do you frequently wonder if his past girls are prettier, smarter, sexier than you, and if you measure up?*
4. *Are you still waiting for him to shed his wife?*
5. *Do you like him less but need him more?*

YOUR BAROMETRIC RATING SCALE

4–5 noes Getting along with men may just come *naturally* to you, you lucky thing! At least, you make it *look* easy! Compare notes with our writers to add a trick or two to your *successful* repertory.

3 noes If you scored well on *three* questions, why not all? You *have* man-alluring skills—find out how to use them to *full* advantage.

2–0 noes Perhaps you feel victimized by uncontrollable urges—or an immature *man.* Don't let feelings of insecurity hold you back. You can move on to happier love affairs by reading the wide-ranging advice in this section.

WHY (SOB!) DIDN'T HE CALL? The way it happens in the movies *I've* seen is boy meets girl, boy chases girl, girl chases boy, then next day or year, depending on how *au courant* the film is, they wind up in bed. Fade out. Next scene, boy calls girl, who mumbles sleepily into phone that she feels *wonderful,* yum-yum; camera moves in on her languid smile that indicates sexual satisfaction . . . and, *zap,* they plunge into sunshiny affair, engagement, and/or marriage.

Hmmm . . . this cinematic myth needs some taking apart. For one thing (soft-focus film embraces notwithstanding), going to bed with anyone for the first time is *not* apt to be the most sensational sex thrill of a girl's life (it takes *time,* lovey), but, much worse, the morning-after call may never come . . . maybe you don't even get a "Dear Jane, I forgot to mention I'm married" note. He (who was *so* tender, so sexy *last* night) simply disappears, never again to return.

My guess is that if one were to conduct a secret poll to discover how many girls this has happened to, a new Silent Majority would emerge. Getting left after loving has happened to almost *everyone,* and the only reason you don't hear of these experiences as often as Big Romances and Wedding Bells is because having the fellow you liked enough to go to bed with disappear is not likely to be a favorite subject of conversation.

It's hard to find *anyone,* even a mother, who'll fall into a swoon anymore at the thought of a couple sleeping together before marriage . . . or even before they *know* each other well. Girls, however, are still *soppy* about sex, tending to subscribe to happy-ever-after myths and regarding sleeping with a new man as the Start of Something. When it turns out, instead, that bed is The End, the sexual-emotional whack in the stomach can leave you gasping.

A year ago I was badly shaken up by a series of just such emotional rebuffs. Are you up to hearing about them? I'd been enjoying the single life, freedom, a good job in advertising, my own apartment with a *real* fireplace and sensational river view . . . and was feeling very with-it and in-control. I'd recently emerged from two semiserious affairs that broke up more or less mutually, and without any badly hurt feelings on either side. (One of the men *was* a bit peevish when I said it was more "sensible" for us to stop seeing each other so much and lumbered out my door mumbling "rotten bitch." But, to be truthful, I was more flattered than injured by this bit of temper.)

The other affair ended when we reached the Marriage-or-Else point. A very serious young doctor had decided I was the perfect girl for him and wanted to do the whole marriage thing. Since my life struck me as quite delightful as it was, I chose Or Else, kept job and apartment, while the doctor, after insisting that I was making a terrible mistake, went off to find a girl who cared more for *him* and less for her freedom.

Then followed a summer romance with a political science graduate-student from Columbia whom I finally dropped because of his endless rambling about the ecology crisis (he insisted I bathe only once a week and complained every time I threw away a paper napkin).

As you see, *I* had been in control of my lovers' entrances and exits— which leads to certain good feelings for a girl. Life was indeed pleasant, until . . . I happened to get dropped by three men in a row! They, so to speak, never called back, and I began checking out mirrors for evidence of the uglies and listening closely to myself to see if I somehow sounded dumb or annoying or unfeminine. I didn't know what I was doing wrong —I assumed I *was* doing something wrong—three in a *row?* My up-to-that-time sturdy ego started crumbling like a butter cookie.

The series of self-defeating adventures began one dateless, boring evening when I decided to try one of New York's East Side "singles" bars. I thought I'd *probably* meet nothing but creeps, but what could I lose? So on to Maxwell's Plum, where a lovely-looking lawyer (and definite non-creep) almost immediately offered an Irish coffee, and, after introductions that New York's singles consider sufficient, but neither Amy Vanderbilt nor my Aunt Evelyn would approve, we spent a pleasant evening of conversation, finishing up in a state of cozy togetherness in my bed. This I expected to be the *beginning* of a romance, not the finish, but the finish it *was*. I'd confidently expected him to call the next day; he didn't . . . nor the day after that, nor ever! At this point I wasn't crushed, merely puzzled and annoyed. This sort of experience definitely didn't fit into my life plan, but then surely it would never happen *again*!

After a week of mild moping and paying special attention to the phone that sat there like a great plastic clam, I put myself together, decided he had been some kind of nut, and set out again. There followed a two-week something—not an affair exactly, but a new friendship that involved sex, dating, quiet dinners in little French restaurants, plus flurries of whispery phone calls. The man, whom I will be happy someday to forget, was a thirty-five-year-old advertising executive who mumbled about his wonderful children and a wife in Bedford Village who loved interior decorating more than him. If only his wife (who was frigid) were more like *me* in bed. One week after we met, he moved out of the Yale Club and into my apartment, and I began to feel all snuggly and cared-for. Then—zap—four days later he evaporated, returning, no doubt, to those children he loved and the wife he didn't. I was left feeling rather *used*; I had been the young swinger who held his hand while he demonstrated to his wife (and himself) that he could still "get" another girl. Swell!

Somewhat battered, I approached my married older sister for sympathy and advice. Elaine had married right out of high school, was raising two children, and had never *had* any problems like mine. "Jan, you're becoming hard," she said. "You should stop running around, get married and settle down." (Elaine divides people into great, simple categories—hard, soft; good, bad; our sort, not our sort.)

I couldn't explain to Elaine that what appeared to her to be aimless (or promiscuous) drifting had for me an important purpose. I was searching for a *relationship* . . . for a man who would make me feel vital and feminine. I wanted to love and be loved, but what I was finding was straight sex, unencumbered by tenderness.

Then at a party I met Allen, a quiet, rather shy man, and decided, between one vodka tonic and the next, that he was for me. We talked for hours, discovered that we both liked cross-country skiing, tennis, murder mysteries, and chiliburgers. Later at my place we sipped coffee and brandy until three in the morning, talked some more, and (surprise!) finished up in my bed.

The next day we listened to records, ate my special chiliburgers, and chattered for the entire gray, lovely, stay-by-the-fire day. He said good-bye, all sweet and friendly, caressing my hair and gently kissing the tip of my nose, and that, my dear, was his final exit. He didn't even call with any funny excuses like he had to go back to his wife and seven children or send a bunch of dusty daisies and a note: "I love you, but the Peace Corps must always come first." Nor did he invite me to lunch to explain that he was already involved. Nothing—he just dematerialized like an enchanted fairy-tale prince.

One Thursday life had seemed cheery and brimming with promise, the next it was pointless and gray. I felt wounded (still do) by the encounter. Instead of promptly dismissing Allen as a "bad experience," my mind would return again and again to the place the pain was. For days my three-in-the-morning relivings of this experience would fill me with combined rage, desolation, and bafflement. I would go over every moment we had spent together, *analyzing* everything. I believed there must be some Secret Reason why he hadn't returned. If only I could reconstruct the moment when I had made my *mistake.*

A few of the brilliant insights I had at this time: I had been too *easy.* If only I had been coy and made him wait before taking me to bed. My delight over our shared interests (like chiliburgers) had struck him as naïve. My apartment was too cluttered and messy. I talked too much and intimidated him by my incessant chatter. I didn't talk enough and had been stultifyingly boring.

I kept going round and round, returning each time to square one, with nothing (no insight) gained. Then for the next few weeks I behaved like a heroine from grand opera. I wore black in deference to my broken heart, stopped wearing makeup (what good would it do to try and be attractive?), skipped jolly lunches with friends, and declined party invitations. Finally, I got very *bored* with being sad. It was, after all, spring; hyacinths were blooming all over New York, and I felt too young and vibrant to keep playing Camille. I went out and bought a nifty pink coat and was myself again.

But cautious.

I wanted to go on living the single life, and, sure, I planned to keep on sleeping with men, but I didn't want my tender little feelings stomped on anymore. I mean, men didn't have to marry you straight off, but they didn't have to go sneaking off like kleptomaniacs. Or did they?

It occurred to me that, since I couldn't go off and live in an Eskimo settlement where love and sex are simple things, perhaps I ought to find out more *about* the complicated urban man I was dealing with. I hadn't been away from the small town I grew up in *that* long. To begin my search for insights, I talked to the six girls who came to brunch one Sunday afternoon in my apartment. We ranged in age from a sophisticated twenty-two to a fat, too-innocent thirty-seven-year-old, and it wasn't too hard to interest all six in discussing the behavior of the vanishing male (now you see him, now you don't). Certainly all six of us knew some, and none of us was shy about sharing experiences.

Helen, a petite photographer's stylist, offered this experience: "I got this tremendous rush from a photographer—you know, Charlie of the runny vermilion sunsets. There were calls, flowers, lunches, dinners, perfectly chosen presents, until, O.K., I go to bed with him. I wasn't mad for him, but he was persistent; sleeping with me seemed to be the most important thing in his entire life, and he was so *nice*. Anyway, he staged the grand seduction scene one night in his studio and then, good-bye Charlie. Just like that. How was I to know that he was Charlie the Collector, chasing me the way a trophy hunter stalks an impala? As soon as I was added to his collection, he was gone. Yes, I went right into shock!"

Mary, my oldest friend in the city, added *her* offering. "Your collector sounds like my Don Juan. His name is Harrison, actually . . . short, going a bit bald . . . you couldn't call him good-looking, but attractive all the same . . . charm oozing from every pore, really *clever* compliments. When he came to pick me up for a date, he had a way of standing there in the doorway, silent for a minute, looking as if he were *stunned* by my beauty. He really was too much to be true, but I loved the way he made me feel and wept bitter tears when he moved on to the next engagement. I had to find out the worst way—by gradually hearing from other girls—

that he lavished those special attentions on *every* girl he took out . . . and to bed."

Francoise, a French girl who'd been working in New York for three years as a designer, asked, "'Ave you evair run up against zose married heroes of zuh commuter train? Zay take off zair vedding rings and stick zem in zair vallets on zuh nights zay stay een town. *Alors,* zay sink zay 'ave a better chance to get you eento bed eef you sink zay are available, vich, of course, is *vrai.* Steel, eet eez a rotten trick. *Bof!* You hear sings like 'nevair call my offeece because I 'ave a *secrétaire* who eez een love viz me and jalouz.' So, you go along viz zees but een zuh back of your brain, zere's a leetle signal going beep, beep, zuh whole time, only you don't leesten. Zen when you sink eet eez becoming a lovely romance, he decides you are getting too demanding and—zut!—zat's zuh last you see of heem."

And so it went with the others at our little brunch . . . Serena and Audrey next in line to talk about *their* men who took off without explanations. Serena's was a secret homosexual. Audrey's—when he *did* call a year later—told her he'd had severe emotional problems at the time she came into his life—hah!—and wasn't really up to sustaining a new relationship.

Serena tried to reason for all of us. "Look, none of us can expect to avoid ever being hurt, but there's such a thing as common sense, I guess. I think maybe you have to *know* the man you're dealing with. Some people you can really *know* in just a few days, but with others it takes two or three months. I've decided maybe it isn't *necessary* to pop into bed with a man just because you're feeling horny and he's a honey bug. He may put on a big act and accuse you of being a prude or, worse than that, a tease, but it's just an act. If he really likes you, he'll wait out a few dates while you figure out if you two have enough in common or whether he's going to be *around* long enough to have an affair with. If he *is* a 'collector' and in a big hurry because others are waiting to be seduced—and dropped —just like you, who *needs* him?!"

I then contributed my sad story of Allen, soul mate for a day. The six of us kicked *that* experience around for a bit, agreed he probably wasn't a homosexual or secretly married or anything, but merely one of your simple, old-fashioned, chase–score–on-to-the-next-girl types. (I *still* don't know. Maybe he did hate my apartment!)

So the little soul-therapy brunch being over, it was time to ask some men: how does the *enemy* explain the phenomenon of the Disappearing Lover?

I questioned my *friends*—of whom I had some by now . . . Good Guys, not Bastards . . . your average nice man that most of us marry someday. All of them admitted, with varying degrees of guilt, they *had* slept with girls in whom they'd had only a minimal or sexual interest. And, yes, they *were* sometimes aware that the girl had a heavier emotional investment than they. Villains! Exploiters! Actually, all I could conclude was that even the nicest, most loving man acts the "bastard" at some time or other. (To be fair, haven't most *girls* played the *bitch*? This is me with my new compassion and insight speaking!) Here's what a couple of them said.

Evans, who has recently become engaged "after ten energy-draining, fantastic, girl-chasing" years, said, "Sex alone isn't going to hold a man. Fifty years ago maybe, when nonvirgins were considered 'ruined,' so a man really appreciated a revved-up girl who 'went all the way,' sex may have had quite a bit of clout, but now that it's considered a treat for everybody, not just a man, nobody's going to feel overcome with guilt or gratitude just because a girl goes to bed with you.

"Of course, many women *still* put a lot more emotional steam into a relationship than a man does. Some girls do it with *everybody* they go to bed with . . . bed automatically has to mean love, marriage, and foreverness. Well, a man doesn't go that far all the time. Eventually, he'll fall in love as deeply and permanently as a woman, but I know a lot of men who've forgotten the names of girls they had affairs with." (And, of course, many women have comparable stories.)

My friend Martin offered these observations: "When a man takes you to bed, in a certain sense he's 'trying you out.' Not just sexually, though that's a part of it—you want to see how well you can *relate* to this particular girl. And if you find there isn't much there, maybe you do 'disappear.' Girls, for God's sake, do exactly the same thing—though sometimes you're not so abrupt about it. You tell us you've washed your hair or have to work or you're leaving for Greece the next day. The trouble is that when a man doesn't come back, some girls take this kind of rejection much more seriously than they should just because sex *has* been involved. They feel they've 'given themselves'—sounds like something out of *Little Women*—or some such nonsense, when, in truth, *both* parties have been experimenting."

Mack, a thirty-three-year-old divorced lawyer, said, "The worst mistake a girl can make is *using* sex to get a man to like her. That is a very bad kind of insecurity and a real turnoff. If I like a girl, I'm going to like her with or without sex. That doesn't mean I'm going to wait an eternity before she 'gives in.' To hell with that! But I will wait a reasonable amount of time. I know girls need to build up a certain degree of trust before they can relax and really respond sexually. To me, this trait is very feminine and appealing. I *like* to wait a little bit myself."

Mike, a never-married, handsome (*not* gay) photographer, was particularly candid: "You're going to hate me," he said, "but I can't help trying to charm most of the girls I take out right into bed. Then sometimes sex leads to a relationship, sometimes not. *I* don't even know beforehand whether it will. I never pretend emotions I don't feel or say things I don't mean. If I tell a girl I think she's beautiful, I *do* think she's beautiful, but that doesn't mean I want to marry her or even have a prolonged affair. I think girls should be more realistic and stop expecting love to bloom every time they make it with a man."

So what's it all about, Alfie, and what *are* we supposed to do to cope with our terror and hurt when a man (sob!) doesn't call back? I guess we try to stop thinking we're a special kind of loser or a "victim." We're simply part of a system (a little bit like "tipping" or the electoral college that have both their good and bad points)! Talking to my friends convinced me that most men (not just the sickies or the Don Juans) *are* still a little *predatory* when it comes to sex. They are still the aggressors, and a certain degree of opportunism is built *into* that role. Sure, a girl can sleep with anyone she wants, but she shouldn't expect banjos and rainbows every time out. Some one-time lovers *are* trophy hunters, Don Juans, latent homosexuals, or married men on the prowl. But a man can disappear and *not* be a superrat. He's just after a different (not necessarily better, merely *different*) kind of girl.

And so I can only suggest that if your ego is demolished every time a bed mate neglects to offer undying love, the only sensible course is to choose your sex partners *very* carefully. Get them pretty much in love with you *before* making love. There's nothing quite so satisfactory as a really "hooked" man.

The other alternative is to be smart enough to realize that sex is often just that . . . *sex* . . . and not necessarily the beginnings of love. (Oh, sex *can* be . . . you can even hope *will* be . . . the start of Something Wonderful, but don't count on it.) When you go to bed with a new man, you are exploring . . . which is an unsure business at best. Uncertain for the man, too—what about the lovers who did come back to find *you* not wanting *them*?

Many girls (including *me* in my more self-pitying moods) are still not entirely free of the clichés of the old morality . . . when a lover disappears, you've been "used" (why, for God's sake? . . . you enjoyed it, too), "seduced and abandoned" (come on, nobody made any promises), or even "slutty" (the double standard raises its hoary head). Lots of girls behave like paradigms of a free-living, sexually emancipated age but have a set of emotional responses little different from Grandma's. And this discrepancy is not only confusing to the girl *and* her man, for the girl it can be absolutely *painful*. It's up to *you* to close the gap between the way you feel and how you act. When you finally accomplish this, you'll know the difference between a Brief Encounter and a Great Love . . . and be able to enjoy both!

WHAT—
ME MARRY?

Don't get me wrong. I love the domestic life. I love coddling eggs for a supper for two. I love kindling the fire when the shades are low and the fi is high. I love the Sunday puzzle with a Sunday man who knows the right answers.

It's just that I'm a Devout Romantic. From my observation, marriage turns men to mush and bliss to blahs. That's why I'd rather be a Cave Woman than a Bride in a Gelded Cage.

Like the cave folk of old, I've carved out a cozy lair in the side of a cliff—mine happens to be in Manhattan—and go foraging for food and furs. I scout the bushes for warm companions, not with a club but with the tenderest of trappings to bring 'em back alive and kicky.

I didn't start out to be a Cave Woman. I was all set to be dominated and adored by some delicious man. I even learned how to iron shirts. What's happened instead is the blurring of sexual roles. Men are opting out of their traditional jobs as ruler and rooster. Such is the resistance to commitment that the simple decisions of where to have dinner and what movie to see can become major traumas.

Rather than watch myself turn into a tight-lipped traffic cop instead of the warm, juicy, grabby lady that I am, there was no choice but to open my own cave. It's a thrilling, exuberant way to live . . . and avoid most of boredom's obvious traps.

The Cave Woman fends for herself, so she develops a sharp sense of her own identity. Challenge keeps her fleet of foot, firm of flesh, keen of wit. The Cave Woman lives every minute to its fullest and savors every second. She enjoys options married ladies don't have, among them privacy on demand and great expectations. Anything can happen and usually does. She is never bored. Exhausted maybe, but never tired. Fighting for survival is basic and therefore her life-style is basic, too.

Living alone doesn't mean loneliness. The Cave Woman treasures her quiet times and uses them with primitive cunning. Alone, with the phone in a drawer, she rests and makes needed repairs on her hunting equipment for future forays.

My own cave has that loved-in look. It smiles and comforts me. In anthropological terms, I'm a Neo-Tactile. I like stuff I can touch. Gleamy brass. Grainy wood. Cool glass. Deep pile. Crisp sheets. Hot baths.

As a Cave Woman, I make my own bed and I don't have to lie when I get into it. I make my own rules and live and love by them. Because I've learned to be responsible for myself, I can feel responsibility for others.

The Cave Woman's mating instincts are sharpened by experience. She becomes selective and wise to the nature of the chase. She understands the territorial imperative and the ways of the naked ape.

She learns how to play the waiting game. When she finally spots a likely mate, she knows how to lure him with her scent and maybe a few strategic bread crumbs until one dark night when, baby, it's cold outside, there comes a craving beast, tired of the prowl and wanting in.

That's when Cave Woman caves in—and sets up the ironing board.

3

YOU LOVE HIM MORE THAN HE LOVES YOU

Donna cries herself to sleep at least two nights a week these days. She's been engaged to Tim for almost a month now, and she's spent a big part of that time in tears. The other secretaries in her office keep a special supply of Kleenex on hand to bring over to her phone when he calls. (Or when he's supposed to and doesn't—which is what usually happens.)

Donna's a romantic. When she was a little girl she dreamed of marrying a man who would send her dozens and dozens of long-stemmed roses. Tim never sends her roses. In fact he hardly pays *any* attention to her.

Donna hoped he'd spend a little less time on business and a little more on her now that they're engaged. But nothing has changed. Half the time when they have a lunch date, he never turns up at all. She still adores him—but doesn't see how she can possibly marry him; of course, she doesn't see how she can possibly *not* marry him, either. So she cries and cries and cries.

Isabel isn't the crying kind. She picks at her cuticles and doesn't eat and sits up until three in the morning watching two movies at once on TV.

Isabel's problem is Patrick, a photographer. She met him underwater off Cozumel during her last vacation in Mexico. "I thought you were a shark," she laughed when he surfaced right beside her, a lobster clutched in each hand.

She didn't know it then, but she was right. He is a shark. And girls like Isabel are his favorite fish. Pretty but still not really believing it; on the way up but still not terribly sure of herself. Well-practiced Patrick knew all the right buttons to push. Said all the things she was longing to hear. Isabel was in love before they even got back to the beach.

After a travel-folder week in the sun they flew to New York together. Patrick had planned to go on to Yucatan, but when he discovered Isabel was a fashion editor he decided she might be useful. And of course she was . . . in every way *he* needed.

Patrick moved right into her apartment, and Isabel was delighted. She left a breakfast tray for him every morning when she went off to work, sent his suits to the cleaners, and lent him cash (until some "expected" checks could arrive). Deep in dreams of happy endings, it's taken Isabel weeks even to admit that Patrick has been acting badly. Standing her up. Putting her down. Making passes at her friends. Using her name and influence to bribe his way around. She loves him more than ever, but she doesn't really *like* him so much anymore. Patrick has taken so much more than he gives.

Carol *has no such ambivalence about Ben.* She knows very well how she feels about him—she wants him to divorce the wife he outgrew long ago and marry *her*.

After nine years of kicking around the world as an airline public relations girl, Carol found that Ben was the one man she'd ever met who made her want to settle down. She dreamed of an old stone country house, breakfast on the patio, and fabulous dinner parties for Ben's envious law partners. The only trouble is that Ben's *already* so settled down (with another woman) she can't seem to grab hold of him anywhere.

They spend a lot of time together and she knows he cares for her, but he always manages to keep things very, very cool. (Ben's an expert at switching the subject whenever he senses she wants to be serious.)

They meet for lunch, occasionally go to press parties, and usually have a drink somewhere just before he catches his train home. (It's practically impossible, Carol's discovered, to start up a passionate conversation in Schrafft's.) Although she spends a lot of energy trying, she rarely gets him to come up to her apartment. When he does—usually on his way to or from business out of town—they are as perfect together in bed as they are everywhere else. But he hasn't the slightest intention of marrying her and she knows it.

Three girls who love their men more than their men love them back. Is it the same with *you*? Tenderly, trustingly, you hand over your heart (on the very best silver platter you can find) only to see it being chopped up for hors d'oeuvres (like Isabel with her photographer), nibbled casually around the edges (like Carol with her lawyer), or (like Donna most of the time with Tim) just left lying there on the plate.

The man who doesn't love back isn't the one who dates you once or twice and then disappears (that hurts, too, of course, but it's blessedly quick—like a needle given by a nurse who knows how). This man's the one who *stays* in your life. You may go with him for months or years, you may even *marry* him, or he may just turn up often enough to keep you from falling for anyone else. Maybe he *means* to be mean. Maybe not. Maybe he never gives it much thought one way or the other. Whatever his methods or motives, the man who doesn't love you *enough* keeps you miserable most of the time.

Is there anything a girl can *do* about this painful kind of mess? Unhappily, there are almost as many you-love-him-more-than-he-loves-you situations as there are girls to be in them, and each one will have its own unique solution. Still, there are some basic rules that make sense no matter which particular kind of heartache you find yourself in.

The main thing not to do is just sit there—crying or drinking or picking at your hangnails or whatever—waiting for *him* to decide he really adores and appreciates you. Because chances are he won't. (About the only thing he's likely to think of on his own is to up and leave—especially if you're always crying or drinking or picking at your hangnails.) You're the one who wants to push the relationship forward, right? Well then, you're obviously the one who's going to have to make it happen.

Equally important is not to try to turn back the clock. Too many girls in this fix hope to return to that first incandescent passion. Make everything just the way it was in the beautiful beginning (when at least you *thought* he loved you, which is one of the reasons you fell for him in the first place). The Greeks said it: You can't step in the same river twice. No way!

They try coaxing ("Let's go to that darling little place with tables in the garden where we went the night we first made love"). Complaining ("Why don't you ever call me 'Muffin' anymore?"). And keeping score ("You know you only telephoned me *four* times this week?"). And of course it doesn't work. This kind of pressure is positively guaranteed to send any lover scrambling madly for the nearest escape. Isabel tried it with Patrick, the photographer, and look what happened to her.

"If I can only get things back the way they were in Cozumel," she told herself, "it will be all right." She revived the little pet names they'd used the very first week, stayed home from the office a lot so they could "be together," began every other sentence with "Remember when?"

But the closer she tried to get to Patrick, the more outrageously he behaved; the more romantic she tried to be, the less he made love to her. The only thing that finally *did* happen was that he left her for a skinny little model he met at one of her champagne brunches.

You can't turn a relationship back. Good or bad, it changes, grows.

But forcing things forward doesn't help any, either, when you love him more than he loves you. Donna was unhappy with the way Tim treated her long before she finally got him to propose. Once he was officially hers he'd change, she *thought,* but she was mistaken.

A man who is reluctant or unable—or just too busy—to show affection isn't going to suddenly start kissing your wrists in restaurants and telephoning every fifteen minutes just because you maneuver him into an engagement.

You can't force a man to love you—you can only try to make him want to. Which is why tightening your grip—a perfectly understandable temptation when you feel something slipping out of your hands—is precisely the wrong move to make in this situation. (It's rather like trying to grab a cake of soap in the tub—the simple pressure of your fingers closing around it makes it shoot off in another direction.)

W*hat you should do—the very first, most basic thing—is let go a little.* Cool it a bit. This doesn't mean breaking up (you may have to do that later, but now it's too soon to tell). Just stop crowding him, overwhelming him with your love—which may be quite a load for him to carry around. No more silly presents, calling him at the office, blowing in his ear every time the two of you are alone in an elevator.

Like a judo defense, this will momentarily disarm him and, at the same time, make you seem more interesting. ("What is she *up* to?" he'll be asking himself—a question no man can resist.) It will also give you a chance to try to figure out just what is (or is not) going on. *Something's* wrong between you. Maybe you can fix it, maybe you can't, but one thing's certain, you'll never have a chance to repair the trouble if you don't find out what it is.

So, try hard to go along with being cool and newly interesting, and also try the following:

1. *Get an outside opinion.* You may just need a fresh look at the agonizing relationship. You're too close, in too deep. Look around to see who you can talk with to get some perspective. His best friend: "Charlie's desperately afraid of *more* financial responsibility. You know his mother's sick and yet, Tina, *you* keep talking about how you hate your job and want to quit it." Your best friend (she may not *want* to tell you what she thinks, so you'll have to insist): "Everyone knows that Jeff likes girls . . . he just does. About the only way you can succeed is not to be jealous but to be a living, laughing, sunny, smiling *doll* in comparison to them all."

You could also ask someone who has handled (successfully) the kind of difficult situation you're in now. Don't think you're the *only* one.

2. *When you're with him, stop talking so much. Listen for a change.* A girl in your fix is obviously nervous. But maybe all the time you've been babbling on about how your cousin's wedding was so beautiful it made you want to cry (hint, hint), he's been trying to *tell* you something. He may even have been trying to say that he loves you, who knows?

Even if you don't get a proposal, though, you're sure to come up with some clues. What is he talking about these days—how the fact that so many girls have stopped wearing bras has certainly livened up lunch hour at the company cafeteria? (Maybe he wants more—livelier—love-making.) A new author he's discovered who lives all by himself in a mountain cabin? (Maybe you've been pushing him about responsibility and material things.) The loudmouth account executive who's just been transferred to his office? (Is he afraid he's going to lose his job?)

3. *Sum it all up.* Ability to state a problem simply is one of the first steps in solving it. Hard as it may be to step outside of something that matters so much to you, it will be an enormous help if you can get some perspective.

One way to do this is by putting the whole thing down on paper. List his good points and not-so-good ones (and the same for you), what you have the most fun doing and what you're most likely to quarrel over, what you think you are each gaining from the relationship and what you may be losing or giving up. Your goals—what would you each like to be doing five or ten years from now? Include everything you can think of, but be honest. Remember by all means that he takes you exciting places, but if he went out in the kitchen and made a pass at your friends' baby-sitter smack in the middle of a quiet little supper party, remember that, too. (Don't laugh. A no-goodnik I was once involved with did just that.)

When you're done, read it all over and see if you can figure out what the basic problem is.

Another way to get perspective is to go away somewhere alone. For many girls this results in instant insight. Others are so miserable missing Henry the whole time that it doesn't accomplish anything. You know which type you are.

Using these methods—either a list, a think-trip, or whatever version of them works for you—you'll probably make some discoveries about him, yourself, and what's happening between you. Here are some of the possibilities (and what to do about them).

The trouble is with him:

• *He's an utter louse and it's hopeless.* You may not express it quite so harshly, but if your friends and the facts point the way (he cheats, lies, beats you up, takes your money to spend on other girls), try to face it; he's a professional rat. The only good things you can think of about him are that he taught you how to dive off the high board and how to do the *merengue.*

Better get away before he does you any *more* damage, and—just as important—ask yourself why you ever tangled with him in the first place.

"The girl who falls in love with this kind of man must do some serious thinking about her need for punishment," warns Dr. Tom Leland, Atlanta psychotherapist and associate editor of *Voices,* a journal published by the American Academy of Psychotherapists.

If this is your first louse, be careful. If it's your fifth, you need help. (More about this later.)

• *He's a bit of a bounder but if you handle him differently he may improve.* One girl's louse is another girl's Valentine. An early louse in my life, then a dashing medical student, is now a docile dentist married to a somewhat dumpy lass who keeps him tightly on a leash in Nutley, N.J. I'm told he even carries out the garbage every night. Obviously, she knew something about handling him that I didn't.

If he's generally a good guy and just behaves badly sometimes (or in some areas), take a look at your role in the affair. He drinks too much? You nurse him like a child at hangover time, tell them at his office it's his asthma again. He borrows money and never pays it back? You never *ask* him for it, saying it's worth anything just to be with him. As a personal guru of mine points out, it takes two to tango. Let him know you expect better behavior and maybe you'll get it.

• *He has problems.* Homosexual tendencies, a sick (and therefore undivorceable) wife, a superpowerful mother. In cases like this the decision is a delicate one.

If he has homosexual leanings, is trying to go straight and in analysis— well, *maybe* you'll want to see it through. On the other hand, if the first you knew of his leanings was when you caught him making a pass at your brother, that's obviously another matter. If his wife has a chronic disease that keeps her helpless—well, maybe. If, like an actor I know of, he's using the fact to get sympathy (and other things) from a whole bunch of girls—well, no.

One point, though. If you do decide to stick with him and help him over whatever it is, keep in mind that once he's over it, he may also be over *you.* You could be a reminder of a bad time in his life.

• *He just can't love very much.* He's perfectly willing to let you love *him,* but he isn't able to love back.

A lot of men simply aren't capable of a really passionate relationship. They may have had mothers who rejected them (and made them everlastingly leery about getting too close to a woman again). They may have been only children (and, lacking brothers or sisters, never learned how to have an equal relationship). Or they may have been taught so well to conceal their feelings that they don't know how to do anything else.

A kind of subhead in this category is men who are totally wrapped up in their businesses or careers, including many (but by no means all) artists, composers, actors, and so on.

A relationship with such a man can be a perfectly good and satisfying one if you accept it for what it is and don't try to turn it into a romantic fairy tale. Dynamic men are often so compelling that many women are happy to be a little less conventionally adored in exchange for being a lot more fascinated. (After all, how much time does Ari actually spend with Jackie?)

• *He loves you but he doesn't want to talk about it all the time.* I know a girl who broke up with a perfectly marvelous man because he refused to send her a card for Valentine's Day. Your man may be perfectly content with you, *showing* you he loves you in a lot of different ways, but he may not want to have to tell you every five minutes. He may be shy, not much of a talker, or—like my friend's former friend—he may resent the fact that you keep *pestering* him about it. (Making the symbol more important than the *thing* is the way he put it.) Stop bothering him.

The trouble is with you:

• *You need unhappy affairs.* You bounce from one bounder to the next, complaining as you go about how *tragic* life is. As far as you're concerned there are just two kinds of men—the nice ones (who always turn out to be dull) and the interesting ones (who always turn out to be mean).

"Our culture has produced a lot of girls like this," says Dr. Leland, "filled with guilt. Unconsciously, they're *looking* for men who will treat them badly. They feel that sex is dirty or that girls aren't supposed to be sexual or simply that *they* don't deserve to be happy. Such a girl may not need to be chained in bed to have an orgasm, but she does need guilt-relieving punishment to be able to enjoy a relationship with a man. Falling in love with a rat is the perfect solution." (Such girls have been helped with therapy, of course.)

Most people feel that every girl ought to be allowed one or two disastrous love affairs (she doesn't have to *want* them). But when you can look back and can tick off at least eight horrible men who've nearly undone you, you have to see there's a pattern, don't you? In that case the trouble isn't really him but *you*, and it would probably be better to check in with somebody who can help (doctor, therapy group) than try to straighten out this particular love affair.

• *You don't love yourself enough.* No man can make you happy if you're not happy with yourself. If you need to be constantly reminded how beautiful, clever, attractive, and *needed* you are, that may be more insecurity than the man can cope with. Do you keep talking yourself down? Then you must *do* something to try to like yourself. (If *you* don't, why should anyone else?) The superficial things are to have your makeup done over by an expert, get a new hairstyle, take courses in a subject that interests you until you get to be really good at it. Many girls have achieved success in business—they tried harder—and "bought" themselves considerably more self-confidence and, concomitantly, serenity in love.

• *You fall in love too fast.* The girl who gets drunk on a man the night she meets him is setting herself up for an emotional morning-after. Take another look before handing over your heart. Try to be a little more sure of yourself—and of him. The signs of trouble ahead are usually there *if* you aren't so anxious for this to be "it" that you refuse to see them.

He leaves a bottle of Scotch in your apartment with a line drawn on it so you can't drink any when he's not there? How *can* you be amazed when he turns out to be a domineering tightwad? He never answers the phone when you're in his apartment? You can be pretty sure that one day you'll be calling and he won't be answering for you, either.

"Be suspicious of anyone who comes on too slick or too fast," warns Dr. Leland. "The man who is genuinely interested will be a little bit worried—about his reception from *you* and about whether he really wants to get deeply involved."

• *You expect too much.* Maybe he's giving you trouble because of what you're doing to him? Maybe you're acting like a spoiled little girl, and the more he gives you the more you demand. Maybe *not*, of course, but it's worth asking yourself. Think about your last two annoyances with him . . . were *you* being selfish and greedy?

The trouble is with the two of you:

• *You met him too soon* . . . "I am forty-four years old and the perfect, ideal husband," declared French singer Charles Aznavour, adding, "I would have made a horrible husband in my thirties." And what's true for Charles Aznavour is true for a great many men. Maybe yours. Maybe he just hasn't aged enough. It's rotten luck but there's nothing you can do but have fun while it lasts (and it will last longer if you don't try to turn it into something serious). Timing is all.

• *. . . or too late.* The same holds true if he's much, much older and married. Maybe he really does wish he'd met you first. But it's too late now. He's basically a decent sort, and while he'd *like* to marry you, he feels responsible for too many people who'd be hurt if he did. For every man who leaves his wife for a more fascinating girl there are still hundreds who'd love to but *don't*.

If you can stand to have just part of him, O.K. If that's not enough, you really should keep looking until you find a man who can give you as much as you need.

• *You're going in different directions.* A friend of mine who roamed through Spain with an actor had the good sense to leave him after six months. She adored him and was having a ball but she knew that wasn't what she wanted to do for the rest of her life. Now she's living more or less happily in California with her chemist husband—and some interesting memories.

If he wants to go to Alaska and you dream of Acapulco, if he's thinking of going around the world on a motorcycle and you want to build a house in Seattle—well, there's nothing wrong with either of you but it's probably not going to work for very long. Face it—then enjoy it. Have some fun and go your separate ways while you still like each other. That basic American myth that every romance has to turn into a permanent thing has *really* got to go.

These are some of the possible situations you may find yourself in the middle of. Discover the one that you think fits you, decide what to do, and then *do* it, even though it won't be easy at the start. (The very act of having *decided* something can be a heart balm.)

If you've sworn to stop pestering him, *stop.* If you're never going to say another word about getting married, bite your tongue when you're tempted. Keep an extra good watch on yourself in the wee, cozy hours and/or when you've had a bit too much to drink. Consistency is the watchword. If your behavior begins to lurch from one extreme to the other, you'll just make him even more nervous than he was before.

The same goes if you've decided to break it off—*really* decided and not just trying to blackmail him. If he's too "expensive" emotionally and you can no longer stand the pain this romance inflicts, then force yourself to go through with it and plan every step of the way. Tell him, as calmly as you can and at a time when you absolutely *must* be somewhere else shortly afterward, that you're taking a "vacation." Then simply don't see or talk to him anymore. Rehearse beforehand what you'll say and do if you run into him unexpectedly. *Don't* fight with him—that shows all too well how much you still care. Act cool and disinterested and keep at it. The hardest part is the beginning, and if you let him coax you (or charm you) into seeing or talking to him "one more time," you'll just be extending the agony. Stay busy, see people, expect withdrawal symptoms (bad ones), but keep reminding yourself what things were like at their worst. You don't really want to go back to *that*, do you?

Whatever you decide to do, don't expect a big, happy change immediately. It will take time—to get used to being without him or to a new way of being *with* him. Either way, though, it will be far better than continuing to love him too much much more than he loves you.

4

I'M JUST A GIRL WHO CAN SAY NO

It's bye-bye time at the old front door! "I certainly enjoyed the evening."

"You mean . . . you're actually throwing me out?"

"I had a wonderful time and I hope we see each other again."

"You mean you're throwing me out!"

Shock. Rage. Sneer. What's the matter with you; it's not as if you're some kind of virgin or something. What's the matter with you; after all, he spent forty bucks on dinner. What's the matter with you; you've done it for other guys, so why not him!

Yes, I've done it before. Yes, I have every urgent hope of doing it again. With style and enthusiasm. But with whom and under what impulse or circumstances is entirely up to me . . . no explanations or apologies required.

Women's sexual freedom is gravely misunderstood by many men. The freedom is actually twofold: the freedom from fear of pregnancy and the freedom of choice. Too many men (generally the type who thinks from the waist down) tend to emphasize the first syllable, *free*, leaving unspoken the last—which becomes an ironic comment on their dim perception, *dumb*.

What the emancipated woman must remember is that sexual freedom does not mean sex on demand. That is not freedom but another form of sexual tyranny. Not only that, the logic is false, and there are further dangers of exhaustion and dulling of the senses from misuse.

For the sexually motivated, sex is no longer a simple matter of saying Yes or No, of being Good or Bad. Oddly enough, women seem to understand the nuances of sexual freedom better than the men who have always had it.

The male vocabulary is still distressingly riddled with expressions of sexual exploitation. Touching and dopey at times, these phrases—and the men who use them—have little to do with The Way Things Are. I'm talking about men who *score* with chicks, *hustle* broads, joylessly set out to add a notch. Repellent and pathetic at the same time, they still operate on the religious belief in dinner as a trade deal and calisthenics as part of the package.

The chief basis of illogic is the assumption that a girl's virginity is like a bottle of champagne . . . and once the cork pops, whoopee, it's an endless party, everyone get in line.

"You do it for other guys, why not me?"

The point is, I don't do it *for* other guys. I do it *with* a man I want. *It* is not dessert. I am not a service station. Nor am I a knothole, health club, roadside rest, surrogate mom, or one of those late-night deposits so cherished by banks.

First Times are still first times for me. The sentimental worship of defloration has not only been overdone in fiction and verse—generally by middle-aged adolescents—but is also self-canceling. It is my conviction that a First Time with a New Man be a voyage of discovery, innocence revisited with the added pride and confidence that come from having known other faces, other rooms.

I insist on enjoying my sexual freedom on my terms, on terms that ennoble me and in ways that respect sexuality as a gift of nature to be exquisitely savored rather than mindlessly squandered.

Yes, I will live through the bad-mouth whining at the old front door. Yes, I will sometimes sleep alone in my big brass bed. Yes, even though I am plenty good at saying Yes, I can also—and *will* also—say No.

When my pinball buzzer throbs and flashes "Yes," it will be "Yes, my darling." But when the icy arrow points to gloom, then it's game called, thanks awfully, go away. Love will come another day.

5

WHY PACKAGE SEX IN A LOVE BAG?

No, marital fidelity is not the greatest human good nor is sex among the unwed the greatest evil. At least that much is accepted by everyone other than the Pope and Billy Graham. But there is a far more insidious and pernicious myth that is replacing those exploded prejudices: Sex is good only when it is ribboned and laced with love.

This new puritanism is so pervasive and effective that it even has the support of almost every hack psychiatrist, liberal don, and emancipated woman. And it is perfectly understandable why this should be so. Western society has not yet recovered from St. Paul and John Knox—the two great misogynists of all time.

The thesis *used* to run roughly as follows: Copulation is an ugly and disgusting business but, since the species has to be preserved, it must be tolerated only within the strict limits of the marital straitjacket. And any resultant pleasure from the act must be repressed by the pure in heart.

The *new* mystique is both more sophisticated and corrosive: Sex is really not all that bad, in fact, it can be very beautiful, *provided* it takes place under the velvet canopy of "love," bringing two people *closer together*. The stakes are thus set high in the "communications game." Once more a justification is sought; it is not enough to copulate and derive pleasure from the act. The *raison d'être* of the most intrinsic and exciting human activity is set outside itself; that is, the gross physical vulgarity of the body. We are back to good old Calvinism once again by an ingeniously circuitous route: The body is base, physical pleasure for its own sake is perfidious; the mind is good, the human soul sublime. Do indulge in sex, by all means, but don't forget it is only a sauce that goes with the main meal of mind, emotion, and psyche.

The sex revolution has thus overthrown one kind of thou-shalt-not demagogy for another. As the charcoal smoke of old-style dirty sex clears out of the room, the diesel fumes of mid-century *communicative* copulation blow in, the air around the bed remaining as poisonous as ever.

Let me make it clear at this stage that I don't think there is anything *wrong* with soul communion in bed just as I don't condemn a wedded couple who produce a baby in love and tenderness. In fact, I am all for them if only these things could happen as frequently and for as many people as television ads and Episcopalian sermons would have us believe. But I do wish to insist that a good time in bed should not have to be *justified* by these tantalizing and (more often than not in real life) unrealizable ideals.

For, consider what happens when the mental obsession with "love" tries to repress the demands of the body. In practice, frequently, the body wins. Partners in the ancient conflicts of emotion against legality, love versus wedlock, change attire; the "liberated" in our new society no longer feel constrained by such obsolescent taboos. Instead, they think up new ones—carnality against emotion, lust versus love—and the game goes on.

No, sex by itself is neither beautiful nor sordid, and it does not need justification by regions of the body other than the loins. What Aldous Huxley called the "business of the bouncing buttocks" can be funny, exciting, sad, tender, or all of these things, even in one session. It does not have to come packaged in a parcel called "love" nor is it evil unless you choose to make it so.

PLEASURES OF A TEMPORARY AFFAIR

6

Tears, fears, wads of damp Kleenex, a reddened eye on the clock and the calendar: "After three months, shouldn't he be more serious?"

All of these soggy symptoms blotch the girl who's missing (and mangling) one of the world's greatest pleasures: a temporary love affair. Wringing her laundry, she thinks only of marriage, of time spent toward a single goal. She's wrong—for two reasons. First, it's worth remembering an old joke: The woman says, "I've given you the best twenty years of my life," and the man replies, "Yes, but I didn't like it." *Moral*: It's often more rewarding—and more fun—to be a mistress rather than a wife. Second, many passing affairs are rare and marvelous; a delight worth having *just because* they can't be translated into marriage. Impermanence is usually determined by a character combination that would be disastrous in the long run. More about that later. Meanwhile, it's high time for today's free girls to shed their preoccupation with marriage, and to enjoy living in the present—with men whom they may not see tomorrow.

The affair that *shouldn't* last forever may or may not be the great love of your life. The man may be married—and do remember that married men can be splendid. They are particularly gay and sympathetic in *your* company, because it's *your* charm and humor that cheers them after years of the wheezing wife, cold knackwurst, and steaming diapers that greet them after a heavy office day; the head clamped with metal rollers

91

on the pillow; the rebuke for the four-letter word shouted after a type-writer fell upon a toe; and above all, the news of the week: "Fish costs more than it used to" . . . "I can't seem to tighten my pores." Frankly, he wouldn't be on your doorstep if his home life was delicious. (And you might as well blame his wife for making it dreary. She's probably older than you, and she may well be depressing in bed. She's *not* your problem, so stop worrying about her.)

But, without meeting her, you can learn one lesson from her: marriage and motherhood make a lot of women boring. It's their self-indulgence that stunts their growth, permits them to repeat themselves, nag, growl, and whine. (It's been said that self-improvement is the curse of the single woman. If so, the loss of imagination is the equivalent for some house-wives.) At any rate, the Thurber women—threatening or repetitive—made themselves that way. Very well—their husbands prefer you.

You may hear generations of invisible mothers muttering, "Men are only after one thing." But it isn't true. In an age where action between the sheets is all too available, your lover wants a great deal more: romance, jokes, glamour; relief from that laundry list of domestic nonevents; often, a chance to pamper *you*—to treat you to the music and dancing and bright lights that you both adore. You'll be touched to realize how sensitive a married love is to your tastes; your favorite wines and movie stars, the little restaurant that you like so much, your perfume, and the comedian who breaks you up. He may even remember that you hate Hungarian food, the fox-trot, and walking trips with knapsacks. All in all, you should be flattered that a man comes to you for the very things that realists condemn: romanticism and thoroughly good times. "It won't last," they say—because it's all so enjoyable. No, it probably won't. So, why not make the most of having fun?

However, temporary affairs are not only geared to married lovers. They're often most appropriate—and diverting—at particular periods of your life. You may be with a man whose appeal for you is enormous—and puzzling. He enthralls you now, but the parts of him that perplex you make the future impossible to imagine. (When in doubt, you're apt to be right: He'll eventually prove to be the wrong man for you.) Or: you may be newly divorced; quite simply, you can't think about settling down so soon again. Or: you may be on the rebound—disentangling yourself from something that *did* hurt you, still rather numb and certainly not ready to invest all of your emotional capital in the very next account. Or: you've just split up with someone you *wanted* to leave; it was your choice, even though you may occasionally miss him. But you can't stay single—who can?—and there's a charming man who wants you.

The fun of the chase, being courted, beginning again—all this renews you. You put on your best for each other, as strangers do. The mutual desire to please is never stronger than at the start of a fresh affair—and two people who are eager to please one another usually succeed. It may be that neither of you is in love, and you're both honest enough to admit it—but not so tactless as to stress it. But you'd rather be together than apart.

As the momentum gathers, there's the reward of getting to know someone who is totally new to your life, who brings many of his experiences and opinions, his personal flavor, to interest and amuse you. One of the best reasons for any woman to have quite a few lovers is this: You'll never know anyone else as well, and each such personality is unique. Remember the man whom everyone thought so remote, so hard to know, who talked to you for hours about the most private (and fascinating) events in his exciting life? Remember the man who rowed you down the river, pressing the soles of his feet against yours until neither of you could stop laughing? Remember the endearing clown whose witty self-perceptions could suddenly cut through his neuroses? They were all so different; you could never have had so many lives—or learned so much— with one person. You were fortunate to know them all; it would have been a shame to miss a single one. A few months, a year or so, with each. By their very contradictions, those chapters of your life highlight the value of variety. Thus, permanence is *not* the test or proof of the validity of *any* love affair.

So, you've begun a new affair. And you're wise enough (we hope) not to tarnish it with references to the future, rings, dishwashers, or station wagons—or *plans*. American women plan too much. They're famous for it. They even plan themselves right onto the psychiatrist's couch—often because they're nerve-racked by trying to live up to an impossible, self-imposed schedule. One girl, admired at college for her organizational talents, planned her marriage so fiercely that the man felt he had to go through with it—long before he was ready to make the decision. As his wife, she exhausted him by planning, and he soon needed relief. On learning that he'd once slept with his secretary, the wife planned herself right onto the plane to Reno.

Your affair is probably part time, even if you're living together. Both of you are likely to have office jobs, or work that separates you. Hence, there are lunches and drinks with others, and meetings and appointments on your own. Even if you do live under his roof, remember the advantages of two apartments; you should hang onto your own. It's good to have a retreat, to put cream on your face or telephone an old beau; to entertain friends that your man doesn't like; or for work if you do it at home. Above all, the separate apartment keeps domesticity from dulling both of you. An affair should *not* be like a marriage.

But if your lover *is* married, then you may indulge a certain amusement —keeping it secret. It's often fun when the world doesn't have a clue. One distinguished British novelist, who thrives on intrigue in life as well as in fiction, kept his girl in an elegant, hidden apartment, saw her only at night, played the games of concealment, down to the details of clandestine notes and giving her a veil to wear. (She eventually tired of the effort, and departed. But she enjoyed it heartily for a while.) If you *like* a bit of guilt and feeling sinful—and many people do—then playing it mysterious will make everything seem sexier.

Naturally, the style of any love affair is open to choice. And if you want to be totally open, that's easy. However, you may not wish to close off the possibility of new prospects. Meeting your brother's colleague (newly arrived in town), or your lover's best friend, may raise a pleasing temptation. But living openly with someone may discourage other men. A girl who was rather bored with her lover was delighted at being pursued by a man from her office—and perplexed when his attentions suddenly ceased. She then learned that he'd discovered that the man she lived with was an old fraternity brother of his, and he promptly retreated. This brand of male-to-male loyalty is prevalent, especially when the woman in the case is *not* the wife. Hence, two apartments may be best for most affairs. That technical distance increases the intimacy of meeting after sundown, adds the formality of good manners, and maintains the ordinary kind of privacy which everyone needs—and marriage usually kills.

What about finances when you're involved with a man you won't remain with? In our society, there's a bungling tendency to confuse love or sex with money; no wonder economics has been called the dismal science. Really it's very simple. Accept all presents, and *don't* paw them over; don't try to squeeze significance out of a pair of topaz earrings or a bundle of paperback books. Accept all treats, accept cash kindly offered for groceries for your meals together. Do *not* get involved in joint investments; someday there may be a horrid wrangle about who actually owns the hi-fi, or whose apartment it really is. Don't be *practical*. Don't try to turn that giant cushion—which you bought because *he* likes to sit on the floor—into the cornerstone of a house. Possessions, and the exhilaration of buying them, mustn't be manipulated to mean a commitment. Giving a lover a bathrobe or a tie is *really* giving—not trying to paste someone to you. But how much should you spend on presents for him? Not much, unless you're exuberantly rich. This is *not* an investment; it's an immediate pleasure. It's more important to put thought, instead of just money, behind your gifts. Will *he* like it is your criterion.

Since freedom of style and choice is so available today—outside of wedlock—it's a pity that so many nervous men and women look to pop pundits or sexual advisers for kitchen-tested recipes on how to make love, how to "mold a relationship," or simply how to behave. A psychology student, who had read stacks of "how to" books, was so eager to demonstrate the number of positions that she could assume in bed, that she lost several lovers with bewildering speed. Eventually, she realized that she'd never consulted the men on *their* tastes, and that her own proficiency had seemed positively bullying to them. Another girl who had digested too many volumes on "behavioral motivations" finally heard that a man she'd wanted had declared she "had no personality." So, don't try to live by the books.

Now that sexual freedom is lavish, it's time for people to be free in their personal behavior—and honest in their preferences. If you have what Colette called "monogamous blood," then it's easy to live in accord with it. But if you're polygamous—and today, more and more of us realize that we are—then be that way. But, there's no need to report that you've been unfaithful. No man or woman ever really wants to hear about what happened behind his or her back. So keep it to yourself, even when you have two lovers who both delight you. Mixed media is unquestionably the style today; it's an honest image of polygamy *or* the variety of pleasures shifting and changing in a love affair. Think kaleidoscope: Life can be that way, if you wish—if you're ready to move with it.

For decades, psychologists, philosophers, and writers have tried to persuade women that playing a host of shifting roles is both natural *and* agreeable. But American girls have been terribly slow to learn. Admittedly, it's harder for a married woman to enjoy the whole cast of characters that she finds herself performing: nurse, chauffeur, secretary, human mattress, and jungle gym. (It takes a *lot* of imagination for her to merit Disraeli's compliment, after ten years of marriage: "My dear, you are more of a mistress to me than a wife.") A girl who's *not* tied down to the fatiguing dailiness of responsibilities can switch from being a seductive temptress to a charming jester and express all of the aspects of her character that can be illustrated by the contents of her closet—from the silver-sequined Harlow dress to the well-cut jeans, the long, romantic velvet coat and the cherry-red rompers. Lovers *like* surprises (a husband may not). Both of you can catch each other's mood, and swing with it: hard rock tonight, entertaining friends tomorrow, then a quiet dinner on your own, a double feature.

But don't jam the wheel of possibilities by accusing a man of not knowing your "*real* self"—it's a line that can speed an exit even faster than "I got all worn out at the white sale today." There's been too much claptrap about being appreciated for one's self alone. It's what you *make* of yourself that beguiles others, and part of the beguilement is being a good actress—a quick-change artist, in fact. There's a slice of ham in everyone, and it's great fun to dish it up. This is the right period for making fantasies come alive, for a while at least.

Of course, no one can switch from her Garbo style to her Lily Tomlin act to standing in for Ali MacGraw on a twenty-four-hour stage. But that's the charm of the passing or part-time affair: you can do it momentarily, because it's *not* forever.

Napoleon used to say that luck was a form of intelligence. He was half right. He was also half wrong where character combinations are concerned. What man you meet—and when—is accidental; luck or intelligence can't control your compatibility. Still, certain combinations must only be temporary, and they are no less valuable for that. Suppose you have a low metabolism and your lover is splendidly energetic; you'll catch his vitality for a while, but eventually it will wear you out. The day that he urges you to take vitamin-B shots and gobble protein tablets will signal that you've both had the best of it. Or perhaps he's a romantic, wraparound paranoid; the possessiveness and jealousy that you both found so exciting does finally become a drag. Or perhaps that brilliant intellect—which stimulated you to read lots of enriching books, taught you so much that you'll never forget—is finally over your head; you pine for big, sprawling, bad movies and science-fiction anthologies. The gifted photographer, with whom you took such fascinating trips (through whose eyes you saw so much that you'd always missed), finally blames you once too often for not being "truly visual"; it's time to stop carrying his cameras around. Or take the psychiatrist who enthralled you for months with his patients' case histories, who finally burst into unmanly tears and said that he'd never been able to "relate to anyone." Any one of these expanded your life and roused feelings that you didn't know you had. But it wasn't for a lifetime, and there's no need for either of you to run each other down.

And, of course, there are charming neurotics, whom you will never cure, despite a period of being happy together. For example, nothing can ever be done about masochists; someone who *wants* his own pain and punishment will make certain he gets it, will precipitate the situation that brings out your unkindest self. (Masochists usually imply that happiness must end by saying that it's all been "so unreal.") These, and others, may finally reproduce the blight of their current or recent marriage in your own affair together; an accelerating vagueness on his part can inject you with the bossiness that he complained of in his wife.

Another much more likely reason for disentangling yourself is geography: Do you *really* want to live with a volcano expert in Iceland, much as you liked hearing his tales about the frozen wastes? Are you *urban* enough for the man whose career will never let him leave the city? Can you lead a *very* public life with a fledgling politician, giving weeks at a stretch to strangers who are duller than anyone you've ever met? Be honest—and cheerful—in recognizing love affairs that shouldn't be prolonged.

Nowadays, women have more chance than ever to savor the delights of the moment. Of course, good marriages are as precious as they are admirable. But no one's born married; there are the periods that come before, between, and after. And love affairs *can* have all of the gaiety and spontaneity that many marriages are apt to exclude. It's time for women of all ages to enjoy using the present tense—today, *tonight!*

7

GIRLS WHO MAKE IT WITH MARRIED MEN We were walking out of a crowded matinee of the hit musical *Promises, Promises,* an unmarried friend whom I'll call Susanna and I. She was reflecting on a much-quoted line from the original, nonmusical version of the show (then called *The Apartment*): "Girls who wear mascara shouldn't have affairs with married men." The implication was obvious—too many tears in the offing. "But that's so out of *date,*" Sue said.

"Wearing mascara?" I joked, thinking maybe she meant everyone was now in false eyelashes.

"No, the whole idea," she said impatiently, "that any single girl having an affair with a married man has to have a hard time, has to be weeping into her pillow every night. A girl who gets into a miserable situation like that *wants* to get stuck," Susanna went on. "She goes into the affair expecting what she *won't* get and not enjoying what she *can.*"

After we parted I reflected on this last statement: expecting what she won't get, not enjoying what she can. What was it that single girls choosing to have affairs with married men (we'll presume the men were reasonably honest and acknowledged they were married in time for a girl to get out if she wanted to) *used* to expect ten years ago, which the girl of today, like Susanna, wouldn't be looking (hoping) for?

Well, usually she expected to get married. Oh, she might deny it, but there was that hope, nurtured through many a long, lonely weekend: *this* time he'll tell his wife, *this* time he'll show up with a big smile and say: "I did it, I walked out." It wasn't always just the romantic fantasies of the *girls* at play here; their married men often *encouraged* these dreams. "My wife doesn't understand me" with all its variations almost inevitably led to "If only I'd met you earlier . . ." or "When I think of our being married . . ." And the married men weren't always faking. Many of them *would* have liked the courage to leave their wives. Sure, some were hypocrites, having fun both at home and away from it, but others really *were* miserable . . . had, through bad luck or marrying too young, picked the wrong woman. These husbands did want out, partly anyway, and with a girl who seemed to offer all they'd been missing in their marriages. The temptation to make that final break, to begin again, grew pretty strong at times. But did they ever leave their wives? Not often.

We know the major reasons: the children (a girl getting involved with an older married man whose children were in college had a better chance), also force of habit. For many married men in their forties, fifties, a new life based on romantic love was tempting, yes, but also scary. They *knew* and were used to their old existence, with all its drawbacks and limitations. Maybe the new life would have worse dangers—also, divorces, alimony, and child support are costly. So these men held back and held back and, finally, the tired-of-waiting single girl of the fifties and sixties took off: the *hell* with it! She was maybe more than a *little* bitter. Would she have gotten involved at *all* if she'd known for an absolute *fact* that there was no chance of marriage to this man?

"Sure she would," says the girl of the seventies. "Or at least *I* would!" And here we see the change. The seventies girl doesn't necessarily expect to marry her married man and, more significantly, *wouldn't* even if he offered. And so she's free of all that anxiety, that bewildered jealousy— who does he love *more*? She knows, and pretty much accepts, that he's partly tied to his wife . . . doesn't really *care* what the reasons are. Maybe the wife is an invalid or maybe he's still a little hung *up* on his bride, but who cares! The point is, he's with his wife legally, and probably ten years later he'll be with her still. But our seventies girl—at least many of them— doesn't *mind,* because she never wanted or needed the lure of eventual marriage to make an affair with this man worthwhile.

I recently talked to one of my close friends who was involved about the married-man/single-girl syndrome. She had been a little cagey over the past summer; friends who tried to see her found her mysteriously busy— she never said why. Then, a season later, she told us: she'd been living with a married man. His wife was away for July and August, and his job kept him in the city. They'd been seeing each other casually over the winter, but that summer, they both realized, offered a chance to be together in a relaxed, intimate way that would never be possible again. And so he moved in with her. "I knew he'd pack up in September. Both of us understood the time limit. I had to decide—did I want this affair for what it was worth for two months or didn't I? I decided I did and I've never regretted it." As Frances described the summer, I, more prudish, could *almost* see what she meant—here was a love affair with sweetness and great emotion, but it wasn't as though *one* of the lovers was taking advantage while one was going to be *dumped* (1960s rationale). There was complete honesty between them (1970s fashion); he didn't have to lie, she didn't have to feel like a discarded corsage.

"Didn't you ever wish he would leave her?" I persisted. "After all, if he was *that* great . . ."

"He *was* that great . . . No, look, I would have married him if I'd met him when he was a bachelor. We got along wonderfully. We'd do things I'd never done with anyone before, practice the guitar together, listen to medieval church music. Now I don't mean to say I would *only* marry a man who loved music the way I do, but just that it was nice and so unexpected to find we shared many pleasures. I hope someday I'll find someone to share them with who's *available*. I think I will."

Ironically, the single girl who goes into an affair with a married man not expecting marriage often ends up having it. This had happened to a girl I worked with. When I knew Amy, she was already married to her guy, and the marriage seemed to have something special going for it . . . the way her husband picked her up every day after work . . . the bunches of violets from him she'd bring in and set in a glass of water. When we weren't too choked with envy to admit it, we girls all agreed this was the kind of marriage *we'd* like. One afternoon I asked her how she'd happened to meet her husband (hoping to pick up a few hints). "He was married when we met," she said. "I wasn't . . . frankly, I never expected to marry him. His wife and I were in college together. She wasn't one of my best friends, just a classmate. When I ran into the two of them again in the city, it was clear they were miserable and never should have married. Still, that was *their* problem . . . I just assumed they'd work it out. So I saw him occasionally, maybe falling in love with him a little bit more than I expected, but never *once* imagining myself as his wife, not even in daydreams. . . . One day he showed up at my door and said he'd left her . . . would I marry him? You may not believe this, but it took me a long time to say yes. I wanted to make sure he wasn't just acting on a crash decision, one he'd regret later. He *did* have doubts, it turned out, but I think not having me leap at the chance to get him, just as I hadn't pressured him *before*, made him certain finally that I was the girl. When I realize how terrific he is to be married to, I wonder how I could have played it so cool."

In Amy's case she got her married man almost because she *didn't* want him or had convinced herself she didn't. Many other girls are perhaps even more sincere about not wanting marriage. They may be between marriages, or having too much fun at their jobs (airline stewardesses sometimes say this) . . . or dating too many attractive men to be ready to give them up. For these girls a married man is a perfect lover because he isn't interested in marriage *either*. Ten years ago nobody would have believed that a man's main appeal could be that he *couldn't* marry. Any girl who got involved with a man like that, so the theory went, must be a masochist. But those were the days when a girl who was unmarried at twenty-two was already panicked. And there were even vestigial traces of guilt and shame for the girl who had been "used" by a man who didn't marry her. (In those days there was still the last of the good-girl–bad-girl categorizing.)

Nowadays, despite the bachelor shortage, there's less panic and virtually *no* guilt or stigma for the girl who's had an affair. If there *is* any, it's in her mind alone, or maybe her mother's, not the man's.

According to my research, girls are choosing to marry later, if they feel like it, because they know that at thirty, thirty-five, and even later, they'll still look good and can still attract men. Nor will the men they eventually marry particularly care that they've had a few flings along the way. (The man may be secretly disappointed if the girl hasn't!) At twenty-four or five, there's *time* . . . why not try a few love affairs that necessarily *won't* "work out"?

"Paul never pressured me," says an attractive friend of mine who recently married, but *not* the man we were discussing. "I can't tell you what a relief *that* was. People always talk about how women are pressuring men into marriage and what a drag that can be for the men. They never *mention* the other side—those bachelors who've had what they consider the requisite number of affairs and are now ready to 'settle down.' After two dates they size up how you feel about living in the suburbs, how much money you spend on clothes, whether your folks are going to be a drag. If they *could,* they'd count your fillings to estimate how expensive their future wife's dentist bills are going to be! Who needs it! I just don't find that kind of pressure flattering."

"So you picked this man precisely because he *was* married and wouldn't be able to marry you? What if he'd been single?"

My friend grinned slyly. "Ah, luckily I didn't *have* that dilemma! . . . I guess I'd have dated him in any case . . . we had too much going for me to let him slip by, but it *was* a plus that he was married. . . . He told me immediately he had no intention of leaving his wife and that certainly didn't unhinge me. We both knew exactly what we were going to get out of the affair—excitement, sex, friendship—and neither of us was disappointed the least bit."

What *are* the "benefits" for a single girl from an affair with a married man, aside from not feeling trapped?

For one thing, my subjects tell me, the married man is usually older and suaver . . . more courtly. He isn't just beginning the long arduous climb up the greasy pole to job success. "The single men I meet don't really have *time* for romance," a beautiful black model reports. "They're too busy trying to succeed. Now I like that . . . I like men who want to make it. I've no doubt these men will, given ten or twenty years . . . but at the moment too much of their energy is going into their jobs. The married man often has economic freedom already. And if he owns his own business, he can even make his schedule. The husband also knows a lot about women. A single man of forty is frequently a professional roué or a mama's boy or both. With *those* handicaps who cares if he's admired by your girl friends at parties or fantastic on a surfboard? A married man of the same age is more likely to have all the *experience* with not so many emotional hangups."

A young shoe designer told me, "The single men I meet resent my success and, frankly, I don't blame them. Probably I *am* a threat. Once I've made it, maybe I'll be more accepted, but now if I meet a man in the same field as mine—and most of the men I meet *are* in my field—I know he's thinking: who needs *this*? . . . a wife who might earn more than he will or be more successful. I had an affair with a wonderful man last year—we're still good friends—and he couldn't have cared less about my success. Actually, he *liked* it. He's the vice-president of a big shoe-manufacturing firm, and he only *encouraged* me. Maybe I offered a stimulating contrast to his wife, who's a homebody. Anyway, he certainly had nothing to be scared of. No matter how high I rose or what I earned, I wasn't likely to top *him*."

The married man, besides being older, more experienced, more knowledgeable about women, can also give a girl a sense of being wanted, cherished, that she can't always get from a single man! "Bachelors who are any 'good' today are pretty rare," says a TV-network receptionist, "so they know their own value. Not to put too fine a point on it, lots of them are wildly egotistical. Maybe they have a right to be. Single men know that any girl who gets them is pretty lucky, so why should they bother killing themselves chasing her—there are plenty of girls to go around! So a single girl having an affair with a single man finds herself, no matter how self-confident, doing *everything* to please him. She has to be a bit of an aggressor, a triple whiz at *everything*, whereas with a married man she can enjoy the feminine privilege of sitting back and being pursued. Bliss!"

Admittedly, a girl may be less shy about *taking* the initiative today. Given a man who attracts her, she isn't reluctant to set out after him, trying, naturally, to be subtle about the chase, so he doesn't quite notice her chasing. "But what girl still doesn't like an affair 'with all the trimmings' . . . champagne, flowers, presents . . . most important, the feeling that she is worth all that devoted attention?" says the TV receptionist. "A single man may be dating six other girls besides you, possibly having affairs with all of them. You *may* win out in the lottery, but maybe you *won't*, and all that competition can be unnerving. With a married man, his wife is hardly likely to be an object of romantic interest or he wouldn't be straying. And it's very unusual for a married man to be seriously pursuing two single girls at once. Too risky, too expensive, and too exhausting! So you know, with the married man, for as long as the affair lasts you are the darling."

Says a wealthy ex-debutante just back from two years in the Peace Corps, "I'm tired of always suspecting the reasons men are after me. If you have money, it's like having a 36-22-36 figure . . . you know men don't want you for yourself alone . . . you *learn* to be suspicious. That's why my last love affair—with a married man—was such a change . . . and a good one. He wasn't rich, but he made me *feel* that he was . . . he showered me with presents. They weren't big things, no jewels from Cartier, but, frankly, I don't *need* jewelry. I can buy it myself. It was Romeo and Juliet. Think of those movies we see over and over again, blotting up a few tears by the end . . . *Roman Holiday, Casablanca, Girl with Green Eyes.* All the heroines in these films had affairs that had to end. Such an affair, in memory, is like those beautiful little scenes you see in old-fashioned Easter eggs . . . never tarnishing, never spoiling. Even girls with happy marriages admit that whether they had a romantic affair with their husband or not, by now the memory of that affair is blurred by the day-to-day routine of marriage. One stage ends, another begins. But the girl having an affair with a married man will never have the letdown of a day-to-day routine. And because the affair can't last, there's a mutual intensity, a shared quality of precious doom, as it were, which a relationship with a single man, with all its open possibilities, usually can't match."

Can all girls successfully handle a married-man affair? Probably not. Some girls still seem to need the security of a written contract, a happy ending hopefully spelled out. Probably these girls, knowing their emotional makeup, ought to move cautiously. But more and more single girls *do* have the self-confidence, economic security, sexual curiosity, and poise to bring it off. For them an affair with a married man is an experience, like a nude swim on a beach at dawn, that shouldn't, no matter what, be *missed*. "And," adds my friend Susanna, "wear all the mascara you like. It's waterproof anyway!"

8

THE LIVING-TOGETHER HANDBOOK

It's Wednesday morning and your weekend date is still using your toothbrush. Or, a chap you've been dating frequently has now brought several essential possessions over to your house—two changes of clothes, a couple of his favorite books, his guitar and autoharp, a suitcase, his walkie-talkies, power tools, banjo, mandolin, a green box full of acrylic paints, two large teacups, his TV, an AM-FM transistor radio, spices, a ten-gallon hat, winter boots, more clothes, a razor, two gerbils, and his towels.

It is safe to assume that yours is no longer a casual relationship. You may be about to embark on a totally new way of life. You may even be living together.

There will be, in this situation, new joys, new pleasures, and most certainly new problems. Ranging from how Christmas cards should be addressed to you, to how to introduce him to your boss, these problems will be subtle and constant. Your taxes, vocabulary, relationships with friends—things which you've been taking completely for granted until now—will suddenly demand an unaccustomed amount of concentration.

You're not *single* any more—but you're not married, either. To determine if this state of limbo can be officially classified as living together, take this little true-false quiz. (If you haven't got time, let *him* take it . . . the results have *got* to be the same!)

1. He/she has the key to your apartment.
2. He/she has the *mailbox* key.
3. You maintain more than one apartment.
4. You maintain more than one checking account.
5. You split the grocery bill.
6. Both your wardrobes are at one apartment.
7. Either of you may answer the telephone.
8. You've lost track of how many of his/her books you have in your library.
9. His/her dirty clothes are in your hamper.
10. You've got a joint bank account.
11. His/her mother hangs up when you answer the phone.
12. You take turns taking out the garbage.
13. You shop for groceries together.
14. Your friends invite you over as a couple.
15. He/she lives out of a suitcase.
16. He/she has at least one dresser drawer.
17. The mailman leaves his/her mail in your mailbox.
18. Your maid knows his/her name.
19. Your answering service takes messages for him/her.
20. You've disposed of three or more duplicates—TVs, stereos, toasters.
21. You've stopped giving gifts to each other every week.
22. You've stopped counting monthly anniversaries.
23. You always say "we" when discussing your social life.
24. He's seen you in curlers. You've heard him gargle.
25. He/she has seen you being sick.

If even a sprinkling of the above statements are true, there's very little doubt, my dear, that you two *are* living together. So let's get on with the practical matter of how to *cope* with the situation.

One problem of cohabiting is that you're constrained to hand out different information (stories, fibs, blatant lies) about yourself or selves to different people. The landlady must be told one thing, the druggist another, your respective bosses something else. In order to help you keep all these stories straight, we have prepared a workbook, which, after it has been filled out, can be posted near your front door for ready reference as you are rushing out. Just substitute correct name or check one of the multiple choices where necessary:

Our real address is _____.

(His Name) is/is not still maintaining an apartment at: _____.

(Her Name) is/is not still maintaining an apartment at: _____.

Our present apartment is: (a) his; (b) hers; (c) one we got together.

The landlady thinks we're: (a) married; (b) cousins; (c) just good friends.

The super thinks we're: (a) married; (b) cousins; (c) just good friends.

The mailman thinks we're: (a) married; (b) using our professional names; (c) strange.

The man at the dry cleaner's thinks we're: (a) married; (b) roommates; (c) sloppy.

(Her boss, if any) thinks we're: (a) married; (b) good friends; (c) has never heard of _(his name)._ _(His boss, if he is employed)_ thinks we're: (a) married; (b) living together; (c) usually late. When _(her boss)_ called last week and _(his name)_ answered the phone and _(her name)_ was in the: (a) shower; (b) bathroom; (c) bed, _(his name)_ told _(her boss)_ that he was: (a) the window cleaner; (b) the doctor; (c) the man from Glad. When _(his boss)_ called the other day and _(his name)_ was out (a) bowling; (b) gambling; (c) doing the laundry, _(her name)_ told _(his boss)_ she was: (a) the maid; (b) his social secretary; (c) Josephine, the plumber. When _(her mother)_ came over the other day to look at the new apartment, _(his name)_ answered the door. _(Her mother)_ was: (a) frightened; (b) angry; (c) pretended to be Josephine the plumber, and/or (a) ran away; (b) made a puddle; (c) sat down in the best chair. _(Her name)_ told her mother that _(his name)_ was: (a) the super; (b) an out-of-town friend; (c) her guru. _(Her name)'s_ last name is _____.

(His name)'s last name is _____. The name on the prescription for The Pill is _(her last name)._ The druggist thinks his last name is: _(her last name)._

Now that you've got the problem of what-to-tell-whom and who-will-think-what out of the way, let's explore what you think, and see how this new living arrangement is affecting your mental processes. We already know what it's doing for you physically, and we're so happy for you! There are bound to be situations inherent in or created by living together, however, that prey on your own old fears, or bring up totally new top-grade anxieties. In an effort to reduce these chrome-plated worries to mere black and white, test your anxiety quotient:

1. He/she will go out for cigarettes and never come back.
2. He/she'll take my dog with him/her.
3. Everybody knows we're living in sin.
4. I'm being followed everywhere by a king-size bed.
5. She is going to throw out all my favorite old clothes.
6. She is going to burn all my favorite old clothes.
7. She is going to clean all my favorite old clothes.
8. He/she hates all my friends.
9. He/she is going to leave me and take the television set.
10. He is a failure.
11. She is a witch.
12. He/she is crazy.
13. He/she is a sex maniac.
14. He/she is not a sex maniac.
15. He/she is going to find all my old love letters.
16. He/she is not going to find all my old love letters.
17. His/her mother will show up at three A.M. with the entire family and a catered meal.
18. The landlord will throw us both out into the cold if he finds out.
19. The neighbors can hear every word we say.
20. The neighbors all snicker at us behind our backs.

There are no right or wrong answers for this list . . . but don't you feel *better* now that you've figured out what's bugging you? With this new peace of mind, you'll be prepared to meet and face that inevitable living-together phenomenon, commonly known as the nutty-as-a-fruitcake period.

There comes a time in every girl's life, especially a girl living with a man, when she trips and falls knee-deep into a moment of truth. This is known as the I've-never-been-involved-with-anybody-like-this, or the nutty-as-a-fruitcake-period. The symptoms of this syndrome range from shortness of temper to a constant feeling that he is a crazy man and you are chained to him . . . for life.

Here is a list of things you may be muttering to yourself, or silently stewing about during this critical time:

He picks at me all the time.

Why does he like me?

How much could he like me, anyway, if he *picks* at me all the time?

What am I doing with this idiot?

There's no way out.

I can't stand the way he lights his cigarette, combs his hair, hums.

He's not my physical ideal.

I never liked (skinny, fat, tall, short, blond, dark) men.

I'm not *his* physical ideal.

He thinks I have bad breath.

Maybe I have bad breath.

Maybe he's not my best friend.

He's getting on my nerves being here all the time.

I'm nothing but a drudge.

He doesn't appreciate everything I do.

I feel crazy.

Maybe I *am* crazy.

Maybe *he's* crazy.

If he's crazy, what am I doing living with a crazy man?

No one has ever talked to me like this.

No one else has ever *dared* talk to me like this.

I've never talked like this to *anybody*.

I must be crazy to put up with this.

Maybe I *am* crazy.

I can't get out of it.

It's out of my hands.

I feel trapped.

I'm not getting any sleep.

He sleeps all the time while I'm slaving over a hot desk.

I know at any moment I'm going to do something wrong.

I'm innocent and he insists on picking on me all the time.

  Patience! The fruitcake frenzy soon passes—or is pushed out of consciousness—because of the more pressing quandary of . . . *parents!*

You have been living together for three months now and your parents have, after the initial hysterics, taken it pretty well.

His parents actually seem *happy* that you're living together . . . though you occasionally catch a hint of subtext that says: "We're happy they're living together so that he'll find out firsthand she's no good, and won't *marry* her."

Note: Simply because your own parents aren't growling or shouting, don't be fooled into thinking they're not *plotting.*

You are sitting in your living room reading a cookbook when the phone rings. You haven't yet quite shaken the habit of leaping for the phone before *he* gets a chance at it, so, of course, you get the receiver off the hook first.

"You don't know me . . ." (the voice at the other end begins). "But I'm Harvey Beemeyer . . . and . . ."

You immediately try to think where you've heard the name "Bee-meyer" before, while Harvey says that he'd like to know "if you're busy or anything" this Saturday night. You decline, saying that you have your shock-therapy session scheduled this Saturday and . . .

By the time you hang up you're positive you've heard the name "Bee-meyer" before somewhere. Didn't your Uncle Al marry a woman whose first husband's name was . . . ? Aha! Your uncle's wife's son by her first marriage!

"Who was that?" your man of the house yells innocently from the can. "That was one Harvey Beemeyer, who wanted to wine and dine me and take me to a chic village joint," you say. "Who is Harvey Beemeyer and what the [mumble] did you tell him?" he asks. "I told him my wheel-chair wouldn't fit through the door."

The phone has started to ring again, and this time it's Mark Dichter whom you haven't seen since high school. "Hi, Mark!" you stammer, a bit more confused than proud to be so popular. You manage to squeak out a halfhearted "What's up?" and rack your brain, trying to remember if he's the same Mark Dichter who in high school had set fire to the teachers' lounge. He was a cut-up, that Mark. Anyway, *this* Mark Dichter, who turns out to be the same one, wants to take you to the zoo Sunday afternoon. When you tell him about your allergy to fur, feathers, scales, and high-school buddies, he says he'll take a rain check.

You're beginning to see a pattern, but it's still very fuzzy.

You've just replaced the phone on its cradle when your mother calls to say that she's just run into the guy you used to go with in kindergarten and he looks just great and asked her all about what you were doing. Well, how could she help but give him your number? Certainly "that man" doesn't answer *your* phone, does he? Suddenly everything is clear. You've been sabotaged by your own mother. Here's what happened:

Your mother became hysterical when she found out you were living with a man you (a) weren't engaged to, and (b) weren't sure you were going to marry. She told your father, who was upset about your being "taken advantage of" but then returned to the evening paper—thereby robbing her of a continuing concrete sense of drama and satisfaction. Mother went straight to the desk, riffled nervously through her address book to look for friends and relatives who had eligible sons, cousins, brothers, friends, doctors, dentists, enemies, or knew of *anyone* who might be free to take you out. She also sat down and made a list of all the boys you used to know, date, write to, go to school with, push off tricycles, or live near. That accomplished, she turned the ancestral home into a campaign headquarters to prove to you that you could have a fabulous social life and didn't need to "waste" yourself on that person you have been living with sans guarantee or license or anything. Since then, your phone, which had been comfortably wearing a two-month coat of dust and living under your bed, has been ringing every fifteen minutes to announce another beau your mother has flushed out of a forest or found under a relative's coat rack to save you.

What's the next step? Strangely, everything seems to have calmed down and fallen into place recently. Your mother sent him a birthday card; *his* mother invited *you* to lunch at Schrafft's. Life is serene and you *should* be deliriously happy. Why *aren't* you? You've rechecked the anxiety-quotient list and are satisfied that those old hangups are *not* what's bothering you. Your temperature is normal but you still feel rotten. Do you suppose . . . is it *possible* . . . you are now ready to *marry* your roommate?

Don't hate yourself. The marriage urge has been known to sneak up on many couples who *thought* they were happily living in sin but then found themselves talking joint tax returns and honeymoons in Megève. If this giddy condition overtakes you, it's probably best to follow the advice of a seventy-four-year-old great-grandmother who recently eloped with an eighty-six-year-old man just one week after they'd gone out on a blind date. She said, "The thing to do is, not to court too long or fool around too much."

In case you are in *doubt,* however, the following checklist may help:

1. Do you forget whose toothbrush is whose?
2. Do you use the same deodorant?
3. Have you started receiving junk mail at his address?
4. Do you say "we" instead of "I" when people ask you where you're going for your vacation?
5. Do you have joint ownership of the cat?
6. If you used to argue about money, have you stopped?
7. If you never argued about money, have you started?
8. Are your clothes *completely* mixed up together?
9. Have you stopped being paranoid about all your friends getting married?
10. Are you meeting new people who know you only as a couple?
11. Do you occasionally leave dishes in the sink overnight?
12. Are your friends asking you how he is, as a matter of course?
13. Are you being invited around only as a couple?
14. Do you find yourself wishing you were married, so you could introduce him as your husband?
15. Are you ready to get married even if it's *not* in a cathedral with four thousand close friends and the President on hand?
16. Have you given up *Bride* magazine entirely?
17. Have you given up daydreaming about what it'll be like to be MRS. HIM?
18. Do you still like him?
19. Are you still happy together?
20. Do people *think* you're married?

Come on, now, you know where all the noes and yeses belong . . . so maybe it's time to follow what we did and really start *living* together!

FUN (AND KINKS?) IN BED The sexual revolution of the sixties seems to have replaced Victorian intimidations with new ones! We're finding out that sexual *freedom* can be *just* as confusing and prickly as the old repressiveness. Archaic guilts and fears stemmed from conflicts with the ordained morality: *Nice girls were virginal when they married. If you were not a virgin when you married, you weren't a nice girl.* Simple logic . . . easy to know, at least, what was *considered* right.

But now nineteenth-century moral and social imperatives are *gone,* and a girl must set *personal* standards. For the old puritanisms ("Sex is for procreation, *never* pleasure"), substitute new, far more ambiguous restrictions ("Sex with the *wrong* person, or for *wrong* reasons, is sick!") Now, instead of repressing your feelings, you're *encouraged* to appraise sexual experiences: Am *I getting* enough out of lovemaking? Is my partner? What would *I like?* Alas, hardly any criteria exist for evaluating new actions . . . thus, the potential for confusion and trauma is *nearly* as great as ever. Fortunately, this muddle is *healthier* than the previous . . . self-expression and emotional well-being *are* possible.

If you're the rare girl who hasn't the *least* doubt about her sexual adequacy and psychological soundness, just skim this section. But, if your bed life is tinged with tension, the straight talk that follows can *help!*

FUN-IN-BED BAROMETER

It's only *recently* that a girl's been *allowed* to have and enjoy sex without guilts . . . nobody expects you to be *perfect* at it, yet. Besides, sexuality-experts say what's important is how *you* feel, what *you* like, not what *other* people do in bed. How well are you handling sexual options? The quiz below might provide some insights. (You have the freedom—work on the wrinkles!)

1. *Does your lovemaking follow the same routine every time?*
2. *Are you timid about letting him know your sexual needs?*
3. *Did you wake up in several different beds this week—and wish you hadn't?*
4. *Does not having orgasms, or having them the "wrong" way, worry you?*
5. *If you're troubled by a sexual problem (yours or his), have you looked for help? (asked someone, talked it over, read a book?)*

YOUR BAROMETRIC RATING SCALE

4–5 noes   Even if you "suffer" from a problem or two, your answers indicate that you can work them out because you're willing to accept help and frank information (like the following) without anxiety.

3 noes   Sometimes you're sexually uncertain, but your basic enjoyment of sex can *motivate* you to clarify feelings and improve physical compatibility.

2–0 noes   If this is your *particular* problem area, perhaps you're simply unaware of the facts, don't know whom to ask. Read every chapter carefully . . . underline situations that apply . . . and try the advice given.

PLAIN (AND FANCY) FACTS ABOUT ORGASM Orgasms feel good. Very good. So much so that nearly everyone wants to have more and better ones. At the very least we want to be reassured we're not missing anything . . . but some of us are. Even minor hangups interfering with sexual fulfillment can be so annoying they may drive a girl to write a medical columnist:

Dear Dr. Hip Pocrates [author Dr. Schoenfeld's *nom de plume*]:
When I am about to have a climax, many times I get a charley horse in my foot or leg. Is there any way to prevent this?
Answer: My limber secretary suggests that daily calisthenics may be useful preventive medicine. Her boyfriend suggests a timely foot massage. She says he spurs her on. . . .

Much has been written about the orgasm (Dr. Wilhelm Reich, still an important figure in psychoanalytic theory, even went so far as to develop an entire school of psychiatry based on this most sought after—and worried over—of human ecstasies), yet the precise definition of the act remains muddied. Dorland's *Illustrated Medical Dictionary* describes it as "the crisis of sexual excitement," which could just as well describe *failure* to have an orgasm. And *Webster's New Collegiate Dictionary* gives this definition: "Eager or immoderate excitement or action; especially, the culmination of coition." Eager? Yes. Immoderate? For lexicographers, maybe. And while lovemaking may culminate with a climax, for many women it culminates without.

Orgasm in the male is easy to identify—it occurs coincidentally with ejaculation; but in the female it is much more covert. And not until the late fifties, when Dr. William Masters, a St. Louis gynecologist, and psychologist Virginia Johnson conducted their in-depth scientific study of human reproduction (the first ever recorded in the annals of medical history), was this particular aspect of human sexual expression clinically observed. In *Human Sexual Response*, the book based on their findings, Masters and Johnson note:

For the human female, orgasm is a psychophysiologic experience occurring within, and made meaningful by, a context of psychosocial influence. Physiologically, it is a brief episode of physical release from the vasocongestive myotonic increment developed in response to sexual stimuli. Psychologically, it is subjective perception of a peak of physical reaction to sexual stimuli. The cycle of sexual response, with orgasm as the ultimate point in progression, generally is believed to develop from a drive of biologic-behavioral origin deeply integrated into the condition of human existence.

What a paradox. Many more women than men have difficulty reaching orgasm, yet a woman's capacity for sex is unlimited compared with that of a man.

Recently, I taped a conversation with a former photographer's model, a beautiful woman I had known for many years. She had managed finally to reach a climax through lovemaking for the first time at age thirty-one, only a few months before our conversation. Nancy confessed she had slept with many men, and though she could find release in oral sex or masturbation, she had been unable to reach orgasm through sexual intercourse. I asked what thoughts had gone through her mind when she made love:

"Well, I'd have sort of a feeling of hopelessness. No sense in prolonging this any longer than we have to, because it's only for him! But, of course, the men never knew that. To tell them would be like saying, 'I'm mixed-up, frigid.' I would never tell. I'd always pretend to have an orgasm near the point when I felt—all right, now it's time for both of us to have our little explosion and end this. Of course, by that time I had managed to reach a climax by rubbing against him or being fondled, but he never knew that was the only one I had."

I thought to myself that an experienced man, especially one who knew her well, certainly *could* tell the difference. I also came to realize that although many women who don't experience orgasm during intercourse fully share the satisfaction of their lovers, this girl was not among them. Her continuing problem stemmed from a deep-seated distrust of men, a hangup she had discovered only a few years earlier. She went on:

"Making love didn't seem the way it should have been. I was really doing it only for the men. I'd do anything they wanted—like an expert— because I thought I had nothing to strive for."

She believed that masturbation had interfered with her ability to enjoy lovemaking. Although Nancy knew self-stimulation was a normal mode of sexual release, she thought the specific way she had done it had perhaps contributed to her problem:

"Maybe it turns out the only way a girl can climax during lovemaking is how she's done it herself. If she's always stimulated herself in a certain way, maybe that's the *only* way she'll be able to reach orgasm. Anyway, I was too shy to tell any man just how I wanted him to touch me. So I'd pretend to be so turned on I couldn't stand it. Then he'd have *his* climax and that would be the end. I'd defeat myself again instead of talking the whole thing out."

I wondered whether Nancy harbored guilt feelings about masturbation. Or if she secretly believed in any superstition which might have inhibited her reaction (she had once told me a story about some advice given by her mother: as a girl of fourteen, Nancy was about to leave the house wearing skintight jeans when her mother told her anything that tight would give her cancer). Or perhaps she knew something about her own body that a clinician couldn't. At any rate, I asked about the first orgasm she experienced during intercourse:

"I was with a man I was very close to in every way. Whenever I pretended I was ready to climax, he'd just go on doing whatever it was he was doing—but he wouldn't have an orgasm himself. So we'd have to continue making love, and I couldn't understand why he acted that way.

"All right, I'd think, so this particular man *won't;* he'd continue making love. So I would pretend again to have *another* orgasm. Maybe he'd think —well, she's having another one. But then he still wouldn't climax for a long time. He just kept making love . . . almost as though he knew." Perhaps he did know, I suggested.

"Then one time I had a funny feeling, a good feeling. I thought—well, my God! This was after we had been together many times. I began to hope again I could have an orgasm during intercourse. I thought to my-self—maybe you can, maybe you can."

Most of her active sexual life, Nancy had either tried too hard or given up in despair. Now she was more relaxed and with a man she trusted:

"I started thinking of him as the ocean . . . that was the image I got: that he was like the ocean, and I could count on him forever. He hadn't failed me; I just felt he *wouldn't* fail me."

There's a popular French song which uses that imagery. Did she think that could have influenced her thinking of him as the ocean?

"I'd never heard of that kind of image being connected with sex. It came instinctively and naturally to my mind. He represented the ocean to me after a time . . . I had faith in him. And I thought if I could com-pletely open myself, if I could relax without worrying about him expect-ing anything, if I didn't have to do any kind of complicated stuff, then maybe—if I didn't have to put on a show for him, maybe he could put on a show for me. Maybe for once I could be submissive . . . passive. Or at least not worry about being so great in bed."

Nancy had decided not to bother about playing the *femme fatale,* an impression she obviously thought important to create:

"I stopped being so . . . so *conscious* all the way through. I had a vision of the tide—and there was a slight fantasy connected with it. I don't think I really had an orgasm that time. But then I started working on the image of openness and the tide all connected.

"By the way, I stopped lying to him after that. I finally told him the truth . . . that I'd never had an orgasm that way. He didn't make an issue out of it, and after we talked I finally opened my body to him . . . I could actually *feel* it opening. Then I decided the rest was up to him. And he did it! It was just amazing . . . the most exciting moment of my life. And from that time on I had regular orgasms."

Of course, many women who have never experienced an orgasm before may attain one during intercourse when deep love and trust—and the mental relaxation these qualities bring—are present (and the longer a girl is with someone she really digs, the better her chances). In Nancy's case, complete surrender to her lover was an act of trust, and at that time the passivity her surrender brought was right for her. But passivity in the bedroom is neither necessary nor desirable for most women. The notion that females should be docile and sexually frigid has all but faded away.

What is frigidity? Masters and Johnson define it the following way: "a loosely applied term used to express female sexual inadequacy, ranging from the Freudian concept (inability to achieve orgasm through coition) to any level of sexual response considered to be unsatisfactory by the individual female or her partner on any particular occasion."

Their definition is broad enough to include every female at some time in her life. At the other extreme, my work copy of Dorland's *Medical Dictionary* defines frigidity as "coldness; especially sexual indifference, usually applied to sexual indifference in the female." But, like Nancy, many so-called frigid women achieve orgasm through self-stimulation, caressing, or oral relations. Difficulty in reaching fulfillment isn't necessarily "sexual indifference"; often the opposite is true. Furthermore, many women who never climax during lovemaking (or perhaps at any time) nevertheless can greatly enjoy sex and the pleasure shared with their partners. But we continue to call them "frigid" for want of a better term.

Alas, sometimes these *labels* cause more psychological upsets than the feelings themselves.

Of course, anatomic variations may cause frigidity in rare instances. Dr. John Eichenlaub, a Midwest gynecologist, believes a high-placed clitoris can lead to poor sexual adjustment in some women. Writing in his book *The Marriage Art*, he says: "If you find it easy to elicit a feminine orgasm by sex play or by genital caress at the conclusion of intercourse, but almost impossible to do so during intercourse itself, a high clitoris is usually at fault."

Frigidity may cause much anguish, but worse afflictions can strike a luckless female . . . as demonstrated by a nineteen-year-old girl's problem with painful intercourse, which led to the following letter:

Dear Dr. Hip Pocrates:

This is extremely important to me. I am nineteen years old and have the Pill so I won't get pregnant. The problem is that I have slept with a boy but never had intercourse because it has hurt too much. Is there anything at all I can do to lessen the pain? I am open to all suggestions.

I thought this an interesting letter and used it in one of my medical columns. My advice was for her to have a gynecological examination to rule out any physical basis for her complaint—implying, of course, that her particular problem usually has psychological rather than physical origins. My very thoughtful medical assistant then offered the suggestion that, barring a physical problem, the pain would become pleasure if the girl were free of guilt and in love with her boyfriend. Seemed like sound advice, so I added my assistant's words as well as sending along the information that in medical lingo painful intercourse was called "dyspareunia." The column ended with a quote from one of my medical-school classmates: "It's better to have dyspareunia than no pareunia at all." But, as I pointed out, he didn't have dyspareunia.

Two months later I received a letter in response:

Dear Dr. Hip Pocrates:

Quite a while back a girl wrote in to you asking what to do about her problem of severe pain during intercourse. Having been through this same problem myself, I felt that your advice was singularly unhelpful, and finally decided to send some of my own along.

She then gave a description of how a girl might prepare for lovemaking, suggesting that she take it slowly and "relax, relax, relax. Sometimes this may mean thinking about something besides sex and what's happening at the moment." Also, saliva was suggested as a natural and readily available lubricant. Not as glib as my reply, but a lot more graphic.

Since few cases of frigidity stem from demonstrable physical defects, treatment must usually be directed toward discovering underlying psychological blocks or altering behavior patterns, or, preferably, both. A complete physical examination is nevertheless necessary to rule out possible physiological causes. Vaginal infections, for example, may reduce pleasure because of pain and itching, and certain medications used in psychiatric treatment have been known to alter sexual response in females as well as males.

Often a woman, unaided, will find the solution to her problem by combining diligence with experimentation. The following letter illustrates such a case and may be directly helpful to some readers:

Dear Dr. Hip Pocrates:

I had the problem of not being able to achieve orgasm through intercourse—although I could other ways—until just five months ago. At that time I began exercising the muscles from my abdomen on down. I found that attempting to clench my vaginal muscles had the side effect of actually stimulating my clitoris. I tried this little clenching experiment while making love, but to no avail: I was very stimulated, but no orgasm—until one day I shifted my position so that maximum friction resulted. That, combined with the clenching, produced a very intense climax for me. Please pass this information on to other young women who are unnecessarily frustrated.

Done. The experiment is certainly worth trying. Even if it doesn't work for all "young women who are unnecessarily frustrated," this method will work for some.

Now, what can help the girl whose frigidity stems from other than physical causes? Well, if it's due to mental hangups, understanding them will take care of the problem, right? Maybe. Much depends upon whom a girl goes to for help. Because legal standards vary greatly from one state to another and diplomas too often turn out to be meaningless pieces of paper, any troubled person should choose her marriage counselor, psychotherapist, or psychiatrist with great care. A good source of information about these practitioners is the mental-hygiene division of county or city health departments. Advice is also available through county medical societies or nearby medical schools.

Another avenue one might take in learning to understand both common and unusual sexual problems would be to study valid sex and marriage manuals. For bedtime reading I recommend:

The Marriage Art, John E. Eichenlaub, M.D., Dell, 95 cents.

New Approaches to Sex in Marriage, John E. Eichenlaub, M.D., Dell, 95 cents.

The Art and Science of Love, Albert Ellis, Ph.D., Bantam, $1.25.

Sexual Expression in Marriage, Donald W. Hastings, M.D., Bantam, $1.25.

You'll notice that three of the four manuals mention marriage in the title, but booksellers don't require proof of marriage. Further, relaxation of censorship has allowed publication of books formerly banned as obscene, many of them hard-core pornography which arouse prurient interest. If you want to read them by yourself or aloud to others to arouse prurience—why not?

Another source of concern for many women is the distinction between "vaginal" and "clitoral" orgasms. Sigmund Freud believed women could experience two types of orgasm, vaginal and clitoral. Masters and Johnson observed, however, that almost all female climaxes were triggered by the clitoris, even when no direct contact was being made. They found three women in their sample who were able to reach orgasm simply by having their breasts stimulated . . . and some few women are able to climax with no physical stimulation whatsoever, relying on their fantasies alone.

Today most sexologists believe that, however the arousal, "an orgasm is an orgasm." No difference in its character can be observed no matter how it is produced. As Masters and Johnson wrote, "The human female's physiologic responses to effective sexual stimulation develop with consistency regardless of the source of the psychic or physical sexual stimulation."

But subjective feelings are quite a different matter. Given a choice, most women would choose an orgasm attained through intercourse. Physiologically identical all climaxes may be, but those reached during lovemaking seem to meet psychological needs in a woman as yet unmeasured. "I know it's supposed to be the same feeling down there no matter how you have an orgasm," my secretary told me, "but it's different up here," she said, pointing to her head. "That's where it really counts."

Many women have found masturbation an aid in reaching sexual fulfillment. Years ago, masturbation was such a forbidden subject it was referred to only as "self-abuse." Little girls were told they would go blind or insane if they explored their genitals, and physicians sometimes recommended preventive measures such as tying the hands together or wearing straitjackets and chastity belts. Today, however, self-arousal is known to be a normal means of sexual release practiced by most women and almost all men sometime in their lives, and sexologists now stress the positive aspects of masturbation. Dr. LeMon Clark, a gynecologist and fellow medical columnist, is quoted by the psychologist Dr. Albert Ellis in *The Art and Science of Love* as having said, "Where self-relief in the male or female brings release from tension, promotes repose, and helps attain relaxation and sleep, it is not only harmless but definitely beneficial."

Masturbation, or automanipulation (Masters and Johnson's term), is also considered good training for successful lovemaking. According to Minneapolis psychiatrist Donald Hastings, "The girl who has been able to masturbate to orgasm before marriage undoubtedly has to some extent 'awakened' herself; she has, that is, trained her sexual reactions so that she will be better able to respond . . . with orgasm after marriage."

If a "frigid" woman can climax through means other than intercourse, then, she can learn to climax during lovemaking, proponents of conditioning maintain. Conditioning, which is most effective when combined with counseling or psychotherapy, begins with the woman nearly reaching climax through stimulation by her partner or herself. Then, at the point of orgasm, the man initiates intercourse. Over a period of weeks or months the actual act itself occurs earlier and earlier, until the woman learns to associate orgasm with lovemaking.

Fantasy, too, is often an important component of sexual enjoyment. Fantasies are controlled dreams or wishes fulfilled through imagination, and if they are sexual in nature, they usually arouse people—turn them on. It's as if a person were directing his own screenplay with himself the star. Or, more likely, *herself,* since sexual fantasies during lovemaking seem to be more common in women than men.

Content of fantasies, and the reasons they are employed, depend on complex psychological factors which vary from one person to another. For women who consciously or unconsciously feel guilty about enjoying sex, whether it's with a boyfriend or husband, fantasizing transports them from an apprehensive situation to one less threatening because it is unreal. Other women may feel uneasy about lovemaking due to some

125

forgotten incidents during childhood, and for them fantasies create a make-believe world where anxiety simply does not exist. Whatever the reason, fantasies are used to increase sexual pleasure, enabling many females to reach an orgasm which they would otherwise be unable to achieve.

Recurrent themes are often featured in a woman's fantasy life. Rape scenes, sometimes involving a member of a different race, country, or age group, are not uncommon. Nor are fantasies of being tied and bound, of beating and being beaten. Group sex, homosexuality, and more bizarre themes have also been reported.

If thinking of the Washington Monument is the only way you can get to where you want to be—why not? Once you know the road well, you can focus on the driver. As for the possibility of fantasies putting psychological distance between a woman and her lover, that is a gap which can be bridged by *sharing*: getting inside each other's head to enjoy a fantasy in common is an especially exciting form of intimacy.

Can sound affect sexual pleasure?

"Vocalizing my orgasms tells me how free the rest of me is," a friend told me the other day.

"What do you men?"

"Comparing the actual volume of sounds I make today with those of a few years ago, I would say I've gone far." And she had actual tapes for evidence.

Few things are more erotically exciting than the voices of love. Given a private, relatively soundproof room, a couple can express themselves as they wish—and one turns on the other. Some women are greatly aroused if they or their partners utter "profane" words. Others enjoy making love to music, often wearing headphones. Sounds a bit contrived —until you've done it.

As for positions in the love nest, not so many years ago there was only one that was sanctioned. The "missionary position," South Seas natives called it, for only missionaries were observed to make love face-to-face. But what are considered the "normal" postures today? Any way that people can fit together for mutual pleasure. A general rule in the bedroom might be: There are no rules in the bedroom. If it doesn't harm you or others—why not?

Take, for example, the experiment performed by a couple who once complained to me that sex between them was not quite satisfactory. He reached a climax long before she did and often couldn't sustain himself long enough to gratify her. Also, there were times when she wished to be aggressive, yet he found it difficult to remain passive.

I knew this couple had an interest in mysticism, so I suggested they practice a little-known form of Yoga called tantric, the Yoga of love. In the "yab-yum" position—look *that* up in your *Kama Sutra*—the couple sits facing each other, the woman initiating all movement. Practitioners of tantric Yoga maintain that after one or two hours of "yab-yumming"— that's right, *hours*—a kind of enlightenment is achieved: the man and woman feel themselves merge into each other to form a "third presence."

Enlightenment aside, the couple I had advised to try the Yoga of love found "yab-yum" particularly useful for their special problem. They claimed that because of the juxtaposition of their bodies, union could be maintained long after he reached a climax.

Because one's general physical health and vigor are usually directly reflected in bed, exercise makes for good sex (and sex is good exercise, too). A regular program of calisthenics doesn't take much time and will make you feel more alive within and without. Also, exercising the whole body seems to increase sexual yearnings, with subsequent sexual response, in some young women—as indicated by this letter I received recently:

Dear Dr. Hip Pocrates:

I often find when I'm exercising in the morning—particularly doing strenuous exercises on the floor like hip rolls, leg swings, bicycles, etc.— I get an overall sexy feeling. If somebody were in the room right then, I'd probably attack him. This doesn't *automatically* make you sexy later on when you're with a man, but I think having your body in shape somehow gives you more confidence that you *can* achieve orgasm. In both instances—orgasm and/or exercise—you are using your body as it was *meant* to be used.

Good point. Having confidence in your body will reflect itself in *all* your activities. Now add to your general routine of push-ups, arm whirls, and whatever else you do to keep in shape, the specific exercise of squeezing, clenching, contracting, then releasing the muscles of the vagina—thereby strengthening them and making them more elastic—and you'll almost surely enhance sexual pleasure for both yourself and your partner. Essentially the same as the exercise practiced by that woman who wrote to me explaining how she "clenched" her way to orgasm, it is also similar to the one often recommended following childbirth and pelvic surgery. And it can be done anywhere, at any time. Right now, for example.

Can technological advances increase the quality and quantity of orgasms? That's not so far-out a question as it may seem at first. For many years scientists have planted electrodes in brain pleasure-centers of laboratory animals (as a medical student I saw films of monkeys wired for pleasure), but when the animals are taught how to turn themselves on by activating the electrodes, many kill themselves with excess. It is conceivable that humans would do the same if they were so wired, just as some men and women kill themselves with drugs.

Drugs, of course, can be used as well as abused, and I think it won't be long before physicians will have a number of aphrodisiacs available on prescription. Two studies have already shown that marijuana users believe the drug increases sexual pleasure for people already turned on to each other (if a couple is turned off to each other, marijuana increases the alienation). Drugs like LSD and mescaline also have the reputation of greatly increasing sexual feelings—again, where people care for each other beforehand—and while some people claim to be turned off by amphetamines, others report that "speed" gives them true erotic stimulation. And though it has been proved that an overdose of alcohol commmonly causes impotency, it has also been demonstrated that in appropriate quantities alcohol relaxes inhibitions of many people by "dissolving" the superego.

I place drug usage for aphrodisiac purposes in the future because at present we don't know enough about their safety when prescribed for sexual pleasure alone. But the idea does have real possibilities. Meanwhile, as we've discussed here, there are plenty of tested ways to achieve increased sexual pleasure. Orgasms are free, and since you can't use them up, why not have as many as you want? Well, why not?

2

I WAS A SLEEP-AROUND GIRL I finished telling her about myself. "And how about you?" I asked.

She smiled faintly through the shadows that a flickering candle threw across her face, fondly reminiscing of a time past. "Oh, me," she said. "What's there to say? I used to be a sleep-around girl. Now I'm not." And she smiled again.

"'Autumn Leaves'?" I teased, irritated for a moment by what seemed her almost sentimental resignation from life itself. "'And the time grows short as you reach September'?"

"I think I've found a better way to go, that's all. Something I didn't believe existed. But now I've found it." She later told me her age: twenty-nine.

We'd just met not more than an hour before in a half-darkened cowtown airport at 4 A.M., drinking a bit and wearily waiting for our respectively delayed flights to be announced. It had been one of those astonishingly swift recognitions that sometimes take place between passing strangers. Perhaps we both immediately knew each other as two big-city people stranded and bored in this dim desert town. At any rate, we were having one of those conversations that can only start up when you're tired and it's late at night . . . the kind that begins swiftly, as if both your lives have been unconsciously rehearsed and made ready in the wings, each of you letter-perfect to play together when you finally meet on some inadvertent stage . . . barings of the soul so immediate and naked in their way that they are brief love affairs, with intensity added—in this case, literally—by the fact that you each have your own plane to catch before dawn.

I was barely eighteen when I gave my virginity," she said. "I didn't give it *up*, and I certainly didn't 'lose' it. God! How I hate that phrase; the damage the idea of 'losing' one's virginity has done to generation after generation of girls. I didn't 'lose' it. I gave it. Bestowed it!

"Funny," she went on, "how we live in an age when everything, including time, accelerates. That was only a little over ten or eleven years ago, but it was still an era when girls used to be taught to think of their chastity as something so delicate and fragile, so . . . infinitely precious. And you had to be careful or some nasty man would come along and you would 'lose' it. Once I asked my mother, when she was beginning to try to get me lined up the way *her* mother got her lined up: 'But if it's so precious, and you lose it, what does it matter if the man is your husband or not?' Then I asked, 'Do boys lose their little things? Why should only girls have to lose? I don't want to be a cripple!' "

"What did she say?"

"First she slapped me, and then she ran out of the room in tears. Two minutes later she came running back and put her arms around me and just rocked me back and forth until I was crying with her. I was only identifying with her unhappiness; I didn't know why she was crying then. But I know now."

"Why?"

"Because—the way only a kid can—without knowing what I was doing, I'd just poked a hole in the nutty mess by which she tried to live. But all my life I knew one thing, and that's what saved my sanity when I was growing up. I knew if they got you to thinking that if a boy wanted you 'that way,' it was a dirty thing, you'd still look on it as something dirty later on, married or not, and you'd be dirty, too."

She paused to put out a cigarette. "And I resented the innuendo that being wanted was wrong. Even as a little girl I felt so . . . so feminine. I *wanted* a man to want me 'that way.' In fact, in every way. I knew then that if I accepted my mother's view, I'd be less of a woman than I wanted to be. And also—maybe this is the worst thing of all—that way of thinking (my mother's way) made men and women see each other as . . . well, enemies. Each was out to get something from the other. But I never wanted to think of men as my enemies. Even when I was the wildest swinger in what was a pretty liberated bunch of people, and even if I went to bed with a man I didn't like much—that happened to me more than once or twice—I'd like to feel he was my friend afterward. When I began to lose that capacity to *like* the men I was going to bed with—" She brushed her hair back. "But I'll tell you about that when I come to it." She smiled at me, a faint, weary, lovely, 4 A.M. smile I remember still.

And then she began again, briskly, as if to spark her flagging spirits. "So there I was, eighteen, engaged . . . wildly, stupidly in love—and, best of all, my fiancé wanted to go to bed with me! He just dropped the hint in one of those two-way sentences when he brought me home one night. I could understand him or not. Well, I didn't answer him then, and I didn't sleep that night, either. But the next day I called my best girl friend and we went shopping for enough lacy and ribbony underwear to open our own store. 'Why all the frills?' Jeannie kept asking as we shopped and I dramatically built toward my terrific revelation. 'Why?' But when I finally told her, she wasn't floored. She was aghast. *Aghast!*

"There I was, thinking she was going to be jealous, maybe just a little. I thought she was someone I could anticipate this thing with, to talk about it with, to giggle over this marvelous wonder that was about to happen to me. But she just turned off. We were never friends after that.

"You see, when I was in my teens, people still thought somehow it was an insult if a guy 'propositioned' you . . . that he was a rat, only 'out for one thing' . . . that it was demeaning of you to let him think for one moment you were the kind of girl who would even dream of saying hello to a man who wanted you 'that way.' But I *always* wanted a man to want me 'that way' . . . to make as passionate a commitment, have as passionate a feeling about me as possible. I certainly wouldn't have settled for somebody who only wanted my photograph to put on his mother's piano in the living room."

The PA system clicked on, and we both cocked a hopeful ear. But the plane announced was neither of ours. Then she looked at me sideways and smiled, because we suddenly were both aware that while we *had* hoped the announcement would be for us, we were also glad to have just-who-knows-how-many-more minutes together: she wanted to tell me her story; I wanted to hear it. She hurried on:

"For a man to want to take you to bed, and then to *actually* take you, and then make it a night you'll always remember . . . that's real. There's something very honest about sleeping with a man. A girl has to learn to judge what a man *says*, to second-guess if he's telling the truth or maybe only *thinks* he is when actually he's just lying to himself. But you always know exactly what the score is in bed. Wanting to sleep with you is the ultimate compliment a man can pay you, except maybe to want to marry you."

She paused for a moment to get her thoughts straight, then leaned in a little closer to me: "But, you see, I didn't want to marry *them*. So why should I insist they marry me? If I wasn't ready for marriage, why should they be?

"Well, anyway, I didn't marry my fiancé. The 'honeymoon' convinced me not to go through with the wedding! Arlie was a nice boy . . . my family liked him, his family liked me, he had a good job, and we'd have a long, comfortable life together playing golf, and maybe I'd join a ladies' club. In the evenings, of course, there'd be TV.

"When I think now of what I would have missed if I *had* played it insanely safe and married Arlie; I'd never have had these incredibly beautiful years since him . . . not the heartbreak or the adventure . . . I'd never have known the freedom of having my own life in *my* hands. The thought frightens me; it catches my breath. So much I'd never have known—"

What happened with Arlie?" I asked,

"We went to his house that night—on the same day I'd done all the shopping with my girl friend. His parents had flown to Bermuda so the place was empty. And when I walked into that house I was proud of myself—proud of Arlie, too, even though at the last moment he seemed to be getting a little apprehensive. But I did everything to convince him that I was a *willing* partner. As I said, I didn't lose my virginity. I *bestowed* it.

"Still, that very first night together, I *knew*. I was a virgin, yes, and had no other man to compare him with. He was twenty-three and I knew *he* wasn't a virgin; he told me he wasn't, and that was one of the most exciting things about the whole affair: I was going to learn how to make love from—don't smile, I was only eighteen—a man-of-the-world! But even at eighteen I was a woman, and I knew my body—what it wanted and what it needed . . . and it was almost like coming to an exam in school when you knew you'd done all your work and you were going to get a marvelous mark; I knew that very first night with Arlie that I was going to get fantastic marks all my life for what was not an exam at all but *pleasure*. And I also realized, almost instinctively, that Arlie was zero, zero.

"I didn't say anything to him then or on any of the few other nights we had together. I didn't *have* to. He knew. He was an intelligent boy, after all. But finally I did tell him, 'Look, don't take all the blame on yourself. Maybe I'm the one who's wrong for you. If you married me, Arlie, you'd never know if maybe there was some other girl somewhere—maybe you'll meet her tomorrow—who was right for you . . . who'd send you off like a rocket. I don't want to miss that feeling myself, and I like you enough not to want you to miss it either.'

"He kissed me on the forehead then, and went out without saying a word. I later heard he'd married and moved away, and later still that he was divorced. After that, when I was living in California, in my PP (Post Promiscuity) phase—I'll explain about that later—he came to town for a sales conference and phoned me, and we spent the evening in bed. Why not? By then I could see him for what he was: a friend. I'd always *liked* him. And without all that marriage tension—" Then she corrected herself: "No, that wasn't it. You see, Arlie had grown up with the male equivalent of all that sick morality my mother had been trying to feed me. So if he took a 'nice girl' like me to bed he had to be guilty, because *he* had 'seduced' *me*. And, of course, no one makes love very snappily under a load of guilt. So what I think it was . . . I think in the years since I'd last seen Arlie I had evolved more into the kind of girl I wanted to be. I'd thought things out for myself and now knew how to unload this feeling of guilt a man has on his back for wanting to take you to bed. I knew how to make it clear he wasn't 'seducing' me but just joining me in what I thought was the loveliest thing in the world two people can do . . . that if anything, *I* was 'seducing' *him*. Of course, we had the best night we'd ever had together. He still calls whenever he comes back to town, and once when I was in Chicago—he lives there now—I called him. We always wind up the evening in bed—and wake up the next morning liking each other just a little bit more. Whenever I think of Arlie, it's with great fondness. But if I'd married him, I'd hate him by now."

When we started talking," I said, "you told me you were a sleep-around girl. So far you've been with only one man. What happened after your affair with Arlie?"

She put back her tired head for a moment and closed her eyes. "Perhaps when I mentioned that," she said, "I was just testing you." She looked at me directly: "There's no such thing as a general, all-purpose sleep-around girl. Different girls go through different phases of sleeping around for different reasons. I went through three entirely different phases of it myself."

"Where are you now?"

"I've just left Phase Three."

"What's that?"

"Wait . . . first let me tell you about Phase One of sleeping around, when I wouldn't have dreamed of having more than one affair going at the same time. Oh, that was a halcyon stage, all right. I was young, happy, with a kind of innocence I realize now was very vulnerable underneath all my supposed experience and sophistication. But, God, it was a lovely time."

"And so who was your 'one man' after Arlie?"

"My boss." Again the reminiscent fond smile, the thoughts behind those pensive eyes turning back into her memory. "James. Jimmy. He was thirteen years older than I, and one of those men who is very good at his job but also physically tuned in, aware of every girl in the building. He was certainly immediately aware of me, and he asked me to lunch my first day on the job. But even while we were talking about which restaurant I preferred, I somehow knew what 'lunch' really meant."

I nodded to the sleepy waiter and he brought us another round. As he set down the glasses, my companion looked at me: "Now you have to remember that though I'd had this affair with Arlie, it had been my first, and I was still only eighteen. I wasn't quite sure I wanted men to see me as sexually as I saw myself . . . and as I saw them, for that matter. Maybe I still had a hangover of timidity from all my mother's noes and my girl friends', too. And, of course, there was this thing about Jimmy being married. I'd felt safe with Arlie . . . he loved me, wanted to marry me. We practically were married. But I knew that starting with Jimmy was a more dangerous, naked game. And so I really tried to stop it; I called him on the interoffice phone ten minutes later and told him I had to work and would have to skip lunch. 'I'm sorry,' he said, 'perhaps another day?' 'I'd like that,' I said and hung up thinking what a dumb, stupid little girl I was.

The next time he asked me to lunch, I went like a shot—and, as I suspected, lunch wasn't just lunch.

"Jimmy was married, but he kept a little one-room bachelor place in town, and that's where we had lunch after only one drink in the restaurant. And *after* lunch . . . well, Jimmy in the bedroom was one of the world's champions, even more of a whiz than in the office. With Arlie, though I'd been the one with less experience, just after a night or two I found myself leading the way. But with Jimmy I had something marvelous. And he did, too. It was really that wonderful thing that can happen between two people if you're both intelligent and don't try to score points on each other. He enjoyed the role of expert tutor, and I was his not-untalented pupil. Simple as that. That's all we had, but it was plenty.

"One of the most tingling memories of our affair was the excitement of not meeting too often in the office, speaking formally to each other on the telephone, almost looking through each other when we'd meet in a corridor. Because the company had this lunatic, antiquated rule about prohibiting what they called 'fraternization,' believe it or not! But though we played it cool with each other in the office, as I said, it was part of our excitement. *We* knew and *they* didn't!"

"When you said a little while ago, 'That's all we had,' what did you mean?"

"Oh, nothing stupid like, 'We only had this physical thing in common.' A lot of people don't even have *that*. But what I meant was that while Jimmy enjoyed playing the role of tutor, after a while I didn't want to be the pupil—the little girl—anymore. I wanted to be more of an equal, to initiate some of the ideas. But he didn't like that. Some kind of power struggle began to upset the works."

She looked at me seriously: "You know how a girl can tell when her girlhood ideas of just what an affair is are coming to an end? When she finds herself going to bed with other men. But that wasn't how I was at this first phase of sleeping around. My unconscious assumptions were still somewhat based on the old conventional idea: that when I was with a man, he should be the only one in my life. In other words, I wasn't yet grown-up enough to be able to take an affair as an *affair*. Instead, I tried to make it into a miniature marriage."

"When did you—so to speak—lose your girlhood notions?"

"Please, let me tell the story my way, O.K.? So, as I said, this power business began with Jimmy, and I found I wasn't seeing him as much, maybe sometimes deliberately breaking a date to show him he couldn't always be the one to say when. And so other men drifted into my life—not necessarily those I liked as much as Jimmy at his best; no single one of them could really take his place . . . but there did begin to be *more* than one man, more than two, even more than three in my life at the same time, and I was juggling them all—successfully. And it was then that I got a hint of what my life *could* be like, what I could *make* of it. I'd show Jimmy, I'd think, accepting a date with one man, making a late date with another. But then Jimmy was transferred to the West Coast and that sort of finished us—I haven't seen him since—and without him around to prove something to I sort of lost interest in those other men, and pretty soon they were gone, too. But I'll always be grateful to Jimmy."

"Exactly why?" I asked.

"One of my girl friends," she said, answering me a little obliquely, "once made a penetrating remark: 'All girls are in the same business. No matter what else they do, they're also in the *pretty* business. That's why they're always competing with each other.' And I'd always accepted the truth of that comment. But with Jimmy—he brought out so much in me, gave me so much sexual confidence and ease, I came to realize that although I was attractive enough to hold my own with other girls, I had another way to compete besides just with a pretty face! I had this natural, unforced talent, and my desire to go to bed was as understandable as Philip Roth wanting to show off his writing in a new novel. Jimmy convinced me I was rare, that I was one of the few girls who unashamedly loved sex and was not going to hide my talent."

"And did your life just keep going on that way, 'triumph' after 'triumph,' with the constant sound of (private) male applause?"

My question made her laugh. Thinking back now, perhaps I most admire her for the moment of laughter at that particular point in our predawn conversation. Most other girls I know would have begun to weep at what she was about to tell me. In fact, the paradox puzzled her, too:

"I don't know why I'm laughing. Now that I look back I can see I was about to be shot down in flames, about to enter Phase Two of my sexual career: the girl who sleeps around in the stupidest way possible. But, of course, I didn't know that then. In fact, I felt positively joyous and powerful. When Jimmy and I were through, I was left with this feeling of confidence that I had finally found myself and was ready to find the next man. Maybe I was overconfident, because the next thing I was going to learn was that I was more vulnerable to jealousy than I'd thought. Oh, I was always as jealous as any girl, but I knew the best way to handle men was not to be too inquisitive, not to play the detective. But I didn't realize there are certain men who deliberately play on your everyday, ordinary jealousy—they enrage it, make it swell, become inflamed, and grow—in order to prove to themselves how much they're wanted.

"Anyway, that kind of man signaled the beginning of what I call Phase Two of sleeping around . . . my next affair, the most disastrous of my life, where I found myself acting unnaturally, totally unlike myself—not wanting to hang on but not being able to let go, and never realizing until years later I was being emotionally manipulated by a Ph.D. of jealousy. Mike was a man to whom women aren't women but—that old phrase—merely notches on his gun. You know the thing about Don Juans? They don't love women, they hate them . . . because these men think women are stronger and need to be broken. Well, Mike was exactly like that. As I said, perhaps I was more vulnerable than I'd thought—and maybe Mike sensed this weakness in me, my vulnerability to jealousy. Men like him can. Of course, they're also attracted to your sexuality—they can scent that, too—so they make *that* their target. Eventually, there went the years of confidence and along came a wrecked ego which I stupidly tried to salvage in the only way I knew how: sleeping around with men and more men. And then, a few years ago, came the low point, when I realized I simply didn't care about the number anymore and tore up my own secret little list. Today I can spot a man like Mike. But what did I know then?

He was about ten years older than I, and, again, we both worked for the same company. He was one of the top executives . . . in fact, similar to Jimmy in many ways: extremely talented in bed, handsome as a movie star, and *definitely* married. But right there all similarity to Jimmy stopped."

"How?"

"Though I knew Jimmy was married, I was never jealous of his wife. She was off in a suburb somewhere and I never even *thought* of her. I knew *I* was the only girl Jimmy was having 'lunch' with—and that was all the security I needed. But Mike—this next one—was an absolutely compulsive and lethal Don Juan. The first, and *still* hopefully last, in my life—if I'm lucky. As I told you, when I was with a man and I was happy, that's all I wanted. My telephone would stop ringing for anyone else. And that's how I thought my affair with Mike was going to be. Well, it went on for almost two of the most heartbreaking years of my life, with me steadfastly maintaining a one-to-one sexual relationship while *he* maintained a him-to-hundreds . . . always telling me how I compared with every other girl he'd ever made love to.

"It's easy to say now: I should have dumped him. Hard. And fast. But a man like that—he fascinated me just like a snake does a bird. And when I hadn't seen him the night before, I'd search the office corridors next day to catch a glimpse of him . . . to see if he had a certain weary, sagging look around the eyes that I knew very well meant a sleepless night in somebody's bed. I often found it. But, of course, all he needed was a martini at lunch to put the sparkle back in his eyes, and if he'd come to my office to ask me out *that* night, he'd look so handsome and healthy I never *could* steel myself to say no. Sleeping with a Don Juan often has this effect on a girl . . . she's shattered by a kind of emotional paralysis, fascinated with a man she hates more than any other on earth and yet loves the most. Sleeping with Mike made me feel, for the first time in my life, as though I were used and degraded. And yet I couldn't stop."

She smiled without mirth. "In the end he dumped me . . . walked right into a party where he knew I'd be, with a girl he knew I especially hated. The sheer shock and pain of being jilted by him lasted almost five years. Five long years! I hated him but couldn't settle down with someone new."

What were those five years like after you and Mike were finished?"

"Let me explain them this way: the funny thing about that nice young girl-next-door you sometimes see in the morning, stepping out so confidently and trim on her way to her good job, newspaper and briefcase under arm, her little sportscar waiting on the lot below to zoom her off into her marvelous future—she may have left a man she doesn't even know sleeping it off back in her apartment. Just because a girl's sex or love life is a little erratic doesn't mean her business life is necessarily going to suffer. *Mine* didn't. In fact, the old cliché about throwing yourself into your job really worked for me. And pretty soon I was that nice young *executive* girl in the apartment next door. I had this lovely place, money in the bank, friends, vacations, and even a robin's-egg-blue convertible. The very picture of the 'good life.' But that's all it was. Just a picture. My early twenties should have been the best years of my life. You always hear that about a woman. But me? I laughed and cried my way through them, and now they're all over, and I'm glad.

"Anyway, my career was rocketing up and up, but my sex life was barreling down, down, down. I was really in pain because of what Mike had done to me, and so I just went cuckoo in bed, constantly looking for the assurance and strength I'd found there *before* Mike. It was sex without affection, without relationship—sometimes angry sex, sometimes in spite . . . but *always* sex. Round heels. Toes up. One-night stands. No matter what other people thought about me, I thought so much worse about myself I just didn't pay any attention to the crummy reputation I was saddling myself with. Everything else in my life—professionally, socially, and economically—was pretty straight and true and foursquare, so I could rationalize like an alcoholic who thinks that as long as he's still holding onto his job everything is O.K.

"And also there was something else in me that wouldn't let me go all the way down. Call it a feeling for health, or maybe the last vestiges of self-respect. Because the men I picked always had a certain degree of worldly success. With the kind of nonstop, violently whirlwind sex binge I was embarked on, if I'd begun to find myself waking up in creepy lofts or shabby hotel rooms, I don't think I could have survived. Maybe it was my career that was saving me. Come to think of it, the fact I clung to my career no matter what else I was doing—that must have been an element of health and desire for survival, too. And so there were champagne nights, and days at the races. Caribbean 'honeymoons,' and weekends aboard yachts. The years spun merrily enough along—so long as I didn't think too closely about them.

"But what was not so merry was the almost constant state of tranquilizer-masked depression I was in and finally losing track of exactly how many men I *had* slept with. I told you about that little secret list I kept? The night I tore it up I cried till dawn. In somebody else's bed. There was this constant knowledge that neither I nor any of the men cared really, and the realization that if I got pregnant, singling out the father would be . . . well, difficult, to say the least.

"Mike had let me down so hard—my defenses against allowing myself to care about another man again as I had about him were so tight—that any man who came along who might have had the capacity to make me respond was turned off. And before long, he'd leave to find someone who could and would respond . . . emotionally. Mine was a busy-busy-busy existence, but in reality, in the midst of all that sex, I felt terrific, enormous sexual frustration. Because a girl is equal to a boy, but she's not the *same* as a boy. She needs an emotional, affectionate framework around sex. And the framework I had been putting sex into could not work for *any* woman . . . it just couldn't be satisfying."

But it mustn't have *all* been grim?" I said. "Or else you wouldn't look back on that past time so fondly? You'd have packed it all in a long time ago."

"Yes," she said. "Toward the end of that phase—Phase Two of my sleeping around—there was one very happy experience. Once again, an affair with my boss. Superboss . . . chairman of the board. It was sheer seduction on my part but mixed up with a there-there-little-girl-come-to-daddy feeling from *him*. Mr. D. was twenty-five years older than I, but the most tycoonish and successful man I'd ever known . . . someone for whom I had genuine regard and respect. That in itself was something of a switch for me by then, and the sweetness of sex-within-a-relationship reminded me of my beginning days, my *really* good old days. Best of all, I had that rare thing a woman wants so much—the pleasure of making someone you care about *happy*. Mr. D., at fifty or so, was absolutely euphoric over the elaborate sexual attentions of a girl so much younger and one who wanted nothing from him except the respect and affection he gave for *herself*.

"Maybe it was on the springboard of that renewed self-confidence from him that I decided to change my life. After a few months I flew to California and got a new job. If anyone ever needed a 'fresh start,' despite Mr. D., it was I. And if anyone was ever prepared to do something about it, I was. The 'something' I did besides get a job was to enter psychiatry. And I guess it really wasn't surprising that, as I began to put my feelings and emotions back into perspective, my sexual patterns started to change, too. For the *better*, like almost everything else in my life. Within a year I had left my *first* new job and become public-relations director of a large industrial firm . . . two assistants and a secretary all my own. Everything went together. As pride in myself began to come back, I moved into a beautiful apartment and used it as a *home* . . . for me and my friends . . .

for entertaining people I liked and admired. Rotten old Phase Two of sleeping around was over."

"And Phase Three?"

Phase Three was about to begin—from the time I was twenty-five until right now. Unquestionably, the best time of my life."

"So how and where did sex fit into everything?" I asked.

"Come on now!" She smiled. "Is success or psychiatry ever a satisfying substitute for abstinence? Of course there was sex, still is . . . lots of it . . . luscious and lovely. And, of course, there were men . . . plural! But always carefully chosen. And when they overlapped? That was usually a signal that an old affair was fading and a new one about to begin . . . or a past affair merely temporarily but lovingly renewed. Above all, these overlaps were handled with care so that neither man knew about the other—and no one was hurt, including me."

"Were your Phase Three men single or married?"

Her smile at me was lightly derisive. "By the time someone like me—in her late twenties—comes into a man's life he usually is married. So two or three of my Phase Three (PP—Post Promiscuity) affairs were with married men . . . nice, loving men who gave as much and took as much from the relationship as I. And that's the key word here: relationship. It was wonderful to be caring again about exactly who I was sleeping with, and how often, and why and where and when. And having decided to do so all in a calm, loving state before time for beddy-by. It was wonderful to have lovers who could love . . . to be friends, not enemies."

Again the public-address system clicked on, and this time her plane was announced. But there still was about fifteen minutes to board, so I walked down to the departure gate with her, and she told me what she felt to be the significant difference between how she'd been in the early phases of her "sleeping around" and in this last phase she called PP:

"My belief when I finally got to my PP period was that I wouldn't get into bed with another man unless what we were about to do had meaning to us both . . . unless there was a loving relationship. Well, some time ago I was involved with a marvelous man, an orchestra conductor, who was the only one on the scene at the time. And one day I got a phone call from Mr. D.—remember him? my board chairman—who was in town for two weeks. Did I go to bed with him as well as the conductor during that time? Of course! Why wouldn't I? I loved Mr. D. and was grateful to him and wanted him to be *happy*. If I'd said no, it would have hurt him terribly, and for the sake of what?

"But the one thing I was careful about was to make sure my conductor knew nothing of Mr. D. And Mr. D., of course, knew nothing about the orchestra conductor, either. He merely assumed there *was* a man. I had a small dinner party with both of them there and, frankly, I can't remember ever feeling quite so glamorous or womanly, and—stand by—*happy* in my whole life as I did with those two men."

I was disappointed by her answer. By now I expected something more from this girl. "And so that's what you meant at the beginning when you said you'd found something better? . . . You meant the ability to love and be loved by two men at once and to sustain a loving relationship with each man?"

She was ready to board now, but—did she see some distress in my eyes? —she stepped out of the line to have a last word with me.

"That was a lovely time of my life," my companion said, brushing a wisp of hair out of her eyes. "A lovely time. But that was my very last phase of sleeping around."

"And what's the state of your love life now?"

"I hope I'm entering it today. A whole new thing built on the capacity to love and be loved by *one* man. I've fallen like a slab of marble."

"And so this flight . . . you're going off to convince him?"

She winked at me, emanating a little of the flirtatious fire that is as unconscious in a girl like this as the air circulating in her lungs. Then she stopped and patted me on the cheek as tenderly as if she had kissed me. "I'll write you," she said, and got on the airplane and flew out of my life.

Because, of course, she never did.

Could *you* successfully handle more than one affair at a time *without* becoming a "sleep-around girl"?

1. Don't get hurt. This is the basic rule from which all others logically derive. Try to keep your motivations high, but your expectations harshly realistic! No, it's *not* easy!

2. Don't let any of the men know about the others. No compulsive confessions on your part . . . he may very well be carrying on more than one affair, too. Don't ask, don't tell . . . and neither of you will get hurt.

3. If a man is married but demands ice-blue faithfulness from you, even on weekends when he is home with wife and kiddies, forget him. He'll hurt you . . . or, rather, allow you to hurt yourself.

4. Just because an affair is over doesn't mean that the feelings you essentially have for each other have ended, too. If one of your old beaux who has been transferred to another town, let's say, arrives on your doorstep for a night or two, don't think of yourself as a "sleep-around girl" just because you go to bed with him. You're not. You've *always* had a relationship, but it was suspended. Now, temporarily, it's not.

5. If you have a long, lovely evening with a man you don't quite feel "that way" about, but nevertheless still find yourself in bed with him—again, don't think of yourself as a "sleep-around girl." It's been said that to go to bed with a friend is "the friendliest thing two people can do."

6. The one big *don't* is this: don't go to bed with a man to show off, to spite anyone, in anger, because you're drunk, lonely, nervous, to win his affection, to hold him. Those *are* sleep-around tricks. *Nice* girls go to bed only with men they like who like them. I don't say they always *do*. But when they do, the man is chosen from that warm, affectionate circle.

3

WHAT'S NORMAL AND WHAT ISN'T

It used to be that a girl would feel insulted if you made the slightest implication that she was not a virgin. Many a girl today would be insulted if you told her you thought she was.

It used to be that men told each other, "Good women don't like it," and, "Nice girls . . . *really* nice girls . . . are frigid." Smoking cigarettes in public was another mark of what a generation, too inhibited even to say what it meant, called "a tramp." And a *lady* would never wear a skirt that showed "too much leg."

Times have changed, haven't they? The Sexual Revolution took place, almost, it seems, one night when no one was looking. Nice girls *did* make love. Sex *wasn't* dirty. When we woke up, it was a different world.

Which brings us to the next point. With the greater freedom everyone feels, with the constant sexual exploration that is going on, a new element is being added to sexuality. Sophistication has set in. The desires of the body are being augmented by the desires of the mind. People can choose the special excursions that give them gratification. Kinks, the squares call them.

Let's understand each other before we go on. This is an article about those secret, unexpressed, and perhaps exotic tastes and desires most people have about sex, but which they may fear in themselves—may fear

3

3

even to express to themselves—and which they fear in their lovemate. However, if you happen to be, for instance, a girl with a taste for men who carry whips, this article is not for you. You, Miss Leather, already know what you want, you have no trouble expressing it to yourself or him, and you're a nut. Get out of here and into some doctor's office. This goes for anyone else whose desires lead to physical damage and degradation. I'm talking here about folks who merely have some slight, last Puritanic reluctance to give themselves up to some of the fancy pleasures that the mind can bring to the body. That is all a "kink" means for our purposes.

The reason I am trying to be so clear is that we are talking about an area of sexuality in which most people feel they must grapple with their fears and desires in the dark (all alone, so to speak, even when in the skin-to-skin presence of the one they love). People who will gaily leap into bed together will not tell each other what they really want to do once they actually get there. Wives won't tell husbands, girls won't tell lovers, patients won't tell psychiatrists, people won't even tell themselves. Won't name out loud whatever secret desire it is that can flip the switch that will turn them on.

Why such stern self-denial? Why such masochism? If your sexual tastes are, as we said a little earlier, not physically damaging or degrading, what have you gained by denying yourself some unusual pleasures just because if they knew about it, the squares would be shocked?

The answer is you've gained the pleasure of not thinking of yourself as kinky. Big deal!

So let's talk about it. What *are* the various little sexual games with which other people have brought themselves and their partners that added sense of delight and pleasure, that extra *frisson* that makes love or a love affair so memorable? (We start with the assumption that by now we all know that all physical positions and contacts that do not cause pain are certainly O.K., and need not be reviewed here.) Let's talk about the ambience of sex, the elements of fantasy, whimsy, playfulness, and imagination that improve the purely mechanical act of sex. These are the ideas that terrify the square, who have their own names for them. Let's go down their terrible roll call:

Caroline and John were married, went on their honeymoon, came back, and settled down. Their sexual life together slowly cooled off, and their marriage became two or three hours of watching the box after dinner together, then a yawn, and good night. An O.K. but tedious life.

John, who was a salesman, occasionally brought lonely, out-of-town buyers home with him for dinner. On those nights, life seemed brighter to Caroline, much more romantic, more erotic—and afterward, alone with her husband, sex was practically pyrotechnic. Caroline, an intelligent girl, had the courage to face what was going on in her psyche.

On those evenings *à trois* Caroline would make up a little fantasy. Alone all evening with two men, she would imagine that both lusted after her, and that she herself desired the two of them. Not that she wanted a trio in bed. But she would enjoy the playful *thought* that she would give herself at the end of the night to the man who wanted her most. (Though Caroline's practical and faithful *conscious* mind always really knew that man would be her husband.)

Caroline didn't waste time being disgusted with herself for having promiscuous fantasies. No one is responsible for these upsurges from the unconscious, and she knew that she firmly intended not to act on them. What she decided to do was use her fantasies to give herself and her husband fewer of those dreary evenings staring at the television set, and more erotic adventure.

She gave her husband a few drinks one night, and just told him about her fantasies. He began to get angry, and then he just laughed out loud. *And told her a hitherto concealed fantasy of his own.* (Because Caroline had frankly acknowledged her sexual urges, he felt the freedom to reveal his own.)

Now John brings a male friend home to dinner whenever there is the opportunity. Caroline cooks a festive meal, the stranger goes home charmed by the warm feeling of love and affection between Caroline and John. That he has been an innocent catalyst for what happens later does him no harm, and brings about worlds of good for Caroline and John.

On his side, before the friend-for-dinner phase began to freshen up their marriage, John had always had a yearning he felt too embarrassed to tell "a nice girl" like Caroline. In fact, this whole desire on his part was an effort to break the antisexual tyranny of "niceness."

After all, what is the old-fashioned definition of a nice girl? For John, because of a repressive childhood, she was the girl you do *not* take to bed. And if you did, she wouldn't like it, she'd hate you later. What John wanted Caroline to do was make herself into an un-nice girl for him occasionally. He wanted her to use dirty words . . . voice dirty desires . . . in bed. (A word to the lexicographers in the audience. I know there is no such thing, technically, as a "dirty" word. Please understand that I'm using the term as a form of shorthand.)

John had never been able to bring himself to ask Caroline to break out of the Nice Trap. He would lose her respect, he felt; she would loathe him, the worm. After all, what kind of creep would ask the girl he married to do such things or say such things. But, night after night, in the privacy of his own mind, he would hope that Caroline would murmur some word or phrase that might enflame him.

She never did, of course, not knowing that was what he wanted. But now that John realized Caroline had been as bored as he had been when they had conducted their marriage along "normal, conventional, healthy lines," he plucked up the courage to voice his desires to her, even to tell her a few of the things he'd like her to say.

And Caroline, now feeling freer to express her sexuality through more than just the mechanical act itself, discovered something more: she *wanted* to say the words, wanted to shout and scream them sometimes. They not only excited John, they excited her. She was tired of being "nice."

So, after years of sexual boredom, just by having the guts to finally tell each other what they liked, this couple has created an exciting, viable marriage. John has a fine wife and admirable hostess by day, and his own private sexpot at night. And Caroline has, at last, the marriage she had dreamed of.

Thinking about John and Caroline, I went to talk to a psychiatrist about idiosyncrasies like these, which might be called the tender perversions. To protect his patients' privacy, I can't give you the doctor's name, but here are some actual stories he told of how people, by admitting what was obsessing them, found the gratification they wanted for themselves *and* their lovers.

Stan was almost the classic case of the fetishist. He was obsessed with breasts and everything to do with them. He had cut out bra ads from magazines when he was a boy, and had kept them in a secret scrapbook. He would literally turn in the street and follow any large-breasted woman he saw. When he spoke on the telephone, he'd doodle drawings of breasts. When he slept with a girl, however, he would urge her *to leave her bra on,* and on nights when he slept alone, he would put a bra he had bought at a department store under his pillow. He was almost more obsessed with bras than with breasts.

Otherwise, Stan was intelligent, hard working, and successful . . . and too sensible to pass up Jill when she came along. He wanted to marry her, but she was a little put off by what she felt was the strangeness of his desire that she keep her bra on, even when they were making love. She never really understood the depths of the problem, however, until one day, before they were married, she found that absurd 38D-cup bra under his pillow. Sick at heart and ashamed, but anxious not to lose her through an imaginary infidelity, he told her about his bra obsession.

Jill spoke to the psychiatrist, who hazarded the suggestion that Stan's passion for bras and breasts was the slightly deflected symbol of a concealed desire (hang on, I'll tell you). According to the doctor, there lingered in Stan some childhood memory of being deprived of what breasts *contained:* mother's milk. The reason he wanted to keep a woman's breasts hidden and covered up with a bra, despite his desire for the woman, was again an infantile fear that if he did see the breasts themselves, there would once again be no milk—and he couldn't bear the disappointment!

Psychiatry might help Stan, but could take years; and, besides, apart from this hangup, Stan was intelligent, kind, and successful in most areas of his life. So Jill decided not to fight her fiancé's kink but to cater to it . . . to give him a pleasure more satisfying to his deeply buried desires than merely looking at breasts and fondling bras, the pleasure that was the secret obsession of his life: to *taste* a woman's breasts.

On her wedding night, Jill came to bed with a big dollop of Hershey's milk-chocolate syrup tipping each breast. Honest!

Stan is still a fetishist. But his fetish is his wife. And they keep a can of Hershey's by the bed. Does that hurt anyone?

Charley and Harriet had known each other since they were children, and in the country-club set in which they grew up it was always assumed that they would eventually marry. This assumption was accepted by Charley and Harriet, too, since they were dutiful, well-brought-up children who never thought of defying their families or convention. So they announced the engagement, in their own dim, unexciting way.

149

These "good children," however, were less than enthusiastic about the upcoming marriage. Both had that chill, slightly inhibited air of good breeding; neither one could break through the frost. In addition, while they *liked* each other, their roles were too much like brother and sister to send off sexual sparks. Neither one could *see* the other as sexy.

So, here are two intelligent people, and they decided to talk the matter over. Unfortunately, discussion was conducted in their well-bred *cordial* way, and nothing came of it. Unable to put into frank words what he really had wanted to say, Charley decided to *show* Harriet the desires he couldn't verbally express.

One Saturday night, when his family was away for the weekend (yes! conventional Charlie actually *lived* with Mum and Dad), he invited Harriet to his house for dinner. He told the servants to prepare a cold buffet, and gave them the night off. When Harriet realized later that evening that she was alone in the house with her fiancé, she stiffened. Charley himself had a bad case of the blushes as he brought out a rented movie projector, a can of film, and turned off the lights.

"You're being very childish, Charley," the girl said as the movie began to roll and she could see what kind of film it *was,* but she would not give him the satisfaction of walking out. Instead, she sat rigidly, with her head averted, not quite looking at the picture. Charley sat, stiff and silent, too, as far from her as possible, not daring to look at her.

But there in the safe, quiet darkness, more and more of the events on the screen began to catch Harriet's interest. Hating herself, squirming with embarrassment, swearing silently never to do such a thing again, Harriet began watching the picture. It was the most exciting film she had ever seen—although the actors were bad and most of the story absurd. In fact, at one point she found herself laughing out loud, and glanced over to see if Charley was laughing, too. He was, and came over to sit beside her. Before the film was over they were making passionate love on the rug, while over their heads the black-and-white movie flickered on.

To this day (Harriet is *Mrs.* Charley now), whenever they feel themselves drifting back into their old passionless ways, Charley rents a projector and another can of film. They almost never see the end.

Frank was going through a long, scratchy, messy divorce. His ex-wife-to-be was being very difficult about it, and Frank figured if she ever suspected there was another woman in the wings whom Frank wanted to marry as soon as he got his decree, the situation would become impossible.

So Frank and his wife-to-be, Jane, never were seen together in public, and only one or two close friends knew they were in love and planned to marry. In situations like this both people need each other's moral and emotional support more than at almost any other time in their lives. They just *had* to be together as much as possible, both to get away from the bruising outside world and to just sit together and tell each other Everything Is Going To Be All Right.

So on cold, rainy nights when other people got drunk or put themselves under TV sedation, Frank and Jane stayed at her apartment and—read dirty books . . . a quiet, private pastime that made them feel more *together*; didn't put stress on Frank's overstrained finances, and didn't hurt *anyone*.

Frank would bring a bottle of wine and a new book (pornographic literature is vast—enough to last the most serious student more than a lifetime). Jane would light the apartment with big, massive candles and start a stick of incense going. They would take turns reading aloud to each other . . . or sometimes they might just hurry through the pages together, looking for new ideas. And so their nights passed . . . in pleasant excitement.

In the months before their marriage would become possible, Frank's job took him out of town a great deal, and, in lonely hotel rooms, he would write Jane long, passionate letters, saying how much he missed her and describing, in detail, his desires for their next meeting. But when he asked her to write him similar letters, telling him of her strongest sexual feelings, she couldn't. While she never thought anything at all of revealing her desires to Frank while speaking to him directly, or reading to him from one of their books, she found that she *couldn't* write them down on paper. Besides, she wasn't much of a correspondent. Her letters were wooden and stiff, and she felt she was letting Frank down.

Yet she agreed that they must maintain a close bond when Frank was away on one of his trips. They both wanted, at all times, to be aware of the other's intense desire. So Jane bought a Polaroid camera.

Frank still writes her long letters when he is away. But, in return, he gets snapshots, taken by Jane with a self-timer (and developed automatically in the camera itself). They show Jane the way she wants him to think of her . . . in beautiful, naked poses of abandon and desire. And the words on the back always say, "With all my love." These photos, like Frank's letters, are the private business of lovers, and nobody else's.

There is a built-in contradiction in sex," my psychiatrist friend told me when I asked him why the human mind is forever inventing new embellishments and curlicues for what is, after all, supposed to be the most satisfying experience-in-itself of all. "The act of love—*making love* is the very profound euphemism for it—does create love. The two people concerned do feel more loving toward each other afterward.

"On the other hand," he said, "the incest taboo is built into human nature. We have laws against marrying too closely in one family, and if first cousins marry, people feel queasy. So the idea of sex attaches itself most naturally and strongly to the stranger. The first time people go to bed together *is* usually the most exciting; *friendship* develops later. After that, the people know each other; they are *not* strangers . . . some of the strangeness that *is* sexual excitement has worn off.

"So, the more a couple knows each other, the more they love each other, the calmer their sexual feelings about each other become, partly based on the old taboo about *not* making love to members of your own family. Their sex lives may be emotionally more satisfying. But that first carefree sexual rapture has gone. Women always daydream about being seduced by a stranger . . . rarely by a man they've already slept with.

"Various little exoticisms people bring into the bedroom *can* make things new again. You try to give *back* to your partner at least some of that lost, first, sexually intriguing mystery."

But aren't there many people who can get along without these extra little tricks?" I asked him.

"Yes, there are," he said. "But how many times have you heard about stale marriages in which the two people live together, year in, year out, and somehow never get around to making love any more? The thrill has definitely gone.

"Put it another way," he went on, "there are many people who have lived contented lives without ever once having tasted strawberry shortcake. Aren't you glad that you have?"

"Then you approve of these sexual games?"

"I approve of anything that is toward pleasure and away from pain."

152

I asked my doctor friend about other exotic touches people brought to the bedroom—what they meant, and what psychological forces they liberated.

Mirrors are fascinating, he said. People, after all, no matter how often they have made love, usually see only one half of what is going on: they can't see *themselves*, nor indeed, the couple as a single unit. A mirror in the bedroom gives both people sudden, unexpected glimpses of areas of performance they have never seen before. The mirror makes them both new to each other again.

Most people have fantasies about the sex act, women in particular, according to psychiatrists. These are little, imaginary playlets or scenarios that harmonize what is physically happening at the moment with an interior dream that seems more exciting than the current reality. Even the cast may be different—at least the casting of the leading man. This, again, is an effort on the part of the dreamer to make the other person new again. "It is not my husband who is making love to me, but that handsome man who runs our elevator." *It is not disloyal to your husband to have these fantasies.* They represent a release of unconscious forces, and, as such, are exciting. Above all, fantasies are not an indication of wickedness. Enjoy them!

If you can, in fact, handle your fantasy life without guilt and you and your lover are secure in your emotions, you can go a step further.

People who realize the power of fantasy in releasing enormous energies of sexual excitement may have a little talk first—explaining what their fantasies are, so that a partner can share and even intensify the power of the imagined scenes. Or they may even *act out* fantasies for each other. As long as both partners realize that these imaginings are the wellings-up of the *unconscious* mind, and thus in no way harmful, disloyal, or competitive, "collaborative" fantasies can be enormously and *mutually* exciting.

There is a great deal of the mind in love, or if you prefer, spirit or soul. The routine bringing together of two bodies is little more than that. Without love it can be boredom. Love, the ultimate form of spirituality most of us know, *is* a fine boredom preventer—the finest on earth. But why put all the burden on love? Why strain love? If your lover's mind or body is secretly calling for some special kind of thrill, why shouldn't he have it? (As long as you observe our prime rule: toward pleasure, away from pain.) If some of these fine techniques we've been discussing come sooner, not later, in love, maybe the boredom will never *settle* in at *all*.

"Again and again," the psychiatrist told me, "I've found that when a person urges his or her sex partner to name secret desires, the partner will first angrily or shyly deny *having* any, but finally will feel relieved and grateful for the opportunity to express and act out these needs."

And the best way to liberate your partner is to liberate yourself first. You have the nerve to know what you secretly want. You know that there is nothing abnormal in sex if it does not cause pain. You can be sure that whatever desires you have, being human, he—being human, too—may very well share. For God's sake, tell each other!

Though it's a fact that most people resort to sexual kinks to keep the boredom out of their marriages, there's absolutely nothing wrong with being a kinkster to begin with—if that's what gratifies you and your partner. It's true. Ask any good psychiatrist!

4

POW! BAM! SPLAT! GIRLS WHO LIKE TO GET PUNCHED Linda, when you get to know her, is an apparently sane, pretty, smart, sweet, tender, delicate girl who just *happens* to be mixed up with that brute Kurt. What is a nice girl like her doing with a vicious beast like him? Most of us have encountered these abused creatures from time to time, perhaps even in our own mirror. Each proudly or regretfully exhibits her bruise-of-the-week and we respond on cue with the desired sympathy: "Oh, you poor, dear, hurt little thing. Why do you take it? Why don't you leave the rat? You can have anyone you want."

And, tears shining in her eyes, she replies, "Oh, but I can't leave him. I *love* him!"

The girl who allows herself to be beaten up is a well-known figure in hospitals, whose emergency clinics spend a good percentage of their time patching up her bruises, especially between 11 P.M. Saturday night and 2:30 A.M. Sunday morning, which seem to be the peak hours for marital and extramarital mayhem. She is quite familiar, also, to the police, who tend to respond to every phone call reporting a man attacking a woman by asking, "Are you sure it isn't just a family affair?" Policemen know from experience that in 99 percent of wife- and girl-friend-beating cases the victim will either refuse to press charges or, if she has done so, will drop them before the case gets to court.

But why, *why* would any girl let a man be so rotten to her? Being beaten up *hurts* physically as well as emotionally.

Like all other idiosyncrasies that create sexual and emotional havoc within our grown-up but not necessarily adult psyches, the yen for violence is a primary behavior disorder that begins in childhood. Kids are often egocentric, sadistic creatures who will go to extremes to achieve pleasure. Though only on a playpen level of criminality, a child will sadistically plot and sometimes actually execute murderous, spiteful schemes to eliminate any man, woman, or beast who might hinder his immediate fun. Children at play reveal their sadism as they torment, beat, insult, wound, brand each other, and steal or destroy possessions.

In time, if subjected to the right training and influences, these junior ghouls will exchange their criminal instincts for a semblance of moral values. Normally, rewards for "good" behavior substitute for the savage pleasures of destruction. Sometimes, though, the controls don't work properly. A child's impulse to "get back" at the interfering world may be too strong to be checked by the normal restraints.

In this case, what psychologists call a "reaction formation" may set in. The child fears that adults will "discover" how bad he is (or at least how bad he thinks) and withdraw their love. He senses his anger is dangerous . . . it can lose him the approval of the grown-up world. Still, the rage he feels must be asserted, so the child diverts it to a less objectionable target —himself! When this pattern persists into adulthood, we've got a full-fledged masochist on our hands. Masochism is a sort of displacement of normal aggressive drives.

A little girl is more apt to conceal her aggressions behind a masochistic screen than a boy. After all, hasn't she been told she's made of "sugar and spice and everything nice"? Violent games aren't for her, nor are the contests and mock battles that provide a healthy outlet for a boy's aggressions. Actually, though, her fiery young ego may not be nearly prim enough to be contained in a girl's proper pursuits, and so she may turn all her anger inward, against herself.

Masochistic tendencies are often confirmed when a child confuses love and punishment. A child's early erotic feelings may have been aroused in situations that were tinged with violence. Dr. Arthur Brandt, a New York psychiatrist who has had extensive experience in treating the problems of young women, says, "A girl often tries to re-create situations that existed when she was a child. For instance, a little girl's early scuffles with a brother or male playmate were exciting, and also punishable by spanking. Occasionally, something in a man will stimulate her memories and revive her desire for advanced tussles, or she may require a strict parental replacement in the form of a punitive disciplinarian lover."

Punishment for "precocious" sexual behavior can also strengthen masochistic inclinations. A little girl frequently becomes outrageously flirtatious in her effort to capture her father's affection and win him away from Mommy. The tiny seductress will jump onto Daddy's lap, encourage exceptional intimacy, expose forbidden areas, and rub, hug, and kiss him with overwhelming ardor. Her behavior may be punished, either by an unconsciously jealous mother or a morally outraged dad. (Adults are often shocked by the unabashed sensuality of children.) The child naturally assumes her own sexuality will provoke punishment, and that this is a normal thing.

An early masochistic fixation may be intensified when children happen to eavesdrop on their parents' lovemaking. The anguished sounds from Mother and some of her positions (if one should ever observe) suggest that she is being punished and disgraced—in the nude. This can pivot into later rape-and-rapture fantasies as the little boy voyeur sadistically theorizes that if Mother is mistreated, *all* women should be whipped, and the little girl masochistically assumes she's due to get it as a part of life.

Teaching a child that sex is dirty reinforces masochistic logic. Girls whose upbringings have been rigidly puritanical feel they *ought* to be punished for enjoying themselves during lovemaking. Only one step away is the classic masochist, who *can't* experience any erotic sensation unless sex is accompanied with physical blows or mental degradation.

A New York psychiatrist specializing in the field of comparative behavior says that "as girls get older they fortify inner guilts with a number of unforgivable, often fictitious crimes. Sometimes the crime is an alleged sexual naughtiness, but usually it is a transgression against Mother, on whom they blame all their faults and tragedies. By seeking and receiving punishment they atone for the harm they wish on Mom."

In some cases, the masochistic girl seeks abuse simply in order to *hurt* her mother and father. "A girl often feels that by being punished, she's punishing her parents," adds the doctor. "By seeking mental, physical,

157

or social degradation she's proving that her parents are responsible. 'See what you drove me to. . . . I'm only getting even with you!'" (GOOD NEWS: When and if a girl finally achieves a friendly relationship with her parents, her masochistic urges tend to diminish.)

Now that we've considered some of the elements in our backgrounds that may in one way or another create an affinity for violence, we can note how they developed some very specific types of human punching bags.

Joanna shows up at lunch with a broken arm, black eye, and cauliflower ear but, smiling, blurts out from behind her pancake makeup, "You should see *him!*"

She's half of a bandaged, well-matched couple who share a common taste for violence—and often, little else! It's only after they have a good fist-fight, a screaming recapitulation of their rotten marriage for the neighbors, at 4 A.M., then a rich cry and reconciliation, that they're able to find true sexual release. Says Joanna: "If you can't fight with your husband or boyfriend, who else is there? Do you think I want a stranger slugging me? Besides, we don't *really* mean it, and it's a good cure for tensions."

Diagnosis: For Joanna and her husband, violence fulfills complementary needs, his to dish it out, hers to take it. She, like her masochistic sisters of every type, has an infinite need to be physically punished and humiliated. He feels he can't establish his dominance over a woman *except* by abusing her. Their battles have a theatrical quality; often they're staged in a public or semipublic setting. But the two of them are "typecast" in roles they cannot escape. They are acting out the warped notions of masculinity and femininity they formed as children.

Rosie proudly unfurls her red, white, and blue welts with patriotic fanfare to show how much she's suffering for her Number One Hero—her man! He can't help it if he attacks her. The world doesn't understand his genius and talent. But she does. Her bruises prove it. Says Rosie, "Do you think Phil would hit just *anyone?* He has a deep need to hit me, which he doesn't even fully understand himself. But I do! I know exactly where he's at!" As she rubs some ointment on a gash, Rosie continues her defense of Phil: "He's sensitive, poetic, and mistreated by those beastly people he works with. But I'm willing to suffer for my Phil." Without her bruises Rosie feels unwanted. Love is definitely more than skin-deep for her—depending on the power of Phil's punches.

Unlike the martyr, the show-off doesn't wear her bruises as medals of honor from her beloved but as badges for her own personal glorification. What she's really suffering from is a case of misplaced or lost identity. Having bruises is her method of being unique, identifiable, different. She wears low-cut dresses to reveal some of her more exotic discolorations. Of a "generous nature," she feels compelled to share with the world every purple passion welt, framed and set off as eloquently as an exhibit of beautiful jewels. The plan works. She never fails to be noticed or to evoke some response—ranging from sympathy and curiosity to laughter or disgust.

An adept show-off milks as much sympathy as she can from each wound, no matter how superficial. She goes through the emotions of considering the well-meaning advice from friends and relatives: Escape from that monster, he'll only ruin you. However, her scars have barely healed when she displays new ones in the same familiar handprint.

When friends finally decide that the show-off, her whippings, and her boyfriend are a bore, she moves on to new sympathizers. Her bashes are meaningless without an audience. She demands admiring glances or shocked *ooohs* and *aaahhhs* for every laceration. True suffering only comes when she is ignored.

Now for a girl who is shapely, attractive, sexy—but, nevertheless, terribly insecure within herself: the female impersonator. She feels particularly inadequate about her femininity, so she tries to exaggerate it—wearing outlandish clothes and makeup and acting like a caricature of a female. Part of the act must include a perfect *male* impersonator: the exaggerated man, the supervirile gangster tough or muscleman who plays rough with dames. (The Bogart success formula for battering the ladies had great appeal for these types.) The female impersonator usually requires a bruiser to give her some scars to flaunt, thereby showing how strong, powerful, and manly her boyfriend or husband is and how ultra-feminine and sexy *she* is by virtue of being his female choice for slugging.

Certain girls, also somewhat insecure about their femininity, are too drab or ugly (or think they are) to attract a high-class woman-chastiser. To make up for this deficiency, they bump into things—do it themselves, as it were—or wear iodine and bandages over nothing; they then *pretend* that some man inflicted the damage. Mousy Rhoda suddenly becomes more interesting this way, and may even snare a *real* puncher.

The "bad girl" is a battered bird with a homing instinct for men who will dole out punishment. If they don't, she changes men. *Nothing* will convince her that she's as pretty or smart or "good" as she should be. The poor thing feels she deserves every blow she inspires, and wants interested parties to realize she's finally receiving the punishment that she's due. Her mother told her sex was bad, and she does everything possible to make Mommy's predictions come true. Often, she's promiscuous or unfaithful, but she strays joylessly, compelled to justify and relieve her own sexual guilts.

Greta raved about her husband but sought action elsewhere. She always had an affair in full swing which she managed to keep from him. To cover her own nefariousness she persistently accused *him* of various misdeeds until, all riled up, he would give her a few good whacks. Then she had a fresh excuse for leaving the blackguard to go cheat, thus building up a new need for more punishment.

Jane sneaked off whenever possible for sordid, degrading affairs with delivery men (on distant routes), shoeshine boys, petty hoods, and anyone else she considered inferior. She had married a marvelous man she felt was too good for her. To atone for the sin of aspiring above her station, she "punished" herself with these lowly, brutal liaisons.

Masochism isn't always pathological," says Dr. Brandt. "Actually, in a limited degree, it is normal. The need to submit to punishment or humiliation and receive a certain amount of pain is part of the female sexual component, as is the need to be protected and dominated. Accommodatingly, a certain amount of *sadism* is part of the male sexual component. Unfortunately, in some cases these tendencies are exaggerated, reversed, and even provide a sex substitute."

Dr. Brandt continues: "In adolescence the accent for boys is on sadism, not love. A boy takes a girl merely to sate his own drive. If things go well, he will become more loving and less sadistic in his sexual needs as he matures. But many men retain a good deal of their derogatory attitude toward women, as confirmed by their terminology. A man 'seduces' and 'makes out' with a girl; 'scores,' 'throws her in the sack,' and so forth. The loving girl is also rated in a negative manner—she 'submits,' 'gives in,' 'puts out,' is 'a sure thing,' and so on." A majority of these men are the male counterpart of that "castrating female" they're always condemning. They can't help destroying or brutalizing the female. Some women learn to accept brutality, live with it, and even like it. Others fight back. Psychiatrists point out that with the accent now on a single sexual standard and more guilt-free sex for women, it is going to be harder to make a woman feel abused just because she's been taken to bed.

Men have fought over women, for women, and with women, of course, since the sexes began. In many ways violence is inseparable from sex. Little spats and slaps or Gargantuan battles between lovers are part of the love scene, and sometimes clear the air. In his book *The Psychology of Loving* Dr. Ignace Lepp states that "lovers who are not afflicted with any sort of perversion bite each other when they kiss, embrace each other in such a way as to make it hurt, and on occasion even pinch or slap each other. . . . The desire to protect the loved one is intertwined also with the need to conquer and possess, so that the two elements mutually compensate each other."

We know that every masochist has a sadistic side, and vice versa. Yet it's hard to visualize that frail, sweet girl who complains of whippings torturing anyone. Nor are there usually any matching Exhibit B bruises on her tormentor. Yet her sadism does come in—via psychological cruelty or subtle interference with his way of life. You don't need to be a shrew to whip a man verbally. The jibes, nagging, accusations, silent digs, and public insults of a hungry sadomasochist usually are inflicted more viciously than any physical punishment she ultimately receives. And there's always holding out on him regarding sex, isn't there?

Who are the ruffians who manhandle women? Cowards, for one. They're afraid to slam a man around so they pick on girls. An emotional weakling, disappointed in himself, society, his work, and ambitions, can, by asserting his physical strength and will over a woman, get his measly revenge. Others are generally opposed to brutality, but, like their partners in crime, are hung up on a twisted idea of sex. Their satisfaction *depends* on manhandling a woman. The sadist, often the victim of a hideous infancy and libido-curdling adolescence, is as guilt-ridden and frightened of sex as the masochist. In fact, he probably has a hidden desire to be beaten and mistreated *himself!* Homosexuals, musclemen, braggarts, and a variety of impotents will beat or mentally torment

161

women they become involved with *in lieu of sex*. The role of mean heel provides these fellows with a shadowy masculinity.

Then there is the docile, peace-loving gentleman who ends up with a witch. After trying everything within reason he finally discovers there's only one way to shut her up—a good stiff back of the hand. Unfortunately, this punishment sometimes turns a shrew "on" and she becomes *more* despicable to insure bigger, harsher doses of discipline.

Girls who prefer whacks to roses all have a fairly sick, neurotic, one-track relationship with their masters. No matter how happy they think they might be in their bondage, or how much they need the spark of battle to sustain their interest, it's an unhealthy, doomed involvement that can lead to permanent injury or be replaced by something worse. All told, the punching syndrome is a narcissistic, exhibitionistic, and immature method of calling attention to one's self. And a good spanking certainly can't help to dissuade the masochist from being one. Nor can sympathy or advice. But sometimes such a girl will begin to care for a real man who is gentle, and thereby mend her broken life. Or one day she may get disgusted enough or mauled seriously enough to pull herself off the beaten path. Usually, however, psychiatric help is absolutely essential to point the way.

Woman-beaters are common throughout history. Before the so-called emancipation of females, wife-flogging was a daily ritual, and indeed persists today in some cultures. But it's not nice to hit a girl, even if she wants or needs the whip.

IV

DYNAMITE EMOTIONS: HOW NOT TO BLOW IT! Think about them . . . anger, jealousy, hatred, love, lust, sympathy, pity, ecstasy, make us flush, blush, tingle, tremble, cry, sigh, laugh, scream, throb, faint! Yes, *feelings* motivate our reactions. They are powerful forces, sometimes difficult to understand. We assume you're hip to the feeling-volts inside *you*, but still struggling (like most of us) to make these energies work *for*, rather than against, your interests.

Insights into emotions are the only keys to psychological balance . . . knowing what makes you feel what you're feeling is the first step toward *healthy* self-control. Certainly we know that *repressing* feeling is dangerous. Some of our writers have learned how to manage certain emotions in order to have happier relationships with friends and lovers, find more *pleasure* for themselves. See if these ideas don't work for you.

EMOTIONAL BAROMETER

If you didn't *have* emotions, you'd be an automaton. Certainly you'd avoid the "lows," but you'd miss the "highs" too . . . what a boring life! The trick is to experience life to the fullest but manage one's feelings to give the *greatest* pleasure and the *least* pain. Perhaps you breeze through one type of crisis with assurance, while a second variety almost incapacitates you. It's possible certain physical and behavioral giveaways are giving hidden-distress signals. Which particular weaknesses should *you* guard against? Analyze your answers to these questions:

1. *Have you said or thought "It's all my fault" more than once this week?*
2. *Did you let your temper explode?*
3. *Did you take more than two (desperately needed) aspirins, tranquilizers, or drinks to erase a headache or lift a mood?*
4. *Are you frequently tired even though you've slept enough, haven't worked overly hard or taken violent exercises?*
5. *Did you feel deeply depressed more than once this week?*

YOUR BAROMETRIC RATING SCALE

4–5 noes   Sail through *this* section with your customary aplomb, remembering, however, there's no such thing as too much understanding of emotional tides—you may learn how to help people you adore.

3 noes   You're skirting an emotional morass. Explore which areas endanger your usual control, and read about what to do *then.*

2–0 noes   If you made a gigantic once-in-a-long-time blooper this particular week, or took this quiz on New Year's Day, you're *entitled* to a sizable share of guilts, moods fluctuations, or exhaustion. Otherwise, emotional management may be your particular Achilles heel.

1

TOOT, TOOT, As she strained over her drawing board,
TENSION, Ingrid suddenly felt the muscles of her neck and
shoulders begin to tighten. *Oh, no!—not now,* she
BYE, BYE thought in panic. A twenty-eight-year-old dress designer fighting her way to success in New York's fashion jungle, Ingrid
simply could not afford to go through *that* again. Less than a year ago,
when pressures at work had piled up, the nerves in her neck had somehow pinched tight, and Ingrid spent a painful, unproductive week in
traction. The doctor warned her it could happen again.

Betty, a senior at Barnard, faced a different panic. With only two days
left to finish her term paper, she could feel that familiar ache in her skull
that would make her lose precious time. Every time she had a paper to
write, she developed a throbbing, sickening, persistent headache that left
her limp and wet with perspiration. It would pass, she knew, and she
would be able to get back to work, but, in the meantime, the hours would
be long and wretched.

For Susan, a public-relations consultant with a social-service agency,
the focus of pain was in her stomach. Walking back to her office, after a
near shouting match with her boss, she could feel her stomach churning.
It was an emotional barometer, reacting instantly the moment anything
upset her. Susan had had an ulcer, which was supposed to be on the
mend, but now when she got that "kicked-in" feeling, as she called it,
she was doubly frightened, worrying about the ulcer coming back. "The

terrible thing is," Susan says, "I know these symptoms are just physical reactions to my emotional problems, but there's nothing I can do about them."

That's what Susan *thinks*—but it isn't so. The first step, however, to beating the symptoms *and* the problem is to understand what is happening to our bodies, why they react differently, affect different organs.

In the three cases above, the symptoms vary, but their underlying causes are identical: Each of these girls is suffering from what they may call "jitters," doctors call "stress," and most of the rest of us call tension. Although tension can manifest itself in many ways and give rise to a bewildering number of symptoms, it is basically a *physiological reaction to emotion*.

The physiological mechanism of tension was first isolated medically by the late Dr. Walter B. Cannon, of Harvard, who described his finding as a "fight or flight" pattern of response. Dr. Cannon's studies showed that whenever someone experiences fear or rage, his body prepares itself for action. (Blood pressure rises, pulse and heartbeat quicken, body temperature goes up, digestion slows, adrenaline pours into the bloodstream. More sugar is then manufactured to feed energy to the muscles. The muscles themselves tighten. In short, tension occurs.) This readiness to fight or flee at a moment's notice is fine for an animal, and was obviously a life-saving feature for primitive man, but today, even though you are exposed to anger- and fear-provoking circumstances and though your body automatically gets itself *ready* to react, you *cannot then react the way nature intended you to*—physically and violently.

"Tension itself isn't destructive," explains Dr. Hans Kraus, who was the late President Kennedy's back specialist and is author of the best-selling book, *Backache, Stress and Tension*. He went on to say:

"Any animal, including the human, will become tense when exposed to stimuli. The crucial thing is how the tension is handled. A musician or writer is often under tension, but this helps him to produce. As it [tension] forms, he has a real outlet for it in his work. The ordinary tensions of the man or woman in business or private life can't be constructive because he or she can't respond to them."

Each emotion-arousing situation brings on physiological changes that mobilize the body for action. If the body does not act, that mobilized energy is trapped inside. As an occasional occurrence, no harm is done.

Yet, when the pattern of being ready for action but remaining passive is repeated or sustained over long periods of time, many different kinds of mischief can occur (since every individual has a different stress organ).

Sandra, a twenty-two-year-old secretary in a large insurance company, had no ailments to speak of until she was reassigned to a new boss. He was every girl's nightmare of an employer. Mr. Big would leave the office and never say where he was going, revise letters after they'd been typed, think of rush projects just before quitting time, and fly into a rage whenever Sandra made the slightest error. She became overwrought, and developed an ache between her shoulder blades whenever she started typing. When the pains became really severe, she saw a doctor, who gave her injections in certain areas in her back to kill the pain, treated her with ethyl-chloride spray, and urged limbering-up exercises. There was some relief, but the doctor hinted—and Sandra realized—that as long as she stayed on that job she was vulnerable to this backache.

"I did the only sensible thing," she reports. "I quit my job and found somebody more congenial and considerate to work for. I won't say the pain went right away, but it did leave and I haven't had trouble since."

Pain can settle in the back, the neck, the calves—as Dr. Kraus says, "The target area for pain can be anywhere." What happens is that when muscles are continually tensed but not allowed relief in the form of action, they shorten, lose their elasticity. Finally, as new demands are placed upon them, the muscles go into spasms—involuntary contractions—or actually tear.

Lack of exercise can aggravate the muscle-pain cycle. If you exercise enough to keep your muscles in good tone, that cycle is much less apt to victimize you.

The muscles of the face, scalp, and neck play an important role in eyeaches and headaches. Under emotional stress these muscles contract. This contraction, in turn, creates the pressure and soreness of a tension headache. Dr. Robert E. Ryan, of the St. Louis School of Medicine, observes that anxiety and fatigue usually precede a tension headache. Dr. Maurice J. Martin, of the Mayo Clinic, studied a group of fifty patients (most of them women) who came to the clinic with headaches as their chief complaint. Their average age was thirty-eight. Some had been suffering for years. All described themselves as being in emotional turmoil.

They spoke of difficulty in finding any meaningful activity outside their home, domination by a husband or wife, divorce, sexual problems (mainly impotence and frigidity), and other conflict situations. Many had trouble controlling anger and hostility.

"Most of the patients tended to be rather rigid, compulsive, and perfectionistic," concluded Dr. Martin, "and to worry excessively about their health, family, or job." At Mayo, as at other clinics, a three-pronged attack is sometimes used with such severely tension-plagued patients: drugs, physical therapy, and psychotherapy. The drugs and physical therapy reduce the physical tension, and the psychotherapy attacks the emotional causes of the tension.

A surprising number of people also have severe mouth and jaw problems brought on by emotional stress. Pain arises from grinding and clenching the teeth, which many people do unconsciously when they're under tension.

"When tension expresses itself habitually in the muscles of the jaw, what essentially results is a charley horse," explains Dr. Arthur S. Freese, an expert on the physical and emotional problems affecting the jaw. "The person may have difficulty opening his mouth, his bite may be affected, and there may be tremendous pain. Pain is always more severely felt in the head and face." During his twenty-nine years' practice of dentistry on the East Coast, he has had many quite unusual cases. In one, the patient was a twenty-eight-year-old girl who, it turned out, bore an enormous amount of repressed hostility toward her father. Sitting across the table from him at dinner one evening, she suddenly felt her jaw click.

"I couldn't open my mouth," she recalled. "Couldn't open it more than an inch without really terrible pain. It was the weirdest thing—as though somebody had locked my jaw. I wasn't even able to take in food." The incident so unnerved her that after medical treatment relieved the condition, she went into psychotherapy. "I'd swallowed up my feelings for so long," she said, "I couldn't swallow another thing."

There are close ties between destructive tension and depression, as well as between depression and fatigue. Keeping feelings locked in, habitually gulping down fear or anger or hostility, eventually causes as much pain to the mind as it does to the body. Your body will cry in one way or another. One extremely striking thing about depressed persons, observes

Dr. Paul H. Blachly, of the University of Oregon, "is the tremendous amount of anger that lies smoldering just below the surface."

Depression springs from many sources. The death of a loved one or the breakup of a love affair may produce it. (And anger, too—if only at the unkind ways of fate.) Disappointments of any kind can bring on a state of dejection—that blue mood. Premenstrual and menopausal tensions frequently bring it on in women. (Whether or not middle-aged men also go through a physiological change that approximates menopause—a topic of some controversy among medical authorities—many men in their forties and fifties do also go through periods of deep depression.)

After spending four years examining depressed patients, researchers at Massachusetts General Hospital concluded that fatigue is the most common symptom of depression.

Insomnia, chest pains, and a range of gastrointestinal disturbances are other unpleasantnesses doctors often find associated with depression. Loss of sexual appetite can occur. Since depression leads to a general loss of vitality, it is often accompanied by a marked decrease in sexual interest. Many career girls have sexual problems whether they're depressed or not, insists Oscar Rabinowitz, psychotherapist and professor at New York's Hunter College. He cites the eternal conflict between job and family, since "society still doesn't condone women expending the greatest amount of their energy output in their careers," a question that leads girls to question their own femininity.

Rabinowitz stresses that sexual problems may reveal themselves in a variety of ways that are not directly sexual. Among signs he considers revealing are irritability, inability to concentrate, restless activity, daydreaming (with or without sexual connotation), or overconcern about one's health.

It's fairly common knowledge now, and accepted by most physicians, that emotional stress either brings on or complicates a wide variety of physical ailments. Peptic ulcers, for instance, as well as colitis, asthma, skin disorders, hypertension, and loss of hair are some of them.

But the links between tension and diagnosed disease aren't very clear even to medical researchers who have been working on them for decades. Take ulcers, for example. When people are under stress they secrete large amounts of hydrochloric acid that eat away at the stomach's lining—and, in those who are susceptible, produce an ulcer. But many other persons secrete excessive amounts of the acid under stress and never develop an ulcer; this baffles researchers.

Stress also triggers heart- and blood-vessel changes in most people—the heart beats faster; blood pressure is boosted, causing the heart to pump more blood than usual. A relatively small group of medical researchers, more adventuresome and controversial than the rest, are convinced that when such symptoms are sustained over long periods of time, they can bring on major illnesses like diabetes and coronary attacks. Dr. Henri Felix, a medical consultant to the French Army, has reported on ten cases of diabetes that occurred in soldiers after they underwent extreme emotional stress.

Studies of coronary heart patients, both in the U.S.A. and other parts of the world, show that in many more cases than coincidence would allow, heart attacks were preceded by periods of great tension. The late Dr. Joseph B. Wolffe, a Pennsylvania heart specialist, offered the provocative theory that coronary patients were trapped in a "nutcracker squeeze"—a dilemma between what they wanted to do and what circumstances compelled them to do—"the tyranny of 'should' over 'would.'"

And it so happens that medical investigators at the University of Oklahoma and elsewhere are examining the possibility that, in some cases, the person who gets sick and dies may actually have "given up"—making a final adaptation to overwhelming problems.

The rate of coronary heart disease is far greater for men than for women (according to the American Heart Association, about twice as great). And more men than women are subject to ulcers. But some medical men think coronary heart disease and ulcers are on the increase among younger women, possibly due to their more active participation in business life—and its accompanying tensions. Men and women are about equally susceptible to most of the ordinary aches and pains resulting from tension. Dr. Ray O. Noonan, of the University of Alabama Medical School, could determine no difference between the two sexes in one obvious manifestation of tensions—sweating.

On the other hand, it's women who go through menstruation and menopause and must cope with the tensions (often psychological) these conditions bring on. But your tensions need not be insurmountable. Try these tension-diminishers:

170

1. Exercise. "It would be great if instead of several coffee breaks people would take one good exercise break during the workday," says Dr. Kraus, whose book on backache offers a series of exercises, some of which are specifically designed to promote relaxation. But stay away from isometrics, Kraus warns; despite their popularity, isometrics are "tension-producing rather than tension-relaxing. They involve many repetitions without relaxation." Almost any form of vigorous physical activity—sports, calisthenics, dancing, long walks, and bike rides, or just plain scrubbing the kitchen floor—can be beneficial to mind and body.

2. Hot Baths. A nice long hot shower or soak in the tub is a fine way, almost all the experts say, to relax muscles strained during a difficult day. And if you do some vigorous exercises *before* the bath, that's even better.

3. Liquor. A drink before dinner soothes a tense and tired body and helps the digestive process. Dr. Joseph F. Montague, a leading expert on health and nervous tension, recommends an ounce of whiskey, rum, or brandy in water fifteen minutes before mealtime because it "has a relaxing, a tranquilizing effect, and it has the virtue of being burned by the body in a relatively short time." (But a drink too many—getting high every time things get tense—creates more problems than it solves. There's a group of people who drink excessively only when depressed; physicians refer to them as "periodic alcohol addicts.")

4. Yoga. Many girls discover yoga and subsequently swear there's nothing else like it for loosening up. "I had this ghastly respiratory infection, wheezing like an old woman," reports Ellen, a young mother who was going through a divorce when these symptoms occurred. "Every joint ached and getting through the night was a torture. I'd wake up fuzzy from lack of sleep and spend the day that way—a blessing of sorts, I guess, at the time. But it was killing me. Then, a good friend pushed me into seeing her yogi. He fiddled around with my neck, had me do some breathing exercises at his place and at home. It sounds like I'm trying to sell yoga, but it made me feel great."

5. Tranquilizers. Doctor-prescribed drugs help take a person off the high edge of tension. As Hunter College professor Oscar Rabinowitz points out: In a time of crisis, tranquilizers help calm a person enough to get him

to deal finally with the root of his problem. People under tension have a tendency to run away from problems, he adds, and withdrawing from life or blaming others is simply another shortcut to more tension, not less.

6. Supportive Therapy. Naturally, all of us have moments of stress and suffer some of the symptoms described in this article. If you can cope with and finally solve the problem causing the anxiety, your symptoms will probably disappear (providing worse problems don't replace the original one). If you've tried all the techniques above and are still suffering from chronic tension, then you may want to ask your doctor to recommend a clinical psychologist. Unlike a psychiatrist or psychoanalyst, who tries to remedy or help the patient cope with personality disorders, a clinical psychologist just gives supportive therapy—*emotional support* —while you and he work together to solve the particular problem that's at the root of the trouble. This may be all you need; don't wait until you fall apart to try it; you'll only be harder to glue back together again. After all, if you take your hair problems to your hairdresser and your physical problems to your doctor, why not transfer your serious emotional problems to the expert who is trained to help you handle them?

7. Hypnosis. A few doctors have begun sending highly tensed patients— those for whom ordinary methods of relaxation will not work—to hypnotists. The purpose: hypnosis to teach self-relaxation. Though the American Medical Association has approved hypnotism as a legitimate medical therapy when practiced by qualified medical people, many physicians still don't feel at ease with it. One doctor admits he sends patients to a medical hypnotist, but does not want to be identified because "the public might not understand." Hypnosis should only be taken under a doctor's supervision.

8. Be Glad You're Female! In general, women have better chances than men for dealing constructively with their tensions. Women are permitted to cry, and tears are a marvelous way to wash out pent-up emotion. Women are also more apt to plunge into physical activity when angry (many a girl does her best housecleaning or exercising after she's fought with her boy friend or husband), and physical exertion is an excellent way of dissipating energy stored up in tense muscles. Dr. Paul Dudley

White, the famous heart specialist, counsels: "To get physically tired is the best antidote for nervous tension."

Recognizing tension in others can help make you—and them—more relaxed. You'll be able to approach them understandingly if you know that stress is causing their unpleasant behavior. Here's how to spot tension . . . in your boss:

- *He or she walks by without a "Good morning," and never smiles.*
- *The lines around his jaw become pronounced; his face seems to freeze.*
- *He spills his coffee, knocks over the ashtray, and then shouts at you to clean it up as though it were your fault.*
- *He resents any interruptions and snarls "Yes?" every time you come into his office.*
- *He'll suddenly lose his sense of priority about work, and make you do trivia while important chores are ignored.*
- *When you ask a question he'll give you an answer, but it won't answer the question.*

. . . in your lover:

- *He doesn't want to talk about anything—not his day, nor your work, nor the future, not even your friends.*
- *His eyes look over your head and stare at some invisible point in the distance.*
- *He gulps down his drink before you have even touched yours.*
- *He can't sit still, doesn't want to eat your home-cooked, elegant dinner and relax, but prefers making the rounds from one bar to another, virtually exhausting you.*
- *His sleep will be restless; his lovemaking selfish and quick.*

. . . in your husband:

- *He'll tell you he's tense, depressed, miserable—and expect you to do something about it.*
- *He'll alternately shout at you or ignore you—and the children.*
- *He picks at his food and complains about what you've served him.*

- He'll bump into the lamp, cut his finger, drop a glass within the space of a few hours, and swear loudly each time.
- His movements will be jerky, rapid, with head bent and face gloomy.
- He won't make love to you, but may get out of bed at midnight to take a two-hour walk.
- He won't enjoy any activity, no matter how hard you try to please him.

Remember, tense people are often quite loving and beloved! They have the ability to care deeply about others. By also caring what others think of them, they are apt to behave admirably and be pleasant to have around.

2

ANGER— Once upon a time, anger was a stepchild emotion,
HOLD IT IN? looked upon as one of those unpleasant facts
of life, like an unaesthetic bodily function
LET IT OUT? ...the way sex was regarded by the Victorians. One didn't raise one's voice, just as one didn't parade up and down the street in the nude. Anger was excusable only if *really* justified —it was all right for a man to get furious at an occupying army, for instance, or some gross political injustice. Women had a harder time finding excuses; even in the face of total catastrophe, tears or hysterics were considered more suitable. Ladies just didn't get angry.

Freud himself spent a good deal of time listening to the complaints of these hysterical (they let go in his office) ladies, and the result was that anger, like sex, at last came out in the open. (Anger and sex, according to Freud, are the only two *basic* instincts.) Psychiatric theory has done for anger what Boswell did for Johnson, or Zanuck for Marilyn Monroe. Now, anger is the star of the show—everything comes back to it in the end. Anyone who has been in therapy finds himself in a hall of mirrors all reflecting anger in various guises. If you have the notion that you are afraid of someone, look again—what *really* is going on is that you can't stand that person and are terrified of your own anger. If you think you feel guilty about spending too much money, look more closely: You spent it because you were angry about something and now you're guilty about being *angry*, not about the money. The therapist appears like a diligent sleuth, digging out hostility and the guilt it frequently causes. What he seems to be trying to get across is that it's *all right* to be angry; the thing to do is channel your rage or, as he would put it, find appropriate ways to discharge it. And be *aware* of your fury. If it seems to go away by itself, don't be fooled—it may just be lurking there, taking on another form far worse than a simple fit of temper or some broken china.

Psychotherapy makes us sleuths about our *own* anger. For some people, the problem of handling anger lies mainly in recognizing it. Take Sheila, a gem of a secretary. Ordinarily a cheerful person, she had episodes of depression, usually just before her period, during which everything went to pieces. Her work became erratic, her appearance declined alarmingly, and tears were always surfacing at the worst times. A little professional help (sought when her job was jeopardized) revealed that Sheila was terrified of becoming pregnant, which would ruin her job, her relationship with her married lover, and, she thought, her whole life.

But beyond this, Sheila was absolutely furious and didn't know it. She was in a rage at the whole situation and particularly at her lover's wife—there *she* was living in her comfortable home, all taken care of; *she* didn't have to go out and work, and if *she* got pregnant, it might be inconvenient but not tragic. In the meantime, poor Sheila was forced to slave in a hot office all day and even be responsible for contraception, while Henry (her lover) nipped back and forth between the two of them! These were the thoughts buried away in the mind of this apparently perfect career girl, who impressed all her friends with her easy adjustment to the Other Woman role. Besides this, Sheila's unconscious crawled with fantasies of murdering Henry, murdering his wife, and—most pertinent of all—getting pregnant so Henry would somehow divorce his wife and marry her, though Henry had never given the slightest indication that he would do such a thing. It turned out, in fact, after further sleuthing, that Sheila had frequently *forgotten her Pill* and almost always just before the onset of one of her fits of depression.

The psychiatrist pointed out that it was up to Sheila to decide if she could somehow discharge all this anger at Henry in some way that would relieve her and yet preserve the relationship, or whether she just hated him too much to see him any more. More fundamentally, Sheila would have to learn to objectively appraise her over-all situation and emotional state. *Was* she really so cool? Was she really the perfectly adjusted secretary? Did she really want the domestic scene? These were all clearly *big* questions and ones that Sheila, being the chronic repressor she was, had managed not to ask herself. She had always thought it important to be cheery and chin-up, no matter what, and she had rather scorned girls who got too oppressed by men. Besides, Sheila was not *used* to thinking of her anger and being on the lookout for it. Sticking it somewhere out of sight was an old mechanism with her, and this was exactly what got her into trouble. As it turned out, giving Henry hell was good for both of them. Henry was enchanted with her for showing some signs of being a normally jealous female, because it proved she really cared about him, which he had begun to doubt. Their affair had a lovely renaissance—and if the future still lies in doubt, Sheila has, at least, stopped forgetting her Pills.

Sheila handled her anger one way; Ruth, an intelligent, high-strung girl, showed hers under a different guise. After the end of her affair with Jerry—an event about which Ruth claimed to be in *complete* agreement, it was leading *nowhere* and *had* to stop—she developed a strange preoccupation with her apartment. She spent almost every free moment cleaning, rearranging, and redecorating it, with the result that the apartment always looked beautiful, but became an obsession in Ruth's life. If she went shopping with a friend, for instance, she felt guilty about buying anything that wasn't specifically for the apartment—she wandered around in the furniture and fabric departments, endlessly strolling, tapping, pricing. If she went to a movie, she hardly followed the plot because she was so preoccupied with the sets and the furniture. When she had anyone for dinner she began to get anxious around, say, ten o'clock, because they might stay too late and she wouldn't be able to restore the apartment to its impeccable order before bedtime.

This problem became so serious that Ruth stopped inviting anybody over—she literally couldn't go to sleep unless an endless number of trivial routines were completed every night; the dishes neatly put away in a certain order, the objects on her coffee table arranged in a special way, every drop of water wiped from the kitchen sink. Then she began to develop little rituals—touching her pillow three times before leaving the bedroom, for instance, and patting each of the living room cushions twice. She was chronically late for work (busy as she was trying to leave her apartment) and preoccupied when on the job. (*Had* she left a glass on the bedside table? Was her toothbrush in its rack?) For, curiously enough, she was rather forgetful about what she had and hadn't done; her mind seemed to buzz in tight little circles beyond her control.

When Ruth *admitted* to herself that, at the very *least*, she could have *killed* Jerry, her severe obsessive-compulsive symptoms (which is what they were) abated somewhat. When she met another man, some months later, fortunately she relaxed enough to let him spend the night without jumping up at three A.M. to clean out the ashtrays.

Look at Millie, a high-school teacher, who never admits to a moment's irritation. She is polite and thoughtful, to the point of unbelievability, always doing things for her students and friends (mostly the hard way). If she doesn't actually make calf's-foot jelly, she *does* make bowls of soup that she brings around when you have the flu. At first glance nothing could be nicer—in she comes, fluffing the pillows, straightening the bed, heating up her soup on the stove—until she tells you how she shopped around for veal knuckles and marrow bones, and walked twelve blocks for leeks, and leeks aren't easy to find, mind you, in her inconvenient but cheap neighborhood, which circumstances have forced her into. Poor Millie, she isn't so lucky as *some* people who can afford to live in expensive neighborhoods—on and endlessly on she whines, until you are ready to throw the soup in her face!

Why did she come? To express her anger at the world and you, of course. Millie might not be heavy on brains, but unconsciously she is shrewd enough to drive you *mad* with irritation. To vent her anger, she carefully picks a time when you are flat on your back, too helpless to throw her out. But, of course, if you accused Millie of being vindictive, she would be honestly amazed. Angry? Not her, ever.

Then there is Ellen, who really does have a problem with her parents. They are very possessive, rigid people who have purposely kept her childish; Ellen has had trouble taking any steps toward independence. When she finally worked up the nerve to leave home (at twenty-five), and found a job and a roommate, she carried off the whole move so well that her friends were secretly amazed. Then, on the eve of her first paycheck, she went into a panic state—lying on her bed and trembling, too fearful to move a muscle. "I was afraid that if I even *budged*, the world would explode," she said. "I could only save myself by being as still as stone." It took her two hours to reach out her hand for the telephone. She called a close friend who stayed the night and took her to a doctor the next day.

In therapy it turned out (as it always does) that what looked like fear was really rage—in this case a rather complex rage. That paycheck meant independence, a kind of power she'd never had; lying there shaking in her bed, she was full of fantasies about how her father would kill her, absolutely kill her, for taking any money that wasn't his. There was a certain amount of truth in this—he *hadn't* wanted her to leave home, he *did* want her to depend on him—but Ellen was overreacting; after all, she *had* left home and taken the job with his grudging permission. What she was really afraid of was not her father's anger, but the depth of her own rage against him. She could absolutely *kill* him for the years of suppression.

Repressed anger, like repressed sexuality, causes all sorts of physical symptoms. Ulcers, certain headaches, and asthma are recognized as having an anger component. So are the hysterical symptoms so common in Freud's female patients—paralyzed limbs, loss of speech, inability to swallow, fits, and so on. There is nothing imaginary about these symptoms, they are real, and if the anger can be released, they usually clear up. One of the most famous cases Freud treated was a girl who suffered (among other things) a hysterical loss of speech while visiting her sick father. In analysis it came out that as she was sitting at her father's bedside, she had heard the sound of dance music coming from a neighboring house, felt a surging wish to be there, and was overcome with self-reproach. She also felt a sudden desire to denounce her father, and the words literally stuck in her throat. This kind of hysteria, so prevalent in Freud's day, has become rarer as society has become more flexible.

The emergence of repressed anger, either in therapy or in the course of circumstance, can be a startling phenomenon to observe—particularly when the angry person *still* refuses to admit its presence. Take Joan, who was married to a real bounder whom she kept trying to reform. She was always full of agonizing, martyred patience, waiting for him to roll in at three A.M. but she never indicated a sign of reproach except for a little lip-biting and chin-quivering. After a couple of years, this doomed union finally broke up, and Joan *still* doesn't know how angry she is. "Ted has a new job and he's moved to California," she tells you through bared teeth. "Of course I'm *terribly* glad for him. He's so *talented*. He's so *bright*. They're *lucky* to have him. I hear he has a new girl. Well, that's simply *wonderful*. I wish him *all* the happiness in the world." While talking she is gouging a hole in the tabletop with her fingernail. Two minutes later, in response to some bland remark about the virtues of travel: "Why is it the men always get the interesting jobs? Look at me—stuck in my dull office without a chance of anything interesting happening, *ever*! And the men get sent *everywhere*! And we all know about men on the road—I'd *die* rather than marry a man who had to travel! In fact, I'd die rather than marry again, period! I've *had* it with men—all of them!" And so forth. But, angry at Ted? Oh, never! Why, she isn't a vindictive person.

On the other hand, there are a lot of people whose problem is *anything* but repression—they are angry all the time. A chronic repressor looking at a chronic sorehead wonders how anybody can be so angry at so many things so much of the time. And soreheads are further infuriated by repressors—they love a good fight. Bickering and complaining is their natural state. Look at Bill and Emily, who are caught up in a continual hassle. Fighting, to them, is a complex ritual or game. Maybe it keeps their life from getting dull. If anyone suggests that they don't love each other or that their marriage is any worse than most people's, they are amazed—Emily and Bill think war is the normal condition. It's nice they are so well suited, but actually they are very unpleasant to be around and they have very few friends. There is something initially fascinating about their running argument, since the couple are articulate and good at playing to an audience, but after a while watching them war becomes exhausting. Among other things, their relentless feuding seems like such a drain of energy—for Bill and Emily don't really get much else accomplished; they just endlessly bicker the days away.

There is another more subtle but effective way of expressing anger, known in the jargon as passive obstructionism. Take crabby old Aunt Jennifer, for instance. She doesn't repress her anger at all—rather, she shrewdly uses it as a tool to make everyone else miserable. For example, she announces to the family group that she'll take care of Christmas—leave it all to her. The daughters and cousins breathe sighs of relief. They won't have to cook turkeys this year, because Aunt Jennifer is (presumably) going to have everybody over to her house (strangely enough—for Aunt Jennifer usually doesn't do anything nice for anybody). But time passes and somehow Aunt Jennifer never gets around to firming up the details. What does this mean? Nobody knows. When Cousin Lily boldly suggest that perhaps Aunt Jennifer isn't up to all the work, she flies into a rage. Of *course* she can handle it; she's a *genius* at cooking turkeys, and, what's more, if Cousin Lily tries to steal her thunder, she'll eat crow, not turkey. But Aunt Jennifer still won't be pinned down and manages to keep everyone stalled and furious by simply doing nothing until around December 23, when the relatives finally forget about her and make their own plans. Since life normally flows forward at a rapid rate, Aunt Jennifer accomplishes wonders in expressing her hostility by merely standing still in midstream.

But *why* is Aunt Jennifer such a sorehead? And what's the matter with Norman Mailer, William Buckley, and Gore Vidal, those talented money-making, professional soreheads? Is being angry the well-analyzed, non-ulcerous, desirable state? Psychiatrists say emphatically not—this is one of the myths that comes out of misunderstanding psychiatry. Psychiatric theories about anger, like those about sex, have suffered a gross distortion in the translation, so to speak. Freud no more suggested promiscuity as a solution for sexual repression than assault and battery for repressed anger. Chronically angry people have, as we say, a problem. Something is dammed up, something is inexpressible, something is driving them mad. If they're men, maybe girls don't like them, or if they're girls, maybe men don't like them. Maybe they never spoke so well, danced so well, ran so fast, or made love so well as they wanted to—maybe they're still furious at a long-dead, too-strict parent who didn't let them show any angry feelings. Whatever causes their anger, it certainly doesn't help them win friends or live productively.

Anger must be discharged—but *constructively*. "The thing to remember about anger is that it is *not* pathologic," says Dr. Robert Michels, a New York analyst. "The pathology comes with displaced or repressed anger. Anger serves a valuable communicative function—to convey feeling to someone you love, *not* to injure them. In other words, you can vote *no* without quitting." The great lesson people must learn is that "anger is not necessarily connected with violence." It is precisely this fear that drives anger underground where it does the damage. We may lose our tempers *without* running amok with a shotgun—and words have never killed anyone yet (at least not directly). "The ideal thing to do with anger," says another New York psychiatrist, "is to try to change what is making you angry." Harness the energy, sublimate it, put it to use. If you can't stand something about your mate, tell him about it—specifically— without dragging in your mother-in-law or how much he had to drink at that party six months ago. The old axiom about how to deal with children goes for adults too: attack the act, never the person. Continued personal attack kills love; it might provide temporary relief, but it doesn't accomplish the real goal, which is to make a change. A person will try to change him or herself only out of love.

Joan, the lip-biting, inwardly hostile wife, would have done better to say, "Now *look,* I love you, more or less, but I can't *stand* all this drinking and sleeping around. It absolutely *infuriates* me when you don't come here at night, and if you have to drink so much, why don't you drink with me, huh? You think I enjoy sitting around here every night with a lemon Schweppes?" Unless her husband was a total, hopeless alcoholic, this might have accomplished miracles. If Joan says this, she expresses her own anger without cracking up the ship; she tells the truth, for a change, letting Ted know she cares about him in *spite* of her anger, a fact about which he apparently has been in great doubt, or else why would he have been desperately chasing every other woman he met? But, imagine, during their whole marriage Joan *never once told Ted she was angry.*

If she had expressed her rage, Ted might have said: "Well, as a matter of fact, what I can't stand about *you* is all the agony and chin-quivering and sneaky hostility, like knotting up all my socks the other day. So if you *want* to drink with me, you're going to *really* drink. No rotten little pink aperitifs. We're going to get *loaded* and then, baby, watch out."

Now, that's *real* progress!

W hat do you do when you're very, very angry . . . in order not to have the anger back up and make you sick later? Do you just let go? No, that isn't advisable (even once a year), according to psychiatrists. Having an all-out, on-the-spot temper tantrum is not constructive. That's the reason high-powered celebrities, with a few memorable exceptions, rarely hit anybody in public, even if crowds are ripping off their Sulka shirts, or photographers have them backed up against a hot radiator. Public displays of anger, even if you're not a celebrity, may give temporary relief, but also cause permanent harm; you often make a lasting bad impression that comes back to haunt you. O.K., since you are not supposed to "bottle up" anger, what do you do? Here are some possible guidelines.

1. Recognize that you're angry when you *are*—no smiling through your gritted teeth, saying "Who *me*, angry?" Recognize the emotion—but that doesn't necessarily mean you should haul off and let fly.

2. Try to figure out *why* you are angry and at whom. The angry situation of the moment may be similar to many others in your life; each time some event triggers childish reactions—a feeling that you're not pretty, that your background isn't acceptable, that people think your opinions are stupid, and so on. Until you get rid of the inevitable childish reactions —and build some self-esteem—you'll probably go on getting angry at the wrong time, the wrong place, and at possibly the wrong people.

3. Forget trying to "straighten out the boss" with a few fiery pronouncements. Frequent big showdowns with employers will only get you eased out of the company, and maybe not at your convenience. Discussion, in the most reasonable way possible, is *in*. Blatant anger (unless you want to back it up by quitting the same day!) is *out*.

4. In personal relationships, you must, indeed, speak up. In this case, an out-and-out blowup isn't the *worst* thing that can happen to you both. Some husbands and wives seem unable to get feelings into the open unless there *is* a situation in which one or the other has been driven to a screaming fit . . . *then* the anger comes pouring out! Even with loved ones, a frank discussion as the trouble was building might have been better. (Reminder: working yourself into a white-hot rage is *not* therapeutic.) If there's a fight, the "sensible discussion" may come a couple of hours or days afterward—when you've both cooled down. If the relationship is a strong one, there is practically nothing you *can't* discuss. Any loved one who won't allow you to be you—with whom you have to hold back your honest thoughts—is an expensive pet!

5. Guideline 4 may *not* apply to parents, parents-in-law, or relatives. Sometimes, people of another generation aren't *up* to all that honesty and discussing-your-anger. You know your own older generation and can be the judge. You may find it's better to stay on safe subjects and tuck your

tongue down your throat when parents get abusive (because who needs one more futile argument?).

6. Stay *away* from people and situations that constantly anger you. That goes for the "loved ones" in guideline 5. If they can't behave, maybe they don't deserve to see you.

3

SECRET GUILTS (AND HOW THEY RULE YOUR LIFE)

An experiment was once performed by a psychiatrist on three patients under treatment—all with different forms of emotional illness. All three were hypnotized and told that when they woke up they would be offered a chocolate bar and that they must not—under any circumstances—eat it. The first patient, a hysteric, revived as the doctor put a Hershey bar on the table in front of him. "Eat it," said the doctor. "Go ahead." But the patient couldn't even find the chocolate bar. . . . He had developed a hysterical blindness for the forbidden object and could only see the empty table. The second patient was given to physical reactions to anxiety, and he got as far as one small nibble of chocolate before he became violently sick to his stomach. The third patient, a psychopath, suddenly came out of his hypnotic trance and, before the doctor said a word, gobbled up the chocolate bar and threw the candy wrapper in the doctor's face.

The point of the story is that only psychopaths are really free of guilt—the rest of us live with it every day. Our built-in controls function like a million posthypnotic suggestions; they have been with us most of our lives, and violation of them can bring on guilt like a hailstorm. Psychiatrists agree that a certain amount of guilt is normal and necessary. . . . However, the amount a person has is frequently unrelated to whether he's actually doing anything wrong. Ever since Freud associated guilt with repression, a lot of people have assumed that anything that is being repressed is, in fact, bad . . . when this may not be the case at all. Compulsive personalities feel the most guilt, and often about things they haven't even done. One New York psychiatrist describes a type of patient who frequently visits him: "A man around thirty-five, who married young and has several children, becomes depressed without knowing why. It comes out that he's guilty about fantasies of his wild youth which he never really had. He's suffering over sins he never committed."

The guiltiest people are often those who would seem to have the least cause—the perfect hostess suffers over some imagined imperfection in her dinner; the attentive escort worries because his theater seats are too far back; the slim girl can hardly let herself eat a piece of cake. Our standards are strictly subjective. The question is not so much whether we *are* guilty, but rather how much and about what.

Men hate feeling guilty and usually pretend they aren't, but women rather enjoy it and often produce festoons of irrational guilts which they love talking about. This doesn't mean that women *are* guiltier—it just means that guilt lends itself better to the female style which admits more readily to fallibility. When a man does admit to feeling guilty about something, he usually manages to imply that social or cosmic forces are really responsible for his whole dilemma. One long-married father of three feels guilty because society requires him to devote himself wholly to his family, while underneath it all, he has biological and lascivious urges not to. Society, he says, makes him feel guilty. A bachelor in his thirties is guilty because society makes him think he should be married, and the fact that he secretly likes not being married makes him even guiltier.

Women usually never blame society or anything else—they take all the blame on the chin. "I'm guilty about this dress," said one woman, "because it cost two hundred dollars and I feel guilty about all the money I milk from my husband. If he'd told me to keep the dress, I would have felt guilty enough to send it back because he was being so nice about everything. But, he told me to send it back so I got mad and kept it. Now I feel worse." Women are the expert rationalizers, but more for the sake of appearing conscientious to others than to convince themselves. . . . The excuses peel away like banana skin. A man will really come to believe that he *needs* the new stereo because he loves music and the kids should be exposed to Bach. And as long as they've been planning to get a stereo, why not a good one? He is, in fact, often alarmed by his wife's terrible honesty: "No, dear, I didn't really need a new dress and I know we're broke. I just saw it and everything went black and I'm guilty." He is far more comfortable with a line of patter about *nothing* to wear, must look right to meet your new boss dear, *won't* buy any spring clothes, and besides, the dress was on sale.

The real male guilts, says Dr. David T. Read, Manhattan psychiatrist, usually center around sex . . . with married men guilty about not sleeping with their wives enough and/or not satisfying them; about still finding other women physically attractive; about losing sexual interest in their wives; and most of all, about being unfaithful. A good many men—married or unmarried—are guilty about being oversexed. . . . They worry about being great attacking beasts when the poor girl is tired, shy, in love with someone else, or in a taxi and doesn't want her dress mussed. The sought-after ideal is the perfect lover for the particular lady of the day and evening, and after marriage there is only supposed to be one of her—an unnatural limitation (many men feel) but a generally accepted one.

Sex, for most women, is an integral part of a whole relationship rather than a potential personal triumph. Rather than feeling guilty if either she or her mate doesn't respond sexually (the problem more likely being with herself) she may be frightened, sad or just irate, because the relationship is threatened, but (often to the exasperation of the man) she doesn't really blame herself.

The guilt of the single girl about *whether-to* or *whether-not-to* (and often either alternative seems wrong) is again because the future of the relationship often hangs on the decision. This classic female dilemma can reduce a girl to mental pulp, particularly if the man has handled it right. If he lunges at her ten minutes after being introduced, she may well turn him down on principle, but if he gives her time to think about sex he indeed furthers his cause. He *is* attractive; she has gone out with him several times; she *might* be in love with him but she doesn't know yet. . . . But maybe the only way to find *that* out is to go to bed with him. Suppose it turns out she *is* and he *isn't* and he leaves her—seduced and abandoned? Or, suppose she *isn't* and he *is*, in which case she would feel guilty? Even if she doesn't believe in love, does she want (1) an affair (2) a lot of affairs (3) marriage—or what *does* she want, anyway? And *why*, dammit, does she have to decide? Everything becomes a problem. Should she wear her black frontless and backless dress and be seductive, or retreat into her orange and green psychedelic shift and be confusing?

The whole conflict can get so oppressive that she might well give in to the gentleman just to have it over with and hope for the best—whatever that is. But she probably won't feel guilty about anything *unless* she feels she has damaged the relationship.

With men and women forever locked in such combat, marriage is still guiltier than celibacy. In sum, however, women struggle against a hundred forces that threaten the security of the marital ship and feel guilty about small leaks, while men struggle against their periodic instincts to crack up the whole boat. At the same time, guilt prevents most men from letting this happen—the husband who goes off for a carefree afternoon playing squash at the Princeton Club pays in guilt feelings for his transgression. His action, you see, violates the popular theory that husbands and wives are supposed to share all activities (a notion that has never before existed in history) and so does collapsing exhausted into a chair each night—and so does not spending enough time with the children.

A wife is full of strange guilts about things like the expensive, ugly slipcover she had made (she is practically ill every time she looks at it and may even perversely feel that she deserves the torture of having to do so); the once beautiful, now burned steak—even though her amiable husband may be the soul of tact about it; the day she wasted shopping and buying nothing while her house waited for its spring cleaning.

When her husband bursts forth from the nest for a fishing trip with the boys (which of course he feels guilty about), her mind scrambles around in a morass of wifely failures that might have driven him away: the house was a mess when he came home; she forgot to order more gin; he didn't have any clean socks; she was terrible in bed the night before; she is getting dull and neglecting her reading; she gained three pounds, and didn't get to the hairdresser. Possibly, none of these things had anything to do with the fishing trip at all, but she takes up the entire burden of blame and in turn lets her husband have it upon his return—mainly because he made her feel guilty.

Husbands and wives both feel so constantly guilty about their children that they blame each *other*. Once upon a time, children had faults and were naughty, but now parents *fail*. This situation burns so deeply that women dislike talking about it. It is compensated for by family outings, heavy involvement in the PTA and other allied penance-doing activities.

On the other hand, practically everybody—married or not—is also guilt-ridden about his or her parents (a situation that parents can't resist exploiting, as if to say, "You see how it feels for a change").

"I'm guilty about imposing on my mother," said one woman. "I'm guilty about making her baby-sit too late. I'm guilty about mistreating her, about fighting with her, and about ignoring her" (which seems to sum up the mother-daughter situation). "I hear my father's voice on the telephone and my day is ruined," said another girl. "All he has to do is say 'hello' and I feel guilty about all the things he would like me to be that I'm not." The classic interfering mother (or mother-in-law) is a relative blessing—at least you can get mad at her. But the silently suffering papas and mammas with aches, pains, and ailments (real or imagined) really carry the machete. All they have to do is disappear for a while to set off a chain of guilt fantasies in their children. "Maybe I *was* too hard on Mother,"—goes the classic guilty reasoning—"after all she *is* sixty-five and has ulcers, and even if she is unreasonable it's because she's old, alone, sick, and broke. Who wouldn't complain? Someday, I might be in the same spot, and maybe I'll invite her for the weekend—after all, I'm all she's got in the world" (usually untrue). Mother arrives saying she doesn't want to be any trouble to anybody, and everybody tries to be obliging, but somehow the usual fight ensues. . . . Mother gathers up her pills and medicines and stalks out, leaving with daughter the usual deposit of guilt and resolutions to do better next time. No one ever wins.

The most profound guilt (and it really is *guilt* rather than simple grief) is brought on by the death of a parent; it must enter the mind of every surviving child that he could have *somehow* prevented the death. If he had only been the perfect son or daughter—or, psychologically, if he hadn't been so angry so much of the time—he wouldn't have *caused* this to happen. This is why, after a death, a surviving child must agonizingly relive every aspect of the relationship, as if in a desperate search for reprieve. . . . There *was* the day we did so-and-so together; I *did* please him (or her) by getting A's in high school; I *did* show my love, *didn't* I?

Anger is the emotion behind guilt, and almost everyone feels guilty about getting angry! But only the sweet-tempered speak of their "rage." "The one thing I'm really guilty of during my life is all the times I ever got angry and hurt somebody," said one lady in her sixties who actually gets mildly angry about once a year. One rather mercurial gentleman says he gets *furious* about feeling guilty. The anger-guilt cycle is rather a chicken-and-egg problem, and possibly temperament determines which comes first.

Indecision (which is a kind of reverse anger, in that its effect is to accomplish nothing and annoy everyone else) causes guilt in a lot of people; so does procrastination and general passivity, or not taking an action when it is called for. All these attitudes seem like crimes against the self. One ex-Episcopalian minister (who prefers to remain anonymous) blames most behavior like this on Puritan ethics, which, to some extent, are based on guilt: enjoying oneself is often thought to be a sin. This belief can be so rigid that "people frequently choose the thing they don't want to do, because it seems *righter*." Such decisions are not as extreme as they may seem. All of us habitually do penance for our fancied wrongs: We go to bed at ten o'clock after a late night out; we starve to make up for overeating; and there's nothing like a little sexual guilt on the part of a wife who thinks she's neglected her husband to get the closets cleaned out and the floors scrubbed.

One girl tells a curious story of being invited to a dreaded party of show-business and literary lions. She felt fat and unattractive; she couldn't stand her dress; her escort was an old friend who wouldn't bother to take care of her and there she would be—a wallflower among the beautiful and famous. She went, however, and to her surprise began to have a very good time, meeting several nice people who apparently considered her quite human. All was going well when she spotted, in a corner, a sort of alter ego—a girl she knew and couldn't stand, who *was,* in fact, looking fat, unattractive, and utterly rejected. Instead of being healthily bucked up by the contrast between *her* success and the plight of this poor castaway, she took her in hand and introduced her to everyone (thoroughly ruining her own evening). She then went home and cursed herself for having made herself pay for an (undeserved) good time.

Closely allied to this peculiar American sickness of the soul (Europeans laugh at these guilt burdens of ours) are problems about making, having, and spending money. Here the thin line of nonguilt seems difficult to find. Men are always guilty about not earning enough money (which is why they keep trying to make more), and if they are married, they are guilty of not being able to give enough to their wives, who themselves feel guilty because they keep wanting more possessions and running through their husbands' hard-won earnings.

The classic story is of the wife who serves her husband some miracle of economy, say a tuna-fish casserole—seeking praise for her cleverness—only to have him explode: "For God's sake! Can't we afford a steak?" A man's money is what makes his image, and he wants his success to show. His wife could guiltlessly serve a California red wine in a decanter, but *he* wants the bottle of Pommard on the table. Not that the situation is ever that simple—he has had that Pommard around for months, waiting for properly receptive guests; a well-traveled colleague rather than his wife's nephew from Rutgers. A certain guilt about showing off is really what has kept the Pommard in the rack for so long. He longs for an ostentatious display, but creating one makes him nervous.

As a man guards his wine, so a woman guards her clothes—that terribly expensive dress in the closet that she hardly ever wears because someone might ask where she got it—and guilt will force her to blurt out the price, the designer, and how she is going without meat for three weeks because of buying it. One lady wears her Pucci with equanimity because she can tell any inquirers that it went for half-price in Rome (which makes her feel better). She explains her brocade dinner dress by going through a kind of guilty inverse-snob explanation: "Oh, *yes,* I picked up the brocade in Damascus for almost *nothing* and this little woman made it up for me for only twenty-five dollars." She is *really* saying, "Just for making me feel guilty *I'll* show you who's been to Damascus, and who's clever enough to find a cheap dressmaker!"

One man treated himself to a very expensive Abercrombie & Fitch sheep-lined coat, which he self-consciously wore to the office where it was admired by a young file clerk. When she asked him where he got it, he gulped, looked vague, and made a great pretense of fishing for the label . . . as though the name of the store weren't burning a hole in both his conscience and checkbook. *But,* he would never feel apologetic about his wife's new Dior, and her explanations about how it came from Ohrbach's (simply a copy) would only annoy him. The husband of the Pucci lady doubtlessly wishes she would shut up and stop implying that he can't afford to buy her Puccis at New York prices. Whether we are put on the spot by the office file-clerk or someone with closets of designer clothes doesn't seem to make much difference—our reaction is completely personal and implies some larger guilt about having money—and having the self-esteem to spend it. We feel guilty about loving ourselves.

A husband can spend money on his wife and a wife on her husband (even though the money is his) without guilt, but the unmarried are in a spot. Unmarried men have vague guilts about spending all their money on themselves, and so do unmarried women. Working for money alleviates some guilt, but if it falls from heaven in the form of inheritance or private income, money can produce all sorts of feelings about not deserving it (some women still feel that their money ought to come from a man), and strange behavioral penances.

One woman, heiress to some millions, leaves her lights burning when she goes out because she figures that it will cost more to turn them off and then on again when she gets home. Private incomes are hard on a girl's love life. Prospective suitors often feel, if she has all that money, she doesn't really need them. At the same time, girls with a lot of money have a propensity for getting involved with penniless men. One such girl says she feels sorry for the poor dears—they deserve a square meal and a few of the simple pleasures so easily available to the rich. It is agony for her to be taken to an expensive restaurant and to be aware of what the cost must mean to her less affluent escort. It would be so easy to slip him a few bills under the table, but that is exactly what she can't do. Moreover, she feels the dinner places her under too heavy an obligation; if she won't go to bed with him later, he will inevitably think he hasn't priced her favors highly enough. It is a relief to be with a man she can pay for. She is guilty about having all this money anyway, and getting rid of a bit of it takes off some of the pressure. The flaws in her attitude are obvious—most men don't like being paid for—men worth a girl's serious attention insist on paying the way. My friend finally met a man who is even richer than she is, and now she talks happily of all the yachts, planes, and estates he has that she couldn't afford at all.

But money that befalls men (in the form of an inheritance) isn't always from heaven, either. One girl shared quarters for a while after college with a young man of means, and she said it got to her when she staggered home from a hard day sweeping the basement of a publishing house—or whatever she was doing at the time—to find him lying on the couch in the living room reading Keats. (Not working never occurred to her.) To top things off, he took care of *his* guilt by telling her all the time how virtuous work was and how he believed all women should work.

It is *de rigueur* for people with a lot of money to affect economy-mindedness (a kind of guilt in their case), and they are not well looked upon when they violate this tenet. One very rich girl gave a cocktail party, during which she had the poor taste (or pure nerve) to model the opulent mink coat she had bought that afternoon because—as she said—she simply couldn't resist it. The embarrassed silence following this gaffe was at least partly caused (in the psyches of the guests) by guilt *she didn't have.*

We even feel guilt for others—we supply it where we think it is demanded, and often as a substitute for action. We have all witnessed scenes that have made us feel guilty even though they had nothing to do with us: the angry man in the restaurant torturing the poor waiter; the cruel nanny and the frightened child; the mean old man kicking pigeons; or even the thief mugging the old lady. What paralyzes us into guilty inaction (rather than interfering) is that we guiltily identify with the aggressor, wondering if our own (suppressed) anger might one day cause us to commit crimes equally hideous.

One guilt-ridden career girl compiled the following checklist of her symptoms. How many do *you* share?

• Although you are a grown woman, you are *hopelessly* responsive to the criticism, whims, compliments of your parents.
• You never just say No to a request. You explain why you can't comply in detail . . . and sometimes when you have finished the explanation you start all over and explain again!
• When you have to say No to an invitation and your reason is not only legitimate but unassailable, you feel that people don't believe you.
• While some people seem to rather enjoy telling their friends disquieting news (her beau was seen at a party with another girl . . . you know definitely his raise is *not* coming through . . . you've been invited to serve on a committee and she hasn't) you *loathe* passing along this kind of information. You will never put down or deprecate anyone to his *face*, although that doesn't keep you from saying some pretty ratty things behind his *back*.

• You want everyone to get along with everyone else—office mates with each other, your boss with his wife, your sister with your brother-in-law —and are willing to do anything to keep people happy together. You often feel as drained as an empty swimming pool because, although you ask nothing for yourself except a peace settlement and are willing to sacrifice hours and energy toward having warring parties work things out, you frequently find you've done no good at all. . . . They're still at it! This leaves you feeling wretched for being ineffectual.

• In the same vein, you like to keep people loving *you*. Sometimes you almost feel as though you were "feeding the guppies" . . . offering bits of yourself to people you like, hoping to satisfy them until you've time to give *more*! You can't stand to have anybody mad at you.

• You feel *terrible* leaving your children for a weekend or vacation although they will be in good hands. You regret (almost as much) leaving your cat or dog and do wish they could understand human talk so you might explain that you'll be *back*.

• You have a compulsion toward honesty. You prefer telling people the *real* reason you have to say No—you're too tired to go to dinner and would rather grab some sleep . . . concerts bore you . . . their idea for a book is not very good and you don't want to spend a year helping them with it—than to hedge or lie or make up reasons they would more easily accept. This is different from not wanting to tell a friend unpleasant news *gratuitously* that he wouldn't have heard otherwise. You've got to tell him *something* here and you prefer not to lie.

• When somebody in the room is putting someone else down, no matter how subtly they do it, and even if the put-down person is a *bore*, you get the message immediately—maybe even sooner than the intended victim —and feel desperately sorry for that person.

• You have finally demanded and *gotten* something you had every right to: more equitable treatment from your boss, improvements in the apartment from your landlord, more affection from your husband, a refund on faulty merchandise from the department store. Then, having captured your prize, you wonder if you went too far.

• The only "people" you can discipline without feeling guilty are your dog and cat, and there's even some question about *them*. After giving them a spanking, you're apt to let them climb right back into your lap and your good graces.

• You wish desperately the cabdriver would raise the window or stop playing the radio so loud but you figure it's just a short ride and you'll stay silent. Suddenly you blurt out your perfectly reasonable request. . . . "*Could* you raise the window a bit?" "*Could* you turn the radio down?" You suffer afterward because you figure the driver is *pouting*.

• When you reprimand your husband, child, cleaning woman, fellow employee, or friend, and the person continues to do the thing he was reprimanded for, you're secretly a little relieved. You'd *already* begun to wonder if he deserved the criticism.

• You are charming.

• You get emotional and usually *lose* in arguments.

• You cry sometimes.

• You are a perfectionist.

Theoretically a good, valid guilt should be backed up by a good, solid wrong. A man *should* feel guilty about being unfaithful to his wife; a mother *should* feel guilty about locking her child in the closet for two hours . . . anything else is neurotic anxiety. But the line between deserved and unwarranted guilt can grow thin, and sometimes fades away altogether as our social prohibitions get increasingly indistinct. Rather than freeing us, lack of guidelines only leaves us with *more* irrational guilts than when social wrongs were more clearly defined. *Should* a woman feel guilty about being unfaithful to her husband if they have a terrible relationship and he is barely interested in her physically? The answer is probably No, but the straying wife is still stuck with guilt about being the wandering partner. One wonders if the straying is worth it. One wonders if *anything* is worth the guilt we all continually feel!

JEALOUSY, MY GOD, I'VE GOT JEALOUSY

Jealousy is a mongrel emotion. Like a mongrel, it's shrewd and tenacious, greedy and sly. Like a mongrel, its parentage is often obscure. But oh those teeth— once they're sunk in you, beware!

Jealousy, despite romantic notions to the contrary, is not a symptom of love; it is rather evidence of a feeling of inadequacy, of lack of love. I know that jealousy is commonly assumed to be a kind of exotic penalty one pays for passion and intensity of feeling. Even good old La Rochefoucauld said, "We are ashamed to admit that we are jealous, but proud that we were and can be."

Well, I say down with La Rochefoucauld! In fact, having once suffered horribly myself from the mongrel's bite (of which more later), I have come to believe that when I am jealous it means either I am: one, not loving enough, or, two, loving the wrong person. And my emotions are typical enough, I think, and represent enough psychological truisms, to safely assume that what applies to me could very likely apply to you—maybe even help you see your behavior more clearly.

To begin with, we know that jealousy as a condition takes many forms. The *Oxford English Dictionary* defines jealousy as "Troubled by the belief, suspicion or fear that the good which one desires to gain or keep for oneself has been or may be diverted to another."

But that's just the end result, really. What we're interested in finding out is how the mechanism works. What *is* it that sets off the "belief, suspicion or fear"? The details—how you first begin to doubt, the way the first dark hints appear, what you do about them, how *he* responds—are as unique and varied as the individuals involved. Nevertheless, there are a few broad and general categories of jealousy which can lead us to an understanding of this painful emotion and what triggers it.

The two major ways in which you acquire your first suspicion that he's been—as the dictionary so fastidiously puts it—"diverted to another" come from either his desires or from yours. In other words, either his behavior is signaling you or you are going out of your way to look for trouble. In the first case, for whatever reason, *he* wants you to be jealous; in the second case, *you* want to be jealous. (For clarity and simplicity I use the word "want" here to cover both a conscious and an unconscious desire. The wanting is not always obvious to the person involved—but we'll explain as we go along.)

Let's group the first kind of jealousy under the heading Operation Undermine: He Wants You to Be Jealous.

Case 1: Susan and Paul have been living together for about a year. When they first met he was still living (though miserably) with his wife and daughter. Later he and his wife separated. Paul is a senior account executive in the advertising agency where Susan works as a stylist. She's about six or seven years younger than he and comes on as total-chic, total-career. Actually, she's a tender, bright girl from Des Moines who wants nothing more than to devote all her love and energy to her personal life—which at the moment is Paul.

But a few months ago she noticed that he seemed to be slowing down his efforts to get his divorce. He had several accounts that took him out of town and Susan noticed that he was away more and calling her less. And when he called, he always seemed to be just leaving a noisy party; didn't have time to chat, just wanted to "check in." Hmmmm.

Of course, by the time he got home, Susan was edgy and desperately anxious to be reassured. But instead of doing the kind, obvious, and *easy* thing, Paul would act aloof, almost guilty. Several times—as was inevitable—Susan would be driven to ask him if there was someone else—why was he acting so funny, was something wrong? And then, of course, snap! the trap closed, the curtain had risen and Susan was behind the footlights in the title role of *Susan, Suspicious Harridan* . . . unable to control her new feelings of insecurity.

How did this happen to nice Susan and attractive Paul? And why? Well, it seems that emotionally Paul was going through something that might be described as a "reign of terror" (all inward, of course, but nonetheless painful and frightening to him). He had suddenly found himself committed to Susan, having barely (and not ever totally, because of his child) escaped from a strong prior commitment. Once the first excitement of their love had passed, Paul discovered he was unreasonably terrified of a future with Susan. Was there any chance his second marriage would be happier than his first?

Not that he had ceased to love her. In fact, it was his love for her that made him act in a mysterious, seemingly guilty way. Fearing the responsibility of not failing *this* time, he was unconsciously trying to escape from the situation. If Susan was unreasonably jealous (he *knew* he'd done nothing wrong), if she was upset over nothing (he couldn't help it if that was the only time he could call) and accused him of not loving her (he *did* call her, after all), then *she* was the one who was unsure and unhappy, not him. And she would relieve him of his fear of failure by failing first herself!

But because she loved him and in her calmer moments was able to see past her own worries to his, Susan discovered ways to ease her fiancé's unconscious fear of being tied down. She began to go out when he was away—not on dates in order to make him jealous, but out to dinner with friends, or to their houses or to the movies. She began to live her own life again and if he did call and catch her at home, she was cheerful and secure. He soon abandoned his mysterious, guilty homecoming air—she had stopped responding to it, so it had lost its effectiveness.

As Susan maintained her assurance of being loved and her pleasure in doing things on her own, Paul was finally able to relax and realize that he wasn't going to be trapped; he didn't need to keep grabbing at pieces of freedom, because he already had the perfect kind of freedom—a bond that exists by choice, not necessity. And Susan, who had forced herself to behave calmly and serenely, in spite of her doubts, discovered the almost magical irony of the fact that the more loved we feel, the more loved we are.

Case 2: In Paul and Susan's situation jealousy developed as a temporary imbalance within the relatively healthy structure of a relationship. However, in some affairs or marriages jealousy is an integral part of their functioning. I met a couple like this. Barry and Shirley live on a seesaw of recrimination and repair because this particular husband is bent on undermining his wife with every woman he meets.

Barry is a young painter who has received just enough acclaim to cause him to abandon his humility but not enough to provide him with much security, certainly not with *financial* security. That comes courtesy of his wife. Shirley is a mousy little dumpling with wispy blond hair and a growing art collection, of which Barry could be considered the primary acquisition. But in spite of her seeming shyness and frailty, Shirley quickly manages to make you aware of her financial muscle.

"Daddy is desperately looking for a pilot for his new Lear jet," she said a few minutes after I met her. "Would you know someone, by any chance?" When I ruefully admitted that I didn't, she sighed and tried to explain how important it was that Daddy continually touch base with his far-flung industrial empire. "He's pretty much the plastics king," she said modestly.

Barry, possibly to offset any real embarrassment at being consort to the plastics princess, is quite blatant about living on Shirley's money . . . but he mocks her and seems to imply that her emotions are more suited to business transactions than to bedrooms. And he makes sure you know that bedrooms are *his* style. Your bedroom, baby, is the feeling he puts across right away. We had hardly met when I found myself backing off. Later I learned from our hosts that he regularly propositions almost every woman he meets. Statistics being on his side, a sufficient number respond favorably and he enjoys a brief fling . . . taking care, of course, that little Shirley either senses, sees, or is told of his latest adventure.

Under these circumstances, there is obviously no way for Shirley to avoid being jealous as long as she stays married to the same man. Jealousy is a condition of the relationship. Many relationships are built on this kind of sadomasochistic arrangement. All that is required is for two people to *use* one another rather than *love* one another and the stage is set. The using can be hidden and unconscious, with details only a psychiatrist could understand, or it can be—like Barry and Shirley—an obvious, more surface, exchange.

Often, even without being aware of it, each person senses the absence of love and feels cheated and resentful and capable of revenge. But because *both* are using one another (which is usually the case, incidentally; there are few real victims in this sort of arrangement. When you see a situation where the using seems one-sided, look again), because this is a *mutual* con, no one has the upper hand. Shirley, via her money, is using Barry to purchase a place in the fashionable art world; Barry, via his talent, is using Shirley to *support* him in the fashionable art world. She maintains her balance of power by means of money; he maintains his by being unfaithful to her. But human nature being what it is, even in the most practical of arrangements a man can be put down and a woman can be made jealous.

All "using" situations are not necessarily so clear-cut as this one. Almost everyone has been involved in one at some point. Whether it's the time you snagged the captain of the football team, or captured the steady of your worst enemy, or had an affair with a famous writer—if you wanted him for his attributes (he has a great body, he belongs to someone else, he's a celebrity) rather than for *himself* (I love being with him), then you are an easy prey for Operation Undermine, for the kind of jealousy which threatens you with the loss of a possession, not a love.

Now that we've looked at two kinds of jealousy brought on by *him*, let's investigate the jealousy you create for yourself. We'll call it Search-and-Destroy.

Case 1: Marjorie has been dating Phil for almost a year. They talk about marriage sometimes but never seem to formalize their plans. Phil is a successful photographer in his late twenties, lean, bookish, attractive. Marjorie is an assistant sportswear buyer, always aware of her looks and fashionable clothes and creates a rather chilly impression at first meeting.

With Phil, however, she has grown to be the opposite of chilly. The distant, independent character he wooed for six months has recently turned into a clinging, complaining, suspicious female, while he—as he keeps telling her—hasn't changed one iota. Marjorie doesn't understand what is behind her new uncharacteristic behavior; she just knows that every time she sees Phil talking to an attractive girl she's jealous.

Because her feeling is so irrational and inexplicable even to herself, it's possible Marjorie may be trapped in the slavery of *projection* and have created the jealousy to mask other hidden feelings from herself. To describe projection simply, it is the act of ascribing to somebody else a despised trait which you in fact have, but which your ego refuses to accept. By projecting this weakness onto another, your conscious self is able to chastise the bad impulse without having to acknowledge it as your own. By the same token, your unconscious can release some of its emotional charge by imagining the impulse as acted out by someone else. Thus projection provides the individual with a temporary moral victory and a partial psychic release.

In your own case, have you ever found yourself talking to someone and thinking, How boring I am! Behind that thought often lies the repressed feeling that the person you are *talking* to is boring, but for a mixture of reasons—you need to charm him for your job, you want to be *kind*, or maybe you just need to pass the time—you unconsciously switch the source of the boredom so that you need not acknowledge your *real* feeling. Probably, in this case, if you acknowledged it, you might feel obliged to *act* (to get up and leave or find someone more interesting) and that might not serve your *primary* original need.

Take another case. When you think you *look* unattractive or badly put together, don't you find that people respond to you negatively? And reversing the scene, when you feel attractive, don't you sense an air of admiration? Now, while some of these emanations you get from others are undoubtedly *true*, a great part of the atmosphere you perceive really derives from your projection of your own inner sense of self. Unattractive feeling, you project that feeling onto your observers; glamorous, you feel their attraction. (That's why it isn't totally narcissistic for a woman to spend a long time dressing. How she *feels* about herself can totally influence her evening.)

These have been examples of the most simple kind of projection, relatively easy to uncover, but when the secret we are hiding from ourselves becomes more important, more guilty, then the shell of the projection hardens. The more intense the initial sense of guilt in the unconscious, the more frightening the possibility of revelation and therefore the stronger the conviction that it—the sin, the failure, or whatever—*must* belong to someone else.

Try giving yourself a little test to see the way projection works in your own psychological makeup. Take a weakness you know you have. Let's take mine! I have a big appetite, gain weight easily, and I must eat carefully. Now, because I find the possession of this appetite unattractive in myself, I'm extraordinarily harsh on people who I think wallow in their gluttony. If I don't let *myself* do that, how can *they*? How *dare* they, in fact? Of course, since this is a problem I'm aware of, the strength of the projection is naturally much weaker than if it were a genuine taboo, such as homosexuality. Often men who have buried a fear that they are latent homosexuals exhibit a violent hostility toward effeminate men.

In Marjorie and Phil's relationship, if her jealousy is indeed a projection of her *own* hidden desires to cheat, it means that *she* is the one who would like to escape and is only accusing him of infidelity and a wish to escape from her in order not to have to face her *own* desires. Perhaps Phil is beginning to bore her, but she's afraid to give up the security of a steady man; perhaps she feels a stronger sexual attraction to other men but admitting it would mean that she's promiscuous; perhaps she's afraid of being trapped into marriage but nevertheless feels *driven* to marry in order to prove her desirability.

There could be any number of other possibilities, but the crucial factor to look for in this kind of jealousy is an unreasonable intensity of feeling that has no apparent basis in reality. In other words, if you have an outwardly satisfactory relationship with a man, in which he behaves in a kind, decent, and reliable way, wherein you have no overt or even subtle reasons for being jealous, yet are nevertheless plagued with suspicions and doubts, stop and look carefully, not at him, but at *yourself*.

When you start investigating jealousy-by-projection, you must be absolutely honest with yourself. List (on paper if it helps) all the obvious good you feel exists between you and the other person. Then—and here is where you must be relentless—list what you really don't like about him. And include everything, even if it seems minor—he giggles and you hate men who giggle, he squeezes toothpaste from the middle of the tube, he has plump hands, he always leaves the toilet seat up—every little or big thing that makes you the least bit edgy or hostile.

When you finish the list and compare the two columns, good and bad, you may be surprised to find that the negative, con side is where all your real feelings are, and the sweet, sentimental pro side was just a lot of paper lace and convenience. No wonder you thought he might have another girl; the truth is, nothing would please you more!

Case 2: Jane and Charles moved to the country two years ago when their third child was born. Because Charles is an architect, they were able to turn a sagging Connecticut barn into a beautiful, spacious house that's as good for entertaining as it is for child-raising. Jane and I became friends a few years before when we were both working on the same magazine. At that time she had an excellent nurse to care for the first two children and was able to stay on the job until just before the third child arrived. Before she quit working, Jane confessed that she was worried about moving to the country; she had always worked and was afraid she'd be miserable and lost being strictly wife and mother.

After they were settled in the new place I saw them a few times but never long enough to have any real picture of their new life-style. Jane had put on some weight, I noticed, and her hair didn't have the great coiffed look it used to, but nothing was glaringly wrong. Then, one day after they'd been in the country about a year, Jane phoned and asked me out for the weekend. Charles would be away until Sunday, she said, but we could have a cheerful country reunion.

The girl who met me at the station was almost unrecognizable. The few pounds she had originally put on must have grown to twenty, the greater portion of which was wedged into a pair of reluctant gabardine pants. Her hair was choppy and short; three stepping-stone children with dirty faces and drooping socks clustered around her.

It didn't take a clairvoyant to tell that something was wrong with her life, so I wasn't surprised when she put the children to bed early and said she had to talk to me. Charles had a mistress, she said. He was coming home later and later, working more and more weekends, and, worst of all, when he was home he never paid any attention to her. He never took her anywhere anymore, rarely slept with her; they didn't talk much, and he never wanted to have people in.

She went on with an endless recital of clues that proved Charles was unfaithful. She even confessed that she'd called a private detective, but had hung up when he'd answered. "Next time I won't," she said. "I've got to find out who the other woman is!"

About that time I felt I had to try and get her to see the situation from Charles's point of view. As tactfully as possible, I suggested that there might not be anyone else attracting Charles; she herself might be pushing him away. It had apparently never occurred to Jane that his coolness was her fault. But, gradually, as we talked about how she spent her days, how she felt about herself, my friend began to realize that she wasn't any longer the girl Charles had married.

The trigger, of course, was their sudden move to the country, leaving behind her a life in which she felt secure and successful. Jane had based her sense of worth almost entirely on what she accomplished in the business world. Her successful career convinced her she was a substantial, creative, lovable person. When she left the job, there were no longer any such clear standards for judging success. Having either ignored or looked down on homemaking as a career, she slowly began to lose her feeling of being competent. On top of her growing insecurity, she was lonely. She had only the children to talk to all day, found little in common with her neighbors. To be honest, she didn't really try to make friends, having years ago decided women who didn't work were boring.

Once she began to feel inadequate, it was easy to act out those feelings. If she was a failure, why bother to organize her day? There was no reason *not* to watch soap operas, to get dressed for Charles at night, to get up and make his breakfast . . . no reason for anything but survival.

We talked until dawn while Jane discovered new ways she had kept herself down and remembered times Charles had tried to bring back her old self. Having failed, she realized that he had simply withdrawn. Once she was able to see that her jealousy about the other woman had been created out of her own failure, she was able to begin to find her old self and look for different standards of success in her new life. Getting rid of her sense of inferiority, she was able to feel lovable again and to believe that Charles could and did love her.

For that is perhaps the single greatest cause of jealousy: the fear that we are unlovable. Out of that fear we build elaborate structures to prove that someone *else* is stealing love away from us; someone *else* is taking what we really deserve. You can see how that kind of focus, away from ourselves, makes it possible for us to hide from our own flaws. But by burying our fears and putting the blame on others, we stifle any possibility of change and growth. If I am the victim, all I can do is suffer. He has wronged me, why should *I* change? What can I do? Jane believed that Charles would love her if it weren't for his mistress. She was unable to bear the fact that there was no mistress, that she wasn't the victim but the villain. The moment she forced herself to say, "He would love me if it weren't for *me*," she began to accept the responsibility.

Now there is a whole *other* important category of jealousy: the agony you feel when you *know* there's someone else, when it's not a trick or a game or part of your relationship, but there really *is* another woman. What then? Well, unfortunately, this time I speak from personal experience—my own grim bout with the teeth of the mongrel.

My husband and I had what I always considered a unique and wonderful marriage. We had two healthy, bright children; we both had jobs we enjoyed, and loved to talk, travel, make love. I used to say to friends, "It's almost too good to be true—we're so *lucky*."

Well, it *was* too good to be true. Shortly after our tenth anniversary David had to spend several weeks in Chicago setting up a new branch office. When he came home I noticed something a little different about him, nothing specific, though. He just said he was tired and we let it go at that. Then he had to take *another* trip to Chicago. And another. And though he complained more and more about the extra work and having to be away so often, at the same time he was becoming more distant.

One night after he returned from another Chicago trip the phone rang long after midnight. I happened to pick it up. At first there was silence, and what I thought sounded like breathing, then a click. Somehow I sensed it had been a woman calling and I thought David knew it, too, though he didn't realize *I* knew. I lay there sleepless for the rest of the night. I wanted to kill *her*, to kill him, to kill myself! Rage kept twisting and grinding in me as I pictured him in bed with her, talking to her, having dinner at her apartment. Who *was* she? How *could* he?!

I don't know how I got through the next few weeks. If David hadn't been in such a state himself, he would have seen that I was distraught, but apparently he thought I knew nothing. The next time he took off for Chicago, I simply followed a few flights behind. As I look back on it now, it's hard to believe I really got on that plane, and if anyone had told me that I would be sneaking after my husband to *spy* on him someday, I would either have laughed or screamed! Me? Sane, secure me do anything so ridiculous? But there I was, landing in Chicago, moving through the airport like a robot, with one thought motivating every muscle: I was going to see this woman, confront her, do something—anything—to change the horrible life we were leading.

Although I wasn't much of a detective, it never occurred to David that anyone was following him, and it was easy to track him down. It's funny now to think of myself lurking in the hotel lobby, hidden behind a newspaper, watching the elevators. Eventually I spotted him leading a fragile, rather pretty young woman into the dining room.

Now that I had them trapped I found my aggressiveness had totally vanished—I simply couldn't march over to them and act like an outraged wife. Somehow, even in my extremity, I recognized that public scenes weren't my style. Also, the rage I'd felt that first night six weeks before had now iced my blood and frozen every normal response. So, calm with fury and resentment, I had myself seated at a table directly across from them.

I think David saw me as I sat down, but neither of us made any sign of recognition. I ordered a double martini and sat there openly staring at them. I felt a delicious flush of vengeance knowing just how miserable my husband must feel, how confused he must be, trying not to let her know anything was wrong. She, poor thing, kept patting his sleeve and giving him a little kiss now and then, obviously puzzled by his stiffness. He managed some escape excuse because they left without ordering. I remained behind on my glacier.

I flew home that night and waited like a vegetable for David's return. The minute he came back I told him I wanted a divorce. He was horrified. He felt so guilty . . . he just didn't know how it had started. She was a lonely kid; he felt sorry for her but now he was trapped and didn't know how to escape. I was adamant. My heart seemed to be sealed off and all I could think of was the image of them in bed together. I wanted to get away, and I did. I left him with the children and fled to my favorite aunt. There I wept and cried and carried on about my beastly husband. She patted me and said, "There, there," over and over, but I couldn't hide in the country forever. There were the children and there was the divorce. After two days I staggered back to try to arrange our new lives.

Some of my fury and hurt had washed away in those floods of tears, and as I began thinking back over the ten years David and I had spent together I remembered something my aunt had said to me, that I hadn't wanted to hear. It was about how I had failed David. She said I hadn't allowed him to be wrong, to be imperfect or fail. Was there so little to our marriage, I thought, to throw it away so easily? If I really loved him, wasn't that love enough to include *all* of him, even his failures?

The reconciliation wasn't easy. (Yes, he gave her up.) There wasn't any instant-heal, but as a first step we were able to forgive each other, and gradually our closeness returned. In the time that's gone by since those dreadful days, I've learned a lot more about the causes and results of jealousy—enough to think it must be avoided if at all possible. That's easier to say than accomplish, perhaps, but not impossible if one works at it. You, for example.

Let's begin not with the *inside* you, but with something simpler—what you *do*. Who you are is something that you can only change gradually, if at all, and it may take the help of a psychiatrist. (They are very good at this!) But what you *do* can be dealt with.

I'll make a prediction here that you can beat jealousy—even the Operation Undermine and Search-and-Destroy kind—with this very cliché, tried-and-true system. The system is that you become highly successful at your work! A lot of free-floating jealousy, even the kind connected with love affairs, just seems to evaporate when a girl becomes a *somebody* in her world. Of course the passage of time, during which you are becoming more sophisticated and learning to dress, talk, think, and project better, has a beautifully therapeutic effect on insecurities, but add to that a really smashing professional success and you'd be surprised at how "normal" and envy-free you become. One best-selling lady author says, "I just rarely meet anybody anymore I *really* think is a lot more wonderful than I am, unless it's a Nobel-Prize-winning geneticist or something. Girls don't bother me so far as my husband is concerned because I'm *convinced* none of them could write a book!" Another says, "Knowing you're the best in your field, even if it's executive secretary, has the most soothing effect on your ego. It seems to fill in all kinds of gaps and holes."

Of course the man you choose has a lot to do with how well you like yourself, and you don't have to be a nut case to fall for an exploiter. I sometimes think *all* girls have one of these men in their lives at some time. Once you get rid of *him*, it's astonishing how unjealous you get. You can sit right next to the most gorgeous girl at the party and know she couldn't get your beloved away from you because your beloved is a loving man who loves *you*.

So finally do remember to be careful about whom you *choose* to love. Never stay with a man who makes you feel inferior. Even though he takes you to exciting places, spends money on you, and gives you gifts, if he doesn't make you feel like the most wonderful, desirable woman in the world—or at least in *his* world—he should be got rid of. Many women mistake a condition of servitude for love. They get involved with a man who demoralizes them, picks on their taste, their dress, their manners— and they both call it "love." Needless to say, that kind of destructive relationship is the most fertile breeding ground for jealousy. You may not be the most perfect girl in the world, but if you have been truly loving and giving while he continues to make you suffer, move on. Somewhere a better love is waiting. In the meantime you may become a little better *yourself*—so you'll have less cause for jealousy with your new love.

V

GETTING IT TOGETHER: Every single day seems
BE A jammed with mini and maxi conflicts; and nobody, of
MAGNIFICENT course, was ever *born* knowing how to
COPER handle them! Since babyhood you've
struggled to get-it-together; indeed, you continue learning
with every new crisis, always seeking *better* ways to analyze, attack, and
solve! This section is about *improving* your coping skills. We hope our
words will pummel you into a productive "Yes, I can!" attitude . . . then
when the next big test in *your* life looms (finishing your first novel, trying
for a more challenging job, dieting down from 170 to 125), you'll earn
high marks, and thrill to joyous, on-top-of-it-all *success!*

COPING BAROMETER

Yes, some people will thwart you at every turn. But others are darling and help whenever they can. Your best rewards for getting yourself together are friendship, respect, support, love. Usually, it's hard enough to please *yourself*, and dealing with others naturally compounds trouble potential. How do you rate on these situations:

1. Were you late more than once? (Count every occasion . . . dates, hairdresser and job appointments, self-imposed deadlines.)
2. Did you create a crisis by letting obligations pile up until they became unmanageable?
3. Have you spent more than a total of two hours seriously plotting revenge?
4. Did you weep or sulk to manipulate someone into giving you what you wanted?
5. Challenged by a competitor, did you abandon the field instead of redoubling your efforts?

YOUR BAROMETRIC RATING SCALE

4–5 noes   Maintain your rather formidable copesmanship by gliding through this section—but watch out for unexpected obstacles *others* can blithely strew along your path.

3 noes   You try, and that puts you well ahead of Miss Average. Which occasions seem too much for you? Concentrate on those for a time before tackling anything else.

2–0 noes   The details of life hassle you. Are you too impatient, seeking automatic rewards, expecting others to ease your way? Grow up! Learn how to smooth your *own* daily routine.

KEEPING PERKY IN A PRESSURE COOKER

What *is* pressure, anyway? People talk about it so much these days that one wonders if it just sprang into being within the past few years, like plastic furniture. Most of us don't remember anyone worrying about pressure particularly when we were children—troubles or worries, yes, but pressure, no. Or before that . . . Grandma raised six children and baked her own bread, but to her pressure was something having to do with the water pump. Grandpa may well have had work pressures, but they were taken for granted as part of the masculine scene, nobody discussed them much— and certainly Grandpa never complained about them. If you worked, you had pressures, didn't you? And you didn't waste time fussing!

Today everybody fusses about pressure, all the time . . . not just busy executives, who immediately come to mind when you think of pressured people, but secretaries, housewives, college students, small children, and teen-age dropouts. The executive's wife complains of the crushing pressures involved in running her large house with three servants; ten-year-olds get ulcers and take Caribbean vacations because their mothers think they need to get away from the pressures of school and all those piano, riding, and guitar lessons; and college students universally feel overworked to the point of collapse. It isn't just a chorus of complaints— it's actual pain such as Grandma never had. What's wrong with us? Are we so much frailer, or has life actually gotten a lot harder?

Both things are really true. Pressure—or stress, as the psychiatrists say, which is exactly the same thing—is simply exposure to a situation you feel you can't control, or any unwelcome emotion, or a conflict. Stress is anything you don't like that you feel you can't get rid of except by making a decision, and making the decision is agonizing. It isn't that stress is so bad in itself—it is often, in fact, the impetus for accomplishment. If pressure seems to be too much sometimes, well, it is, after all, a part of life, and nobody thinks life is a clambake—or *do* they? A great deal of the complaining sometimes seems to emerge out of an enormous disappointment that life *isn't* a clambake when it's *supposed* to be—everybody said so! A lot of people, particularly young ones, *expect* to be happy without even working for it—the fallacy in the American Dream. Grandma never had any such notions. She knew life was hard and you had to work for everything that was worth having, and she thought trouble was good for you, in a way—you grew wise and strong through adversity. How any other belief ever got so popular is amazing when there is so much evidence on Grandma's side. Stress is one of the unfortunate side effects of our fast-moving age, like the backaches man started getting when he stood up straight. We *are* frailer than we once were; however, rather than going back on all fours, we treat the backaches.

Since stress will be with us forever, like the air we breathe, what really matters is how we handle it. "A lot of us aren't coping with pressure very well," says Dr. Richard Glavin, New York psychiatrist. "There is a lowered frustration/anxiety tolerance level today," he says. "Many people believe that no uncomfortable emotion should be tolerated. Some of them even feel that to be alive is in *itself* a stress. This 'existential stress' just shouldn't be." He cites a typical case. "In comes a girl who has just graduated from college and broken up with her boy friend. She's upset and depressed. She says she can't stand it when she walks along the street and realizes that *nobody gives a damn about her.* I said, 'Why *should* anybody give a damn about you? Why do you expect them to care? Is *this* what you came to me about?' She's functioning well. She graduated with high marks and has had a couple of good job offers. There's nothing really *wrong* with her. Do you go to a psychiatrist when you break up with somebody?"

The striking thing about pressure is the way it varies in its effects on people: problems that one person might hardly notice, or could handle with equanimity, can be devastating to another. Look at Jeanette, for instance, who to all outward appearances should have little to complain about. She is married to an immensely rich man who provides her with anything a girl could reasonably want, such as an enormous apartment and a couple of full-time servants. Jeanette is not married to her husband *just* because he's rich—she has, if not a perfect marriage (which is fiction anyway) a fairly good one. She and her husband get along well most of the time, go to a lot of places, and do a good deal of traveling. She does a little photography, at which she is fairly good and semiprofessional . . . she has a splendid mane of chestnut hair and marvelous legs . . . and she *complains* all the time about *pressure.* To hear Jeanette talk, you would think she had more responsibilities than U Thant. Nobody, nobody can begin to understand what it's like to run a big apartment and a household staff. Bernard (her husband) is a *maniac* for perfection, though one would never suspect it from meeting him. He can hardly stand the sight of a piece of lint on the rug. *She* must look perfect all the time, which involves *so* much shopping and those *endless* fittings! And the dinner parties— well they *do* entertain a lot, and to hear Jeanette describe what she goes through for each party makes you understand why she is so uptight. Bernard is a gourmet, so she rushes uptown for rolls, downtown for *pâté,* midtown for fish, and though she doesn't cook the food, she *plans* it and engages in a personality duel with the cook that would leave anyone shaking.

You listen to Jeanette, and you wonder, now exactly *what* is she com- plaining about? Hard work? Luxury living isn't *that* hard, though she makes everything more difficult than necessary, and it isn't that she's lazy or against being busy—quite the contrary. Pleasing Bernard? She makes him out to be far fussier than he is. What the problem is, and *all* it is, is the way she *handles* stress. In a life that another woman would find incredibly easy, Jeanette feels driven and oppressed. A rigid, compulsive person, she must handle her life by constantly creating emergencies. The rug! The lint! The *pâté* disaster! The qualities of screaming perfectionism that she attributes to her husband are mainly her own. It is as though Jeanette has a kind of hate-love relationship with stress—she can't stand it, and she can't stand to be without it. The stresses she is feeling are probably more within her marriage relationship (which is such loaded territory, she doesn't want to examine it) and certainly within herself, though she constantly implies that somehow, somewhere, there is a pressure-free life—she has fantasies of beach huts in Tahiti. One doubts that she would find such a life-style possible. She would be just as tense in Tahiti, running frantically around the beach to find just the right mangoes to satisfy Bernard's supposed perfectionism.

On the other side of the coin is Celia, who avoids stress at any price— she is terrified of it. She is single and must support herself for the most part; she does get a small allowance from her family and finds that she can scrape by with a part-time job. Celia *tried* a full-time job on a magazine for a while and couldn't *stand* the pressure. What pressure? Oh, all the rush-rush-rush and the tempests in teapots and the sinister lady editors who were always in a hurry and all the silly decisions and the gossip. She had a terrible time; she would get unbearably *sleepy* right in the middle of some enormous office crisis when everyone else was screaming and phoning and arguing and perspiring. Celia just wanted to creep off in a corner and curl up. And she was so *tired* at the end of every day, absolutely exhausted, with no energy left to do anything in the evening.

After a while Celia quit the magazine, which didn't seem to sadden anyone unduly, and now she works part-time at a foundation as a kind of secretary-girl Friday. The job is dull and doesn't pay much, but she feels safer there. She lives in a dingy walk-up in a doubtful part of town where her friends (the few she has ever made) hesitate to come, and if they do, it's hardly a glorious experience. Everything is in shreds and tatters, Celia included. Her love life, too, is cautious—no real involvements, ever, just short relationships with men who don't threaten her too much. If the relationships ever start to deepen and intensify, Celia pulls away. If you asked Celia what she hated most in the world, she would probably say *decisions*. No matter how shadowy and peripheral her life, there always seems to be *some* decision haunting her. Even trying to decide something as simple as which movie to go to frequently immobilizes her so much that she ends up not going to any movie at all. She broods as she lies awake at night (though she has no trouble sleeping in the *daytime*) over the fact that she can't seem to get away from stress no matter *what* she does. She has just as much decision trouble now as she did when she worked for the terrible magazine—the only difference is the subject matter. Now she worries less about her job and more about little problems; it often takes her at least half an hour to make up her mind what to put on in the morning, and usually when she *does* decide, the dress has a hopeless rip or half the buttons off! Everything seems *so* difficult—she used to be a cheerful person when she was much younger, but now she feels sad all the time for some reason.

Celia and Jeanette would be appalled by Andrea, who *thrives* on pressure. It is a tonic to her, a spur to activity. She always has been and probably always will be Miss Extracurricular. In college she was the girl who ran everything. Now she manages a demanding job as an office manager, marriage to a man with another demanding job, a course in Japanese, tennis lessons, a hospital committee, and lectures on the stock market, besides activities she doesn't even *count,* like daily Yoga and refinishing furniture. You can't have lunch with Andrea because she doesn't *eat* lunch—she's always off to the gym or the tennis courts with a container of yogurt in her purse.

Andrea isn't any sort of masochist. She simply loves to be scheduled, loves to be organized, and really comes alive when facing a jam-packed day that would make some of us want to jump out the window. Luckily, Andrea has a husband who knows how to make her stop—for with all her efficiency and organizational ability, this is the one thing she doesn't know how to do. It is almost as though she is afraid to pause for a minute, as though the *real* stress came from sitting still and thinking. And she does react strangely when taken away from home and all those activities. Recently, she and her husband went to the Virgin Islands, and Andrea *slept* around fifteen hours a day, whereas at home she survived happily on seven hours' sleep. Her husband thought she was just worn out from her busy life, but it's more likely that she couldn't face such an unstructured period as a vacation.

Rachel attracts stress in a completely different way from Andrea—she thrives on disaster. She is invariably in the middle of some highly dramatic, soulracking, complicated personal catastrophe, all of which she confides to anyone who will listen. Compared with other girls', Rachel's romances are hair-raising. To hear her tell it, she never *asks* for these things to happen. There she is, minding her own business, spending a perfectly pleasant evening with a perfectly nice young man, and all hell breaks loose. He suddenly and without warning attacks her in the Chinese restaurant. He bursts into tears and confesses that he committed a murder half an hour before. Rachel's role in all this is that of the frail little creature bravely holding up the sinking raft while the storm rages all around. She invariably gets deeply involved with these supposed Mr. Normals, during which involvement there is never a quiet moment. There are sleepless nights, frantic phone calls, paralyzing discoveries, suicide threats, and general hysterics. She swears that all she wants is a little *peace,* and if only she *could,* she'd get away for a while, but somehow it never happens.

Possibly Rachel's greatest delight lies in other people's gasping and saying, "Oh, Rachel! How horrible! How can you bear it, you poor child?" But all this has been going on for some time, and people don't commiserate so much any more—they are beginning to suspect, as a matter of fact, that a good deal of what Rachel says isn't even true. Rachel *does* exaggerate (and often fabricate) the stresses she experiences. She creates or makes up emotionally charged relationships to prove to her friends and herself that she exists, as a frantic bid for attention.

The stress and tension that Jeanette and Celia apparently can't stand— and what Andrea and Rachel apparently thrive on, though it's not really as simple as that—*can* be an excellent thing. "Stress is also happiness for some," says Dr. Glavin, "if it's the right kind." It may be true that for most of us, the busiest times in our lives are the best. Of our four stress-ridden girls, Andrea—Miss Extracurricular—is probably the happiest. She might overdo it, and one might question her motives, but she knows very well that for the most part we *all* function better in a structured situation. It might be said that the trick of getting something done is having an abundance of something to *do* and having to do it by a certain time, too. Things do get accomplished under pressure. Uncomfortable as they may be at the time, there is something about deadlines that is absolutely essential to human productivity. Time limits *force* decisions. Decisions make us what we are (for we are, at least according to the existentialists, *made* by our decisions and subsequent actions), which is probably why decisions are so painful—we forge ourselves at every fork in the road.

By this standard, Jeanette, married to the millionaire, also functions very well. Fuss as she might, she does what she has to do and does it well. There is nothing really pathological about her—she is a garden-variety compulsive. But Celia, who has practically dropped out of life and goes to such lengths to avoid stress, is in real trouble. She accomplishes nothing—not work, not forging relationships with men *or* women.

Every department of her life is well under par, and she is badly in need of psychotherapy. As for Rachel, she accomplishes nothing either, really. Her energy is being entirely taken up by a self-destructive pattern (she doesn't *have* to be involved in or pretend to those battering relationships, does she?) that brings her neither profit nor pleasure nor leads to any real intimacy with another person. They are neurotic histrionics, carried on mainly where other people are around to observe them—when the person who *really* should hear them is a doctor.

But why is stress such a problem? Why do we each react so differently to the pressures in life? The ability to handle stress, which is absolutely necessary for functioning in a competitive world, develops in early childhood. We teach our children how to handle stress, right from the beginning, by deciding a hundred times a day how much frustration the baby can and should tolerate: do I pick him up or do I let him cry? (Whole trends in child-raising have swung on this one point.) We draw the line, each according to what we are, somewhere between smothering and negligence. We teach the baby independence by trying to build up his tolerance to frustration, bit by bit. As he grows bigger, we indicate to him by our words and actions what we think is real stress and what isn't.

What might have caused the low-stress threshold that Dr. Glavin speaks of is the wave of permissiveness that started in the thirties and lasted until only recently. If you pick the baby up every time he cries and let the child *have* a tantrum and give him more or less anything he asks for, when he (or she) gets out in the world, he will not be very good at handling the frustration, disappointment, boredom, and exasperation that are reality . . . the tensions of an office, the pressures of a love affair or marriage. The adult will always be thinking in one part of his mind, "But Mother said I was supposed to be *happy,* and now look—I have to work to support myself [or do all the housework or be lonely or not get what I want or whatever]."

Besides, the world *is* a lot harder to live in than it used to be. Grandma lived in a fairly predictable, well-ordered society. She knew who she was and more or less what to expect (which wasn't much). Today the world turns ten times faster, and girls grow up expecting everything—not only happiness, but success through hard work. Our world is competitive. We feel that time is flying and we must pack in everything while we can; we must try to be brighter, more beautiful, sexier, and more accomplished than the next girl—there is no room for second best in *anything*. In Grandma's time Celia, for instance, might not have been the misfit she is now; she might have been somebody's maiden aunt, a little dotty (smiling vaguely and falling asleep all the time) but tolerated because she had a useful function around the house. By today's standards she is a loser. Stress and its accompanying ills are the by-product of our nervous, highly geared life, and our success in this society depends on recognizing pressure when we see it and handling it properly.

How is *your* pressure tolerance? Everyone has what might be called a stress level—a very individual point beyond which he or she will not be pushed without damage. The damage varies enormously—headaches, fatigue, skin rashes, ulcers, colitis and other gut disturbances, asthma, high blood pressure, back pain, insomnia and hypersomnia (sleeping too much), dizziness, fainting, seizures, and migraines are some of the things that doctors attribute at least partially to stress (some of them have physical causes besides, but stress certainly doesn't help them). Any of these symptoms calls for medical treatment and possibly psychotherapy aimed toward a reassessment of one's whole life.

As we have seen, the idea is not so much to try to *reduce* stress but rather to find a balance between one's highest possible level of productivity and a tolerable amount of stress. It's also important to recognize the difference between good stress and neurotic stress. Is the amount of stress you feel appropriate to whatever you're doing, or do you go to pieces over nothing? Here are a few more questions to help you measure your stress level:

• Are you satisfied with the way you function on your job? Or do you always seem to be six steps behind, running frantically to catch up?

• Do you sleep well, or do you lie awake for hours compulsing about things? Do you sleep too much? Eight hours is enough for most people.

• Can you keep your mind on what you're doing, or are you always worrying about something *else*? Can you concentrate? When you've read something, do you know what you've read?

• How often does your stomach go into knots? Occasionally, like before the Big Evening, or several times a day?

• How do you handle big decisions versus small ones? For instance, do you make a well-thought-out, rational decision about your job and then go to pieces over a restaurant menu?

220

- Are you organized, or do you let things go and then attack them all at once in a frantic rush of activity, possibly making a botch in the process?
- Do you enjoy activities other than your job? Do you enjoy life in general? How about your man—do you enjoy being with him, or does he send you into agonies of conflict?
- Do you get any exercise? Besides the obvious advantages for the tummy, it's an excellent way to relax—the best quick stress-discharger there is.
- Are you bored? Does life just seem like one damn thing after another?

If you think you need some reorganization, here are a few guidelines:

- Probably you're *afraid* of pressure, even the good kind, but are capable of withstanding more stress than you think. Try to think of it as a part of normal living, not your enemy.
- Try to increase your pressure *tolerance*. Force small decisions. You'd be amazed at the amount of time you waste trying to decide unimportant matters. Make up your mind and stick to it, right or wrong. You'll feel absolutely purified. And most of your decisions will be right.
- Get organized; schedule your life—not rigidly, but enough to handle the essentials. When you get used to doing things routinely, you can add more activities or projects you *want* to do. You have more time than you think.
- Most importantly, try to find *your* combination. Are you a doer not doing enough, or a more passive type pushing yourself into all sorts of anxiety-provoking situations because you think you should take on more? Decide whether you can or should try to tolerate a difficult situation or whether you ought to get rid of it. Maybe your boss really is impossible. He might not be to another girl, but if you spend half your life brooding about him when ordinarily you get along with people quite well, then get another job—this one just isn't worth the pressure. There *are* psychotic bosses. Or, are you slogging along in a dull job because you don't think you can ever do any better? Push yourself and find out. You might find *that* kind of stress invigorating. Know what you are, know your capacities, and don't try to be something you're not.

HOW TO HANDLE THE COMPETITION

Chris is such a whiz at writing advertising copy, the agency wants to transfer her to New York—and she's so terrified by the whole *idea,* she's just about decided to quit and marry Good Old (boring) Harold. . . .

The man at the rental office promised to hold the apartment—the one with the fireplace and garden where they *would* take a St. Bernard—until Bobbie could get downtown, but, by the time she did, this lady-wrestler type was already there, insisting that since she'd arrived first, the place was legally hers. . . .

Inga left Julian alone at the party for the barest minute—just long enough to check on how her new eye makeup was holding up—and when she returned, a girl she'd never even *seen* before was grinning cozily up at him with her arm around his waist. And Julian was grinning back. . . .

Competition. All *over* the place. Another by-product of the overpopulation problem perhaps. There simply aren't enough great men, jobs, apartments, or even taxicabs to go around—which means that, whatever it is you're after, you can be pretty sure somebody else wants some, too. Like it or not, we're all involved (at least part of the time) in a grown-up version of musical chairs.

Competition isn't a bad thing. Properly handled, it can inspire us, spur us to do our very best, help us to become the person we're capable of

223

becoming. Healthy competition stretches our abilities, broadens goals, and, in the process, is even exciting. (So says a now superfamous lady executive who, early in her career, went ahead and tackled the kind of job Chris is planning to turn down: "It was wild. There were two other girl copywriters, and we all worked on the same cosmetics account. Competition was absolutely fierce to see whose magazine or television copy was going to be picked, and yet we adored each other. I think it brought the best out of all of us." Adds a top model, "It's satisfying to know that you can get into the jungle and survive.")

Of course, competing doesn't, unhappily, always work out so satisfactorily. (Some girls *don't* survive in the jungle, and some head back for the safety of camp the minute the path looks menacing.) We all know girls who just can't make themselves compete for *anything*. The slightest scent of a rival sends them scooting into their shells like turtles. ("Oh, well," they mutter, almost convincing themselves, "I didn't want it anyway.") And then there are the girls who do just the opposite—get so carried away with the business of competing, they lose track of what they're competing *for*. (A roommate of mine once *married* a man just to steal him away from a cousin she'd always hated.)

Many of us can cope wonderfully well in one area (always first with the latest kinky fashion), only to fall apart over something that looks much easier to manage (can't get through a busy cafeteria line without five people getting in ahead of us). And there's more than one girl who's ready to fight like a python over the last cheese Danish on the coffee cart, yet will practically *help* you walk off with her dearest man.

What's the problem? Why can't we all just run merrily around the chairs, like we did when we were children, and get in there and grab for a seat when the music stops? Why does a brilliant girl like Chris prefer unchallenging co-workers (and pallid lovers, like Harold, who don't threaten her) to the excitement of being among the top professionals in her field? Why does Inga, who's made it in the glittery world of theatre (at twenty-two she's the lead in an off-Broadway smash), collapse completely when another girl makes the slightest move toward her man? (Instead of swooping over with a proprietary toss of her gorgeous red hair when she saw Julian with that girl at the party, Inga slithered off to the den, examined the host's pre-Columbian art collection for much too long, and, when Julian didn't come after *her*, went home alone in a taxi.)

224

And then there's the brilliant and well-known scientist I met at a dinner party last year. What made *him*, fascinating company as long as the group stayed small, turn into a stumble-footed cliché-mouther when more than four people joined the conversation?

How we cope with competition is determined by a number of different elements, among them parents, brothers and sisters (or lack of them), and, for heaven's sake, even *genes!* People used to believe that all babies were pretty much the same emotionally (waiting like lumps of clay to be "molded" by Mommy and Daddy with assists from relatives and nurse-maids), but we now know that certain personality traits come built *in*. Some of us are placid, some are aggressive, others impatient and kvetchy from the day we're born—probably even before! Heredity, then, is part of the reason we head into the fray or away from it, join the hockey team instead of the sewing club, and, later, opt for NOW rather than the PTA.

But genes account for only some of the way your personality is shaped. What happens later can overcome and even reverse original tendencies. Especially important are brothers and/or sisters, step- and half-brothers and/or sisters, and (in this multimarriage era) other, confusingly assorted possibilities. (Yes, your childhood *did* take place a long time ago, but the size of your family—and your rank in it—has a lot to do with you *now*.)

Younger children obviously learn early about holding their own against older brothers and sisters (which tends to make them compete more easily when they grow up), while the baby of a big brood usually holds a favored spot that makes competing almost unnecessary. (My husband had a really great great-aunt who well into her seventies was still saying, "I'm the baby of the family" and expecting special attentions.

Were you an only child? If so, you're probably not as good at open competition as Bobbie, who grew up in the fuss and scramble of a large family and had no compunctions at all about yelling right back at the lady-wrestler type until she *got* the apartment the rental agent had promised to hold for her. (Only children, however, may develop into experts and succeed at the most dangerous sort of competition—the quiet, under-ground kind—staying late at the office to turn out more and better work than rivals, rather than making loud noises at monthly meetings.)

Children are fiercely competitive (musical chairs is popular because the game allows them to be pushy out in the open without getting grown-ups mad), and early sibling squabbles are the first training grounds for coping with competitive conflict later on. How much success you had keeping your first doll away from your grabby older sister twenty years ago may influence the way you handle the grown-up girl who's after your job this very minute.

Sometimes, even when you're young, the stakes are much higher than a favorite doll. That's the way it was with Inga, the beautiful actress. She was only five when a kindergarten playmate stole her father away. Of course, it was the little girl's *mother* who actually did the stealing, but at that age all Inga could see was that Daddy had gone to live in her school-mate's house, and no matter how good or how appealing she tried to be, she couldn't get him back. Having lost the competition for the first really important man in her life, Inga now believes she can't hold on to any other man she cares for. And so she doesn't even try, letting them get away rather than face the humiliation of a fight she thinks she's sure to lose.

"A real dread of humiliation is a basic problem for the girl who has trouble competing," says Dr. Howard Halpern, New York psychotherapist and codirector of the New York Student Consultation Center. "She has experienced lost pride as a child—probably caused by a parent or an older brother or sister—and is terribly afraid of putting herself in such a potentially damaging situation again. Some mothers and fathers make the mistake of forcing their children into situations they aren't ready to handle. Starting school too early or going to supercompetitive camps where losing is shameful can permanently impair a child's confidence."

Such forced competition, often accompanied by criticism when the child fails ("What did you break *now*, Little Miss Butterfingers?" "Why can't you be like your sister?"), leaves scars that are a long time healing. Too much protection, though, can be just as bad, since the child never gets any *practice* at fighting to win.

How well you handle competition in the area where we are all most vulnerable—love and sex—is also determined by parental influence. Even without doing anything as extreme as running off with a schoolmate's mother, a father who belittles or ignores his daughter will make her feel insecure about her ability to hold a man. Constant reminders from Mama—"All men are rotten"; "They're only after one thing"; "Sleep with him before you're married and he'll never respect you"; and other such tidbits of traditional misinformation—can make a girl drop out of sexual competition. Why fight for such a tainted prize?

Finally, luck plays a part in shaping the ability to compete. Chris, the girl who's afraid of the high-pressure job, had a good, loving relationship with her parents. But when she was young, the family moved to a new suburb and Chris changed schools. She was much brighter than anyone else in her grade, and her classmates hated her for it. Every spelling bee and science award that she won made her that much more unpopular. Chris gave up trying to be the best; mediocrity wasn't as exciting, but it was safer. In a way, Chris is still hanging back, seeking the safest jobs, men, life, because she's afraid that shining and standing out will mean rejection again. Those early school years left a big dent in her ego, one she may never repair.

Bad luck, of course, can strike after childhood, too, and even a sturdy pysche can wilt a bit after a really smashing blow or a lot of little jabs. You may, like a friend of mine, graduate from journalism school and head jubilantly off to the big city to become Brenda Starr—to discover that a major newspaper folded two days before you got there, flooding the job market with top pros. You may introduce your roommate to your boyfriend, then watch them turn all glowy at the sight of each other. Such disasters *do* happen, and a girl can't help but be affected by them—but they're only as dreadful as you *let* them be.

There's no real need to let bad luck at five or twenty-five go on influencing you *forever*. Whatever your feelings about competition, or anything else for that matter, you're not stuck with these attitudes. Whether you compete too little, too much, or too erratically, here are some ways to handle competition more easily and turn into a *permanent* winner.

Accept yourself. All right, you're *not* and will never be as beautiful as Raquel Welch, Elizabeth Taylor, or even your little sister Sallie; what are you going to do about it?

"I once had a patient," recalls Dr. Halpern, "who was constantly moaning about how marvelous her sister was, and finally I said to her, 'You're right. Your sister *is* better-looking than you are, and you can either spend the rest of your life resenting her looks or face it and go on from there.' Some things can't be changed and we just have to make them irrelevant."

Every girl would love to be beautiful, and it's painful not to be (and sometimes it's painful to *be* very beautiful) but what matters really is what you do with the looks you *have*. Liza Minnelli isn't a breathtaking beauty. Neither was the girl I saw one winter weekend by the Caribe Hilton pool. Short—a little dumpy, really—with a nose too big, chin too receding, mouth too wide. She had two good features (most of us have one or two), her eyes, which she'd done everything possible with, and gorgeous hair, which she let glisten and swing in the sun. She wore pale lipstick, really sensational eye makeup, but, instead of trying to compete with the surrounding bikinis, she wore a covered-up, black ribbed turtleneck suit. There were a lot of good-looking girls around the pool, but this was the one people, including the man at her side, were watching. Actually, she wasn't only *not* beautiful, she was downright plain, but this girl's *attitude* (her charm, confidence) had you convinced she was something special. I don't know who she was or where she got the confidence, but I salute her. She's the best example I have ever seen of what the French call *tirer le maximum*, making the most of what you have.

The same basic principle can be applied to any area where you may not feel up to the competition: instead of brooding over what you *aren't*, get busy with what you *are*.

Specialize. Get to be an expert at even one thing—crewelwork, marine aquariums, macramé, organic cooking . . . better still, be highly valued for your *professional* work. A sense of accomplishment can greatly increase your basic feelings of adequacy and help strengthen you for later, different kinds of competition.

Diversify, too. Be interested and *involved* in many areas besides your few specialties. The girl who invests all her emotional and intellectual resources in a single stock is not only a bit of a bore, but she also has nothing to keep her going if whatever supports her confidence (man, job, fellowship grant, etc.) sinks somehow away from her.

Plan ahead. Anticipating competition (without being *paranoid* about it) can work marvels at keeping you calm when the battle trumpets blow. Planning ahead means pretty much (with a few off days) looking the prettiest you can most of the time and being the most self-disciplined person you are able. You'll find that *getting* the man or job you want is only half the battle; you're going to have to hang in there (like being ready for the other woman *before* she strikes). Planning for competition means not letting yourself blow up two dress sizes once you're married, taking courses, doing work now that will make you smarter in your field two years from now. Short-range maneuvers are important, too, like not going off and leaving a man you care about alone for hours in a roomful of ravishing (and ravenous) females. You wouldn't leave a Rolls-Royce with the motor running on a busy street corner, would you? Check your eye makeup *before* you get to the party (remember Inga?), and don't get too far away from him. Mild possessiveness is part of acceptable, successful competition.

This kind of quiet, anticipatory strength with a man or job is murderously effective. Staying on guard not only makes life more interesting, it also keeps many of the more commonly horrible contretemps from ever *happening*. (Like having a black belt in karate, you have a certain assurance that makes people hesitate before challenging you.)

Know when *not* to compete. You could have any one of a number of fascinating men, but you've decided you want Robert Redford. This isn't a realistic goal for several reasons: (1) He's taken. (2) The chances of your meeting him are not very good. (3) Are you sure you could really *stand* being married to a movie star? (It isn't easy, you know. For one thing, girls like you are lurking everywhere.)

If you still want Robert Redford and none of this makes the slightest bit of difference, you may be one of those girls who can't *stop* competing. You know them: they have to be waited on first at department stores, win *every* argument, make a pass at every job and/or man that turns up whether they really want it/him or not.

"The girl who seeks competition *all* the time feels just as inadequate as the one who is afraid to compete," says Dr. Halpern. "She just has a different way of expressing insecurity. She may have a big reserve of hate, probably from a mother or father who belittled her or made her compete at things she wasn't very good at. Some parents force a child to attempt something she can't comfortably do—going to a dancing class with boys, making a speech at school, taking tennis lessons—in hopes of 'curing' her. This kind of pushing doesn't work, of course—you can't make someone stop being shy by saying, 'Get in there and don't be so timid.' The constant pressure on the child leaves a residue of vindictive feelings which result in a need to compete with *everybody* for *everything* later on." (Like the lady I know who has a mink midicoat, two houses, and a boat and is always trying to outmaneuver you for the biggest piece of chicken or the last slice of cake.)

This pent-up anger is similar to that which drives some girls toward destructive competition with men. Overaggressive girls are basically resentful of men and struggle with them for control, says Dr. Halpern. Some of these ladies compete in business (although most of us are just in there trying to do our *best* and not competing with men more than with ourselves), but a far greater number reserve their aggressions for love relationships.

"Certain types of frigidity are a kind of competing with men," declares Dr. Halpern, "with the girl refusing to let herself go and have an orgasm because (consciously or not) she considers this 'submitting' and letting him have the dominant role." Needless to say, the bedroom is the worst possible (most destructive) place to compete, and girls who do are *sure* of ultimate loss (a wrecked relationship).

Stop constantly comparing yourself to people better than you. Having an idol or two to spur you on is a *good* thing—the prod of admiration for another can make the difference between just sitting there and going out and *doing* something. (A well-known writer once told me he gets himself going by reading other people's best sellers until he gets so fired up he goes up to his office and begins work on one of his own.)

A sure way to start each day feeling perfectly rotten, though, is to stand before the mirror muttering a little refrain about all the people who are better than you are—Betsey Johnson is more creative, Jackie Onassis more famous, Margaret Court plays better tennis, Catherine Deneuve is more beautiful, and so on. Ponder instead (if you *insist* on this kind of point-check system) the possibility that a number of people might just wish they were as clever or as high-cheekboned—or, square as it sounds, even as young and healthy—as you.

Don't compete against the whole world. "Watch out for having to be best at *everything*," warns Dr. Halpern. "Beware of too many 'shoulds.'" I *should* be the best-dressed, the most beautiful, married before I'm thirty, the best party-giver. The girl who does things because she *should* instead of because she *wants* to doesn't have much fun. Also, when you insist on being best-or-nothing-at-all, you severely limit your alternatives.

Keep remembering that *you're* the only one who sets standards for yourself. Other people are usually happy enough with you as is . . . or, anyway, at your *realistic* best. Think of your own friends. Did you pick them because they were terribly gifted or beautiful? Do you fault them if they aren't? Of course not. If you do get annoyed with them, it's because they hurt you or do something unkind that they can *help*. And they feel the same about you.

You and Roger have a great affair going—until you meet a girl he used to groove with and discover she's a cuddly sex-kitten type. You're long and lean and couldn't be cuddly if you covered yourself with Angora fur; so now you feel *inadequate*. ("What can he see in *me*?")

Too many girls get caught up in this absolutely pointless retroactive competition, trying to outdo people who are long gone (the wife, for instance, who *used* to have their man). Unnecessarily painful—even more important—the exercise is totally unproductive. No *need* to compete with people who are already out of a situation you are (or want to be) in. Roger's ex may look supersexy, but that doesn't mean she *was*, and even *if* she was, he obviously now prefers you, or he'd still be with *her* (at least as long as you don't keep pointing out how inferior you are). Then was then and now is now; accept this and *live* that way.

Don't be afraid to lose . . . or win. Competing *does* involve the risk of losing, but not winning isn't the end of everything. Instead of considering failure a judgment of your worth, try thinking of it as a lesson. Richard Nixon isn't the only one who got a powerful second chance. Losing hurts, but everybody loses sometimes—even the people you madly envy. Think of the problems you were upset about two years ago—aren't there at least a few competitions you're *glad* now you didn't win? (That dentist from Burbank? That job as a go-go girl?)

Some girls (like Chris in school) don't compete because they don't *really* want to win. "These girls dread winning even more than losing," reports Dr. Halpern. "They don't feel strong enough to put themselves in a position where they will be either envied or disliked by others—particularly other *girls*. If that's your problem, you need to be reassured that any animosity incurred by success won't be as strong or as long-lasting as you fear." Actually, just *allowing* yourself a conquest or two can break this syndrome.

Another reason some girls won't let themselves win is that they've gotten to actually *enjoy* losing. "The role of the underdog, the poor sweet victim, with all the built-in sympathy it garners, can get to be a comfortable one," Dr. Halpern points out. "Girls will sometimes spend the energy they could use in healthy competition trying to be the biggest loser instead."

Don't be afraid to fight. Many of us come from a culture of Nice. Nice little girls, so the old litany went, don't (fight with their sisters, raise their voices, argue with a teacher). They don't (most importantly) lose *control*. Sometimes, though, all this self-control can be crippling, causing us to stand quietly by being genteel (i.e., Nice) while something we've earned or someone we love is deftly wrested from us. We should instead be in there slugging it out.

If you're unused to competing, one way to be battle-ready is by trying to win at small things (start with something as trivial as a game of gin rummy). I remember as a child hearing that we were going to be asked at a party the next day to make as many words as possible from the phrase "Happy Birthday." I tried it the night before (why, I don't know), got up to some incredible number of words that I kept in my head. Naturally, I won the prize at the party. Even if you've started late, small wins build up your confidence gradually. Once you've established the little-victories habit, you can go on—keeping the earlier dos and don'ts in mind—and try your hand at larger ones.

After you've conquered your original apprehensions (or misapprehensions), you usually find that actually getting into the fray (win or lose) isn't ever as bad as *worrying* about competing. Trying your very best, even if you fail, is—like loving—better than not having tried. And winning, of course, is *best* of all!

3

THE BEAUTIFUL, ELUSIVE ART OF SELF-DISCIPLINE

Hannah went off her diet in a bubble bath this time. Hiding her round, plump self in a comforting cloud of Mister Bubble, she ate through two pounds of peanut brittle in half an hour. Hannah wants to be an actress. She has talent and contacts (her aunt is a well-known star), but she's so overweight that she rarely is right for any part. She was doing pretty well this time (lost thirteen pounds in just three weeks), but since the bathtub binge, Hannah swears she'll never diet again. Rationalizing that fat girls will be loved *anyway,* she moans to her roommates, "I just don't have the willpower." The roommates have said nothing—so far. They're both fond of Hannah, but they don't know how to tell her they don't like living with the baby hippo she's promising to become.

Then there's Cindy. She makes good money as a pop decorator—the Beautiful People love what she does to their bathrooms—but she just can't keep her budget in order. Actually, Cindy doesn't *have* a budget. Every time she sees something she likes, she buys it on the spot; that is, she charges it. Cindy has thirty-five credit cards, keeps them all in a little alligator case she bought (charged) at Mark Cross. She's worked up a lot of clever gambits to keep her many creditors guessing—sometimes she "forgets" to sign her checks, other times she mixes them up (Abercrombie's gets a check made out to Ohrbach's, Ohrbach's gets one made out to Bloomingdale's, and so on and on and on). She manages to stall people

233

rather well this way, but she knows she can't keep it up forever. Sometimes, Cindy gets so upset at the sight of all those windowed envelopes on her pink marble writing table that she bolts out and treats herself to lunch at La Grenouille (she signs the tab, of course).

Barbara's another one. She finally got her analyst-in-training boy friend, David, to make love to her on his brand-new patient's couch. A graduation present from his parents, David's couch is one of those very official black leather jobs. The instant she saw it, Barbara was determined to be on it before any patient—partly because she's jealous of David's work, partly because it seemed a fun thing to do. David disagreed. It would be, he insisted, "unprofessional." "Come on," she pleaded. "I've got problems, too. Do you care more about some old patient you've never even met yet than you do about me?" For two weeks he said No and then one sleepy Sunday morning when she'd stayed overnight, Barbara saw her chance and grabbed it. Snuggling close as they woke up, she kissed his eyelids, smothered his protests with playful fingers, then ran naked, laughing, down the hall to the room he had set aside to be his office. Half asleep, off guard, he followed, and Barbara got the new kick she wanted. David felt irritable the rest of the day, and they ended up having a terrific row. Barbara finally left in tears.

And Joanne. Only two years out of college, she has a good job at a top public-relations agency. She also takes toddlers from New York Foundling Hospital to the park once a week. Joanne was absolutely horrified the morning she woke up—like some Bowery bum—lying in her own vomit. Staring in disgust at the fouled, flowered sheets, she tried to remember what had happened at the press party the night before—and realized she must have been so drunk when she got home that she hadn't even *known* she was sick. "Never, never again," she vowed, forcing down a cup of coffee before stumbling off (late) to work. But that very same day, at a client lunch, Joanne downed four bloody marys.

Poor little ladies, those girls who can't say No—to themselves. Each one lets a lack of self-discipline keep her from the life she *wants*—and could have. In this age of instant indulgence, self-discipline, on first thought, may seem a bit out of style, more suited to monks in some musty old monastery than to a free-living career girl. Think again. In our go-now, pay-later world, good old-fashioned self-discipline is actually more important than ever before. Today's girl on her own, relying less on much religious and family discipline in her life, had jolly well better be able to take on the task herself. If she doesn't, the possibilities of all things without limit can be disastrous. Running off after the butterflies, she may never notice the cliff. Besides, it isn't the way to get what you *want*.

Perhaps self-discipline, like so many other stuffy-sounding principles, simply needs a new image. Instead of thinking of self-discipline in terms of what we *can't* have, it's probably time to start looking on it as a tool to help us get what we're after. For example, self-discipline may mean saying *"Merci, non"* to the mousse au chocolat, but it can also mean slipping smoothly into a sexy size six. As New York psychoanalyst Dr. Emanuel K. Schwartz says, "Self-discipline is really self-interest. It's the ability to accept the demands of reality and to cope with them."

The art of self-discipline is based partly on habit. Take our "luscious lush," Joanne. *Joanne is no good at disciplining herself because she's never had any practice.* The darling only child of middle-aged parents, Joanne never really had to think for herself until she was twenty-one. A doting mother anticipated all her needs. Life in a convent boarding school and, later, a small Catholic college was equally undemanding. Whenever it was time to do anything, a bell let her know. CLANG! Wake up. CLANG! Go to breakfast. CLANG! Study Hall. CLANG! Recreation period. Although you'd never have guessed it (she always *seemed* so well organized), Joanne didn't know Thing One about managing her time or her life when she first came to New York.

The first year on the job she did so well (under supervision, of course) that she was given a big promotion—and she was now on her own. That's when Joanne started to sink. If a nun with a little bell would appear at strategic times, Joanne would gratefully do what she is supposed to do— leave the press party, forgo another drink, get to her next appointment. As it is, she's always vaguely wondering what to do next, not quite understanding what it is that's going wrong. Joanne hasn't learned yet that it's time for *her* to take over the bell.

While Joanne never had to make her own decisions, Cindy, as a child, was expected to make quite a few. Little Miss Charge-a-plate had a father who was a career Army officer. He believed discipline was everything and it was never too soon to get started. Cindy was on a strict budget by the time she was six. Out of a small allowance she had to pay for toys, books, everything she needed. She even had to give her mother ten cents a week to do her laundry. Instead of "learning the value of money," as Daddums intended, Cindy turned into a spendthrift the very instant she got the chance. *Cindy's lack of self-discipline is a rebellion against the overcontrol of her childhood.* Instead of channeling all her nonconformist feelings into her work, where they pay off (the idea of putting wallpaper on the floor was just one of Cindy's coups), she has let "paying back" her parents become more important than her own best interests. She's going to "show them," even if it means messing up her life.

Gimmee-gimmee-Barbara's equally damaging willfulness stems from still another source. A wispy middle child in a big, competitive family, Barbara spent her early years feeling lost in the shuffle. Whether it was second helpings, new dresses, or her mother's time, Barbara never felt she had quite enough. Now that she's on her own, she's determined to get what she wants, when she wants it. *Barbara refuses to discipline herself because she still feels deprived.* Girls like Barbara find it hard to postpone gratification. They grab out for what they want like a baby reaching for a lollipop—or the blade of a fan—with no thought to the consequences. Way down deep, they feel they deserve more than others do.

Hannah, on the other hand, doesn't feel she deserves anything— enough to fight for it, that is. Although she makes hoop-la about going on (and off) diets, Hannah really *wants* to be fat. It protects her from having to compete—for success or men or anything else. While each of these girls' problems indicates an emotional disturbance, Hannah's is certainly the most severe. In fact, *Hannah's lack of self-discipline is a symptom of deeper disturbance.*

"If a girl is afraid to realize herself," explains Dr. Schwartz, "if, for some reason, she wants to work against her own interests, she may use self-indulgence as a way to go about it."

This is precisely the problem with Hannah, whose feelings about herself—and her career—are very confused indeed. Instead of taking after her glamorous aunt or her equally dramatic mother, Hannah favors her father's side of the family—a double disaster, since her parents were divorced when she was very young. "The only thing he ever gave you was that receding chin, sweetie," her mother was fond of pointing out. Surrounded by dazzling beauties, feeling helpless, lumpy, unable to compete, Hannah retreated into her own flesh. While she's not a beauty in the traditional sense, Hannah has something even more valuable to an actress—a really individual face. But being merely "interesting" in a family of glamour girls doesn't seem good enough to Hannah, so she continues to hide. If you could somehow give her a magic self-discipline pill, it wouldn't really make much difference, notes Dr. Schwartz. She'd simply find another way to sabotage herself.

Hannah's self-image is so bad she probably can't change without professional help. Girls like Cindy, Barbara, and Joanne, though, very certainly can. And so can you, if you feel the need. How do you go about it? Here are some ways that work for the career girls who've tried them:

1. Look where you're going. Take time out, perhaps some quiet, rainy Sunday, to spell out your long-range goal. "In ten years," ask yourself, "what do I want to be doing?" Even if you think you know, ask again. Early ambitions often need revamping. The owner of one of my favorite boutiques—if she hadn't stopped to think about it—would still be teaching school, and I know a magazine editor who decided in mid-career to start over and be a psychologist. Too many people, though, just drift along, paying less attention to their own destinations than to that of a mid-town bus.

2. Think about how to get there. Once you think you know where you're heading, give some thought to helping yourself along the way. Vow to be head of the department? Take night courses in your field. Want to marry a millionaire? (It could happen.) Study up on stocks, learn languages or vintage wines or something you can use to impress Mr. Money should you run across him—and in the process you may very well find someone else to love. A long-range goal gives you much-needed direction, but there's no law that says you can't stop off along the way if something else looks more interesting. What if you don't know what you want? Explore new subjects, try new things. Find out.

3. Avoid the all-or-nothing approach. Avoid wanting it all now. Be careful, careful, careful not to set up goals you can't handle. If you swear to lose five pounds a week, never to drink too much, to be married by the time you're twenty-five—or else—you're sure to be stuck with a bunch of "or else's." Take it one pound, one night, one man at a time, and you'll be much more likely to get the happy habit of succeeding. Don't spend too much time thinking about the glamorous and successful woman you'd

like to be and comparing her with the grubby, insignificant, $110-a-week worker you are *now!* If you do the work in front of you each day with care and devotion, you will get to *be* the other woman. (It's about the only way you *can*.)

4. Trick yourself. Any gimmick goes in your battle with yourself. If charging is *your* weakness, leave the credit cards home except for approved-in-advance expeditions. Always late? Try keeping your clock a half hour ahead. (Ridiculous, of course, but so is always being late.) *Don't* have fattening stuff in the house.

5. Treat yourself. If procrastination is your problem, the reward system can also work. Give yourself caviar, a candy bar, a new wig, or whatever for a job well done or a temptation turned down. A researcher I know keeps a little basket of goodies, which she dispenses to herself and others in time of great trial or emergency. Once, when I had reached absolutely The End of what had looked like a great romance, she brought me a little bottle of perfume when we met for lunch. It really helped. Another friend, a painter, sent herself a postcard after her first show, which hadn't exactly left the critics breathless. "Your paintings are ahead of their time," she wrote. "But don't worry. You *will* be discovered." Silly, yes. But soothing.

6. Trap yourself. If tricking and treating don't work, you may be the type who needs trapping. Instead of telling *yourself* you'll have that report done by Tuesday, tell your boss. You'll be absolutely amazed at how much more likely you'll be to actually do it. This gambit is equally effective in any appropriate combination—like your landlord and the rent or your boy friend and stopping smoking.

7. Issue ultimatums. For some situations, only an ultimatum will do the job. Take a travel-writer friend of mine whose long-distance love affairs were beginning to result in sloppy copy. She finally issued an edict to herself: No going to bed with *anyone* while on a working trip ("I was beginning to get involved with people I wouldn't have looked at twice if I had met them at home," she confessed, "just because it all seemed so glamorous.") She's about to marry a wealthy and interesting man who admits he first got interested in *her* because she was so "bloody hard to

get." Your dilemma may be a different one, but the identical tactic may be applied: No eating *anything* between meals unless I eat five stalks of celery first. And so on.

8. If all else fails, enlist outside aid. Don't be embarrassed to get help if you need it. Many successful people *depend* on such support. A top science-fiction writer has her publishers give her a fake deadline—which they both know she'll break—so that by the time she's begged for and been given a couple of extensions she finally gets the manuscript in on time. The actor husband of a college crony of mine has her literally lock him in his study and promise not to let him out until he's memorized a certain number of pages of his latest part. Once again, your problem may not be the same, but your solution to it can be. Your roommate might volunteer to answer the phone every night until that-rotten-scoundrel-you-know-you-shouldn't-go-out-with-but-whose-voice-alone-makes-you-go-all-misty finally stops calling. Your parents would probably be delighted to keep your birthday check (which you want to save for a ski weekend but you know you'll spend on clothes you don't really need if you get it in your hot little hands) until later. And if it makes you feel a bit childish, all to the good. Maybe next year you'll be able to hold on to it yourself.

9. Check up on yourself. On a regular basis (but not so often that you feel like a bug in your own microscope) check to see how you're doing. Once a week, say, to see how your diet is coming. Once a month to see how your budget is coming. Once a year to see how your career is coming, or your love life. Along with such periodic checks, try to keep your basic goals in the back of your mind *all* the time. Before you do anything—order that fourth martini, stay out all night, hop into the bed of any man who attracts you—stop and ask yourself, first, "Will this hurt my long-range goal?" Basically, it's a matter of priorities, and it is wise to keep in mind what yours are.

To supplement these hints, listen to six prominent women talk about their particular self-disciplinary regimens:
• Leontyne Price, opera singer: "My work requires the same physical and mental attitudes as an athlete's. It's like oiling up the gladiators to go into the arena. Before a performance I get eight or nine hours of sleep, I

exercise, and I like massages to get the blood circulating. I'm not able to go out and carouse, which I normally enjoy doing, because seeing people takes a lot out of me. I concentrate on being rested—the unrelaxed body is a very bad thing for a singer."

• Marietta Tree, former diplomat: "At twelve I was an unpromising child, so my father gave me the most important advice of my life. 'You have neither brains nor beauty,' said he, 'but, nevertheless, you will manage if you are dependable. It is really very simple: Just be sure your word is good. Turn up at nine o'clock when you say you will. If you agree to call five people on behalf of something, then call all of them. Everybody will be impressed and give you more credit than you really deserve.'"

• Jacqueline Grennan Wexler, college president: "As a young religious I subscribed to the whole notion of asceticism and denial. That's not the kind of self-discipline I vote for now. Today, I'm much more interested in the self-discipline where one invests, not denies, one's self. There is no sense in any kind of denial except that which is a logical extension of what you want to do. You may go to bed early at night so you'll be sharp in the morning—that's a pragmatic decision. But I don't believe in self-discipline for its own sake."

• Polly Bergen, actress, executive: "The main thing for me has been discipline about keeping appointments. From my early days as a band singer, later as an actress, and now as a cosmetics-firm executive, I realized that lateness is costly and a waste of time for you, as well as everybody else."

• Betty Furness, consumer-rights specialist: "I think anyone who works and is even moderately successful uses self-discipline in her life and work. Good work habits have to be acquired. We aren't born with them.

"I try to balance one thing against another. When I'm working, I don't stay up late. When I'm on my way somewhere, I weigh time against money. If I have time, I take a bus or walk. If I have no time, I taxi."

• Eve Nelson, executive: "All good ideas take some down-to-earth practical thinking. So, I learned to discipline my creativity to face budgets, expenses, and details. Combining imagination and practicality is unbeatable!"

All the gimmicks and gambits suggested above do work, but the key to them is caring. People who really care—about themselves and their dreams—are the ones who are willing to sacrifice, to give up something they want for the sake of something else they want even more. Only you can decide those priorities for your life.

4

ARE YOU "I'm a late starter; it's taken me a long time to get it
GROWN-UP YET? together." That was Jane Fonda talking, at age thirty-three, and only
recently had life begun to *move* for Jane—the career, the all-her-own
beauty, the intelligent use of celebrity-power.

Maturity!

Are you still with me? There are some words that just don't interest
people, and "maturity" is one of them. Probably you suffer a reflex re-
vulsion to the word, thanks to some high-school hygiene teacher who en-
crusted it with onerous responsibilities, boring duties, and overall un-
pleasantness. Even if you're not wild about hip lingo, there are reasons
for doing away with the word "maturity" and substituting the new phrase
Jane Fonda used. Because "getting it together" is pretty wonderful!

However marvelous it may be, though, maturity, or getting it together,
isn't something that you reach—once and for all—like a full-blown plant!
How often have you said to yourself, "Someday I will get mature . . . and
then *zap!*—I'll meet Mr. Smashing and we'll buy a brownstone." Or, "If I
can only grow up . . . then *bam!*—I'll stop hating my mother!" Whatever
your vision of a mature you *is,* you may be thinking of realizing it suddenly and forever. That's impossible! Maturity considered that way—as
an end—implies *the* end . . . after which could come stagnation. Maturity
is an *ongoing* process. Of *course* you want to meet Mr. S. and perhaps
marry him—but after *that,* you want to know how to live with him. And
of *course* you want to stop hating your mother—but after that, you want

241

to deal with her (and others) in a way that gives you happiness instead of guilt and pain. You want that glorious, nothing-like-it feeling of being on *top* of experiences instead of standing there while life hurtles down on you like an avalanche. You want that headiest of all pleasures—the freedom to be *you*. And the way to get that freedom is summed up very well in the phrase "getting it together." When you marshal as much of your potential as you can, you *grow*. And once a certain objective is achieved, you do *not* stop there and shrivel like a neglected aspidistra . . . rather you grow some *more* toward *new* goals.

Now, "getting it together" is selective, for what you want to get together are only the *useful* parts of you. The rest—self-destructive patterns, self-pity, all-consuming jealousies—are hangups you discard!

Probably you *know*, roughly at least, what your own problems are, and yet you may be clinging to destructive, anti-growth patterns. Why should you be doing this? Well, psychiatrists, behavioral scientists, and other experts on how people act say that we often hang on to nonproductive kinds of behavior because they worked for us when we were *children*. Now everybody knows that having tantrums and hollering "Me, me, me!" is a reversion to babyhood. But there's a lot of less obvious kid stuff you can start weeding out (there's that *plant* imagery again) of your behavior. I'm not talking about severe psychological disturbances but simply stubborn, sticky, little-girl patterns that you should have chucked long ago with the ballerina-length prom dress. Here goes:

Nobody loves me: According to many psychiatrists, most or all of the *other* undesirable, reverting-to-childhood behavior patterns (we'll get to these in a minute) that grown-ups sustain are outgrowths of this early feeling of rejection. Noted psychoanalyst Karen Horney, author of *The Neurotic Personality of Our Time*, called this condition the "basic anxiety" ("the feeling a child has of being isolated and helpless in a potentially hostile world") and built a whole theory of personality around it.

Even with reasonably "normal" people, "nobody loves me" is a basic complaint now and then. If you're *smothered* by this feeling, however, you might take a look at what you really mean by "love." Are you equating it with attention (the kind babies want and need)? O.K., so Monroe has never once given you a present: what, specifically, does that *prove*? Maybe he shows his love by treating you like his equal, by genuinely *liking* you. Maybe he thinks you *know* he'd die for you if necessary. Perhaps he has no money . . . or maybe he *doesn't* love you. Perhaps your friends have stopped "loving" you, *too,* because you've driven them all to unlisted phone numbers with your self-pitying tales of how Monroe never gives you presents.

"Nobody loves me." Why should they? Maybe you're doing something unlovable. Or maybe they're unloving people and you should find some new, more affection-giving friends.

Nobody understands me: Are you making yourself clear? Is it possible that you *want* your true needs to be concealed in a muddle of confused and confusing behavior? Dr. Haim Ginott, a child psychiatrist with a keen (and compassionate) eye for kiddie ploys, points out in his book *Between Parent and Child*: "When a child is in the midst of strong emotion . . . he wants us to understand what is going on inside himself at the particular moment. Furthermore, he wants to be understood without having to disclose fully what he is experiencing. It is a game in which he reveals only a little of what he feels, needing to have us guess the rest." The child, through this maneuver, is testing the love and tolerance of his world. Presumably, an *adult* already knows the world is a comfortable place and doesn't *need* to block other people's understanding with a series of self-created hurdles. I say *presumably,* because so many of us *do* resort to this babyish testing. These are various forms of it; one is wordless crying (translation: "Guess why I'm crying"). Or, YOU: "I feel so depressed." HE: "Why?" YOU: "I don't know; I just can't explain" (translation: "If you love me, you'll be able to guess how I feel without my saying it"). Obviously, this logic collapses under rational *adult* scrutiny.

You think nobody understands you? Don't worry, Dr. Ginott does.

It's all *my* fault: Children often have excruciating feelings of guilt, many of which are unnecessary. As Dr. Ginott notes, misguided parents can often make a child's feelings seem *unacceptable* to him. *If* a little girl is made to feel that anger is wrong, she will feel guilty for *feeling* angry. On the other hand, *adults,* having reached adulthood, should have learned to *accept* their negative emotions.

Grown-up anger and other "bad" emotions are healthy as well as unavoidable. Better find a way to express them rather than feel guilty for *having* them. Somewhere between sewing a sampler (repression) and kicking in the TV screen (too violent expression) there is an outlet. Impose on a trusted friend to let you cry your mascara away; keep a diary, preferably typed (you can get a lot angrier and get more said on the typewriter); write hate letters, cool them for a week, then tear them up. Writing unprintable satirical poems works well for me. A friend of mine talks to a tape recorder. We can *all* mutter to ourselves and curse out loud. No fair abusing the waitress or elevator man (redirecting your anger against an innocent person) or smoking three packs of cigarettes a day (turning anger back against yourself).

When you don't (or can't) let out nasty emotions, you are *left* with your guilt, the nastiest feeling of all. Guilt leads to *self*-hatred, which leads to self-destructive behavior, which leads to *more* guilt . . . and there you are stuck on an (essentially childish) treadmill.

Dr. Albert Ellis, co-author of *A Guide to Rational Living* and a practicing Manhattan psychologist, gave the best answer I've ever heard to a chronic self-blamer. PATIENT: "Doctor, I feel so guilty." DR. ELLIS: "You *are* guilty."

People confronted with such an accusation generally show a sudden amazing ability to separate true from false guilt. ("Now see here, it's true I was too harsh in criticizing the new trainee's work, and maybe it was even my fault that she quit her job, but I'm certainly not responsible for her *divorce!*") The genuine part of the guilt can then be accepted and dealt with—by apology, reparations, or simple dismissal, with the understanding that you're sadder but smarter.

Try Dr. Ellis' technique on yourself when you feel guilty. Say, "You *are* guilty, you miserable bitch," and see if you can't come up with an effective defense against your own self-accusal.

I love my new baby brother so much I could just kiss him to *death* (and that goes for all my grown-up rivals, too): One of the things children frequently feel guilty *about* is hating their new baby brother or sister, the rival for parental love. Grown-up girls are no strangers to rivalry either. We have sexual rivals, rivals for job promotions and for the affection and esteem of people we like. Sometimes our competitors are inanimate objects ("Does he really love racing that car on weekends more than he loves *me*?"). And some of us are our *own* worst rivals, needing desperately to come out on top of an imaginary competition with an ideally perfect self ("I've got to do this *just right!*").

You should be able to acknowledge feelings of rivalry without feeling ashamed. If you simply damp them down, you may start acting like one of these girls whose stomped-on competitive feelings surfaced like a bloated whale when pressure hit:

1. Judy was spending a weekend in the country with her husband, her husband's closest friend, Emilio, and one of Emilio's numerous girl friends, who also happened to be *Judy's* closest friend. Perhaps the relationships already so approximated a family that strong feelings of rivalry were *bound* to emerge, but everybody was having a good time until Emilio broke out the Monopoly set. After about two rounds of play, during which the men cheated outrageously (all within the rules of adult Monopoly, where anything goes), Judy threw down her play money, pounded her fist on Massachusetts Avenue, and shouted, "I'm not playing anymore—you're all so damned *competitive!*" Judy herself, of course, was the one really driven to win, or else *why* did she explode in such a (childishly) angry outburst!

2. Elaine attracts friends like a pot of honey attracts toast. She's seductive, witty, sympathetic. One day a friend phoned Elaine to chat, and Elaine seemed sullen and hostile, responding in monosyllables, clearly annoyed with the caller. It seems that *this* friend had struck up a friendship with *another* of Elaine's friends, and (baby) Elaine didn't like that. Though she refused to admit it, she wanted the people she discovered to be hers alone.

3. Anna bores her husband and her friends to *distraction* with her endless bad-mouthing of other employees in her magazine's art department. It's not that she doesn't *like* them, she insists—they're just *incompetent*. When Anna sends a memo to her boss, it is decorated with eye-catching little cartoons and drawings, of course. *She,* obviously, is the clever one. Anna is *not* a driving career woman, eager to see her co-workers get the ax. Actually, she plans to stop working soon and have a baby. Her problem is simply a need to be the "favorite" (the baby) among a group of symbolic brothers and sisters.

What to do about anxiety-causing feelings of rivalry? First, examine them to see if you really are competing with someone for a prize only one of you wins. You'll find this is rarely the case. Most of the time there is plenty of love and approval to go around, and your feelings of rivalry are directed against *imaginary* competitors. *Keep* your competitive spirit in order to get the best out of yourself, but stop with the jealousy feeling. Irrational jealousy can undermine your very best efforts.

Rational jealousy (you really *are* threatened by a rival) can often be dissolved by telling the person whose love or approval you need just how you feel. (Only *spare* him the details of how you throttle your pillow in fury every night!) "Darling, I feel so lonely when you leave me for these sports-car rallyes every weekend." (He may take you with him next time if you seem interested.) "Mr. Osgood, I hope you'll understand that I'm doing my best to adjust to Jeannie after eight years of running my own department—it's not too easy." (He may assure you you're fabulous, tell you Jeannie is the sole support of a sick mother and father, or take you both to lunch.) "George, it's pretty clear you only see me when Alicia is away on modeling assignments in Europe." (If he says yes, that's the way it is, you'll at least have the information you need to deal with the situation . . . give him up or accept his terms. Only remember that "Why don't you love me more?" is the unanswerable question.)

This direct approach is usually received gratefully by the other person. "Darling" may have felt you didn't give a damn about his consuming interest in cars. Mr. Osgood may have wanted to but not known *how* to approach the question of your resentment tactfully. George may be dying for a showdown. Your friends and lovers may be suffering from throttled feelings, too, and if you come right out and *tell* how you feel, their tension may dissolve with yours.

But you promised! (And I'll hold my breath until you make good on it): *A promise is magic, sacred, like invoking the gods or signing your name in blood.* Not true—except to children. An adult knows that promises have to be broken. A girl friend can't deliver the blind date she promised you with her client, the movie star. Harold promised to take you to Vermont, but he got the flu. Maybe Oscar even makes empty, *pointless* promises . . . "I swear I'll never do it again" . . . when you know he will. In this case Oscar is in the wrong for *his* childish behavior . . . but don't you add to the sum of silliness by throwing a fit when he *does* do the hated thing again. In none of these cases is breaking a promise on a level with war crimes!

My father went to Yale (A little status lie can't hurt): Chronic lying, says Dr. Ginott, is a way children express what they *wish* were true. ("I got a real live elephant for my birthday.") However, we (grownups) should be able to distinguish wish from fact.

Connie is ashamed of her second-generation Italian parents—their lack of education, the knickknacks on their mantelpiece, meals in the kitchen. She *never* takes anyone to meet them. When asked about her mom and dad, she gives a fictitious description of a Yale classmate of William Buckley's and a member of Mary McCarthy's Vassar Group, then changes the subject *fast*. Of course, she can never remember to whom she told what, and she doesn't know how she can ever get married, because the man, on meeting her parents, will discover her nest of lies.

Connie goes further than most of us. But every time you tell a little lie for no reason at all except that you wish it were true ("I got a $1,500 raise." "Of *course* I can finish this by the fifteenth." "Everything's *fine* with Freddie; he wants to marry me but I don't want to marry *him*") you are taking a step backward into babyland. Ask yourself, "What is the worst thing that can happen if I tell the truth?" (You will probably find out you don't *need* all those lies.)

Sex (tee-hee): Some very grown-up-*looking* ladies go around acting like tittering children when it comes to sex. They think, talk, read, dream (O.K., can't be helped), watch movies about, and worry over sex like a Victorian gentleman surreptitiously meeting the boat train to pick up the latest privately printed porno from Paris. They giggle about sex with their girl friends, seem unable to discuss anything but their love life (how the sales manager has the hots for them). At the end of parties, in the middle of smoky living rooms, they often engage in lubricious solo dances to Rolling Stones records.

Of *course* sex is endlessly absorbing, exciting, new. Everybody thinks about sex more than he'll probably admit, but are you a fraud? Do you have the deepest-slashed necklines in Seattle or the see-through-ing-est blouses in Pittsburgh, fling around *all* the suddenly acceptable four-letter words at dinner parties only to blush, mumble, lie, and evade when your lover wants to take you to bed? If you're flamboyantly sexy out of bed and shy as a water lily *in*, you're probably playing a baby game of peekaboo with the real world.

247

Never give a friend an even break (when you can *manipulate* him instead): This little girl learned in childhood that she can get what she wants by manipulating Mother, Daddy, relatives. So she plays her friends off against each other, eavesdrops, and gossips. She's the General Giap of office guerrilla-warfare; her love life is plotted as intricately as a detective story, and she has an arsenal of tricks for harassing, embarrassing, cajoling, impressing, threatening, and even blackmailing friends (to get what she wants). Failing with those tactics, she may even *buy* them with gifts, favors, affection.

A certain amount of shrewdness about human nature is invaluable, and there's nothing wrong with a man-alluring trick or two as long as you don't make conmanship your life's work. Ultimately (like in a marriage), the real you has got to emerge and hold on to loved ones *without* tricks. Besides, a first-rate man isn't often going to tumble for even your sliest deceptions.

I'll be so good you'll *have* to love me: Some children figure they can win love by never ever doing *anything* unacceptable, no matter how much they want or need to. (Dr. Ginott calls them the "Too-Good-to-Be-Trues.") The adult Too-Good-to-Be-True operates the same way (oh yes, she's as much an operator as her sister the Manipulator, though she may not know it).

With her men she may be a super listener, unquestioningly loyal, self-sacrificing to a degree that sickens not only her less perfect friends but the man as well. (June's boy friend seemed to be straying, so she turned up at his apartment at 8:00 A.M. with The New York *Times,* a bag of *croissants,* a bunch of violets. This is the honest truth. What's more, this girl really believes she's doing the right thing.) The office Too-Good-to-Be-True never has four-year-old schedules peeling from the walls of *her* cubicle, is always the boss's sycophant, won't easily take a chance on a new idea for fear of doing (gasp!) The Wrong Thing.

Another goody-good girl is Miss Perfection, whose hems are *always* the right length, whose voice is *always* modulated and rational, whose nails *never* break, who drinks six glasses of water and exercises ten minutes a day without fail, creams her hands three minutes before bedtime, eats the same breakfast every morning at her desk with graceful gestures of unwrapping, stirring, sipping, and who goes through life in a trancelike aura of organization and calm. (My problem is hostility to this creature, who makes everyone around her feel about as together as Professor Irwin Corey with a hotfoot.)

The Too-Good-to-Be-Trues are like children who never learned that the world won't collapse if you don't please those in authority all the time. Spending so much energy repressing their rebel (selfish!) feelings usually makes them very exhausted people. If you're tired all the time, start wondering if this is why.

If you don't love me, I'll kill you: Expressing disproportionate hostility is just as infantile as denying that you feel hostility at all. "I'll make him regret this if it takes the rest of my life" is a baby's rage, not an adult's response to loss. You might spend five minutes to a couple of days figuring out how to do him in, but more than that—or actually going through with such a plan—is, well, to use a real technical word, crazy. So is vicious Virginia Woolf picking at the ego of a person who displeases you, especially in public! If you let hostility eat you up, you're bound to make cannibalistic attacks on other people. And anyone who'll stand for this sort of behavior is bound to be as babyish as you!

Exhibiting some of these baby patterns (or even—God!—all of them) doesn't necessarily mean you should ring for the men in white, even if you are well into your twenties. Although physical maturity follows the clock (menstruation almost always begins between twelve and thirteen), psychological maturity comes to different people at different ages. According to Dr. Keith Conners, Director of the Child Development Laboratory at Massachusetts General Hospital in Boston, you may "mature" as early as sixteen or still be struggling at twenty-five.

Growing up is nothing if not a highly personal, intensely individual matter . . . you must proceed in your own way and at your own pace. But, whenever or however maturity happens, there's no mistaking the girl who's really arrived! She has a full (and powerful) set of emotional responses, but the intensity of her feelings is matched by the intelligence that guides them. She's not lost in endless burrowings into her own confused self and so has time to really pay attention to other people. Inevitably, she has charm, not the frantic, look-at-me kind but rather a compelling attraction that draws others to her.

A "together" girl is beautifully, glidingly in control. She can find her way out of a conflict without losing anything important—like honesty or a sense of self. She also knows the way *into* good relationships, whether they be girl-girl friendships or man-woman loves, because she understands other people's needs as fully as she grasps her own.

"Getting it together" won't make you *more* talented, or better looking, or brighter, but *will* make whatever real resources you have glitter (instead of being obscured by a fog of emotional confusion). So if *you're* still slogging around in adolescent muddles, come out into the sunshine and grow *up*—you'll like yourself better, and so will everybody else.

5

LATE AGAIN? THE SLOWPOKES WHO ARE NEVER ON TIME!

Mary Lou's job supposedly begins at nine, but she never makes it before 9:25. Each morning she enters the office in an agony of embarrassment, mentally rehearsing the marvelous excuse no one ever asks for. *If only someone would say something,* she thinks.

Joan is so late for her dates with Jeff that he makes cracks about her being the only girl "who can go out with me and stand me up too."

Cynthia has given her husband her solemn promise that "this time I'll be ready in *plenty* of time," but at the last minute something goes wrong with her hairdo, her hemline, her false eyelashes, or her nail enamel—and, again, they miss the opening curtain.

All of us are late *once* in a while, but what makes the chronically late girl late? Let's look at some of the more prevalent reasons:

Vanity lateness: Traditionally a woman's problem, today some men are also prone to this variety. Insecure about her appearance, yet wanting to make a smashing impression, a girl fusses with her makeup, tries her hair with and without a hairpiece, changes her mind five times about what dress and what shoes to wear. If her lover or husband is present, she may ask him how he thinks she looks; but, when he tells her she's beautiful, she won't listen. A girl who worries inordinately about her appearance can't feel convinced a man would rather have her be on time, looking like a frump, than late and ravishing. Ten, twenty, thirty minutes later, she is still fussing.

Status lateness: An important executive in a business firm will often feel that he, or she, has a right to be late. In some offices there is an actual "pecking order" of lateness: First the minor employees, then the junior executives, then the bosses are expected to arrive. When the top man comes to the office and finds that one of his assistants is not at work yet, he is apt to be angry—not because the man is late but because he *presumes* to be late. At other companies, it is not the top people but other valued or trusted employees who feel it is their privilege not to arrive on time. At social gatherings, the most wealthy, celebrated, or socially prominent guests are apt to be the last to arrive. Their lateness underlines their status and says, "My time is more important than yours."

Coquettish lateness: Harriet knows Ron is waiting on a rainy street corner; she knows they ought to get an early start; yet she dawdles until she is five, ten, fifteen minutes late. When she arrives, she says to herself, smugly: *See, he waited!* Ron, though wet and angry-looking, is inwardly somewhat pleased that she made him wait; it proves, in a way, that she is a desirable creature.

Antagonistic lateness: Candy is ready to leave for her date with Charles, but she's just not in the mood yet. She resents Charles, feels he's wrong for her; yet, somehow, she's unable to refuse when he asks her out. *Let him wait,* Candy decides. She gets out the iron and ironing board and starts pressing a dress for tomorrow. Thirty minutes go by—*how much do I really hate him?* Lateness can express hostility!

Incentive lateness: Carole may have forty minutes in which to turn in a report, or two hours to get ready for a date, but she dawdles along until she thinks: *omigosh, I'm late!*—and turns on the speed, finding exhilaration in the excited last-minute flurry. Such people are "stretch runners" who work well only under pressure; it gives them a sense of urgency and excitement they lack.

Busy lateness: Suzy dates four different men, studies Russian on her lunch hour, stays overtime at the office to help her boss; at home, she cleans out closets at the same time she sets her hair in steam rollers and will faithfully try to write six old friends (two of whom are in the hospital) only half an hour before her date is due to pick her up for the evening! Like most ambitious people who reach out for more than they can handle, Suzy will no doubt accomplish much in life—but not punctually.

The forms of lateness we have been talking about are more or less "normal," because the people involved are aware of their motives for being late, and because the lateness itself is within socially acceptable limits. When she was making one of her last films, Marilyn Monroe was often as much as two hours late on the set; with director, co-stars, and a full production crew standing by, Miss Monroe's tardiness was costing the movie company about ten thousand dollars an hour! The "reason" for Miss M.'s lateness, according to newspaper reports, was that she was anxious about her appearance and would not leave the house until she felt that her makeup was perfect and every hair in her coiffure in place. Hers must have been a truly monumental insecurity. We have no way of knowing what Marilyn Monroe's unconscious drives and motivations really were, but on some level her lateness *must* have been meant to test those around her: *See how important, I am! They all waited for me. . . .*

When lateness gets out of hand or becomes a puzzle or an emotional problem to the person who is late, we must assume that some degree of unconscious emotional conflict is involved. The girl who is habitually late to work, for instance, may be unwilling to recognize that she actually dislikes her job (if she faced this truth, she might be forced to make major changes in her life). By being late, she is expressing her distaste for the job: *This is how I feel about you! If you don't like it, fire me!*

On the other hand, a girl might have (without being fully aware of it) a crush on her boss. In this case, her lateness is a form of flirtation, forcing the man to take special notice of her. If her boss becomes concerned, she is unconsciously delighted to have aroused a reaction.

Feelings of neglect, of being unwanted, can also drive someone to lateness. The shy, self-effacing woman who has suppressed her desires to relate to others in a positive, outgoing way may find herself becoming a problem to her friends or employers because of her inability to keep to a schedule. Because others are concerned about her, if only out of annoyance, it becomes a "victory" and satisfies her subconscious wish for greater emotional involvement. Other shy girls are perpetually late because they know at a gathering they will be required to act more outgoing than they can comfortably be.

The girl who habitually makes her date or husband wait (or who forgets the date entirely and stands him up) may have an unconscious desire to alienate the man and break off the relationship. Or, she may be motivated by a strong unconscious *attraction* to him. Human motives are often devious.

What can a girl *do* about her lateness problem? First, she should realize that her lateness represents a *reluctance* to face whomever or whatever she is late for. This reluctance may spring from severe, deeply rooted emotional conflicts, in which case she is probably acutely unhappy and in need of some form of psychotherapy. The chances are, however, that a little self-awareness and more open communication with others will go a long way toward resolving her difficulties. Just being aware that there *is* an emotional link to lateness can be a help. The chronically late girl should also make an effort to express her emotions more freely. If lateness is causing a problem between herself and a friend, lover, or employer, she should talk to them about it. It's surprising how easily an honest, open discussion often can clear up wounds and resentments.

SIX-WEEK CRASH RECOVERY PLAN FOR A NEW DIVORCÉE You stare for a moment at the document in your hand. It's very legal looking, and yet, to your surprise, very *ordinary* looking. Banal. Just a few sheets of white paper bearing the caption "Certified copy— Decree of Divorce" (or words to that effect), followed by two names. Yours and his, or his and yours. Complainant and defendant.

The document informs you that, in the eyes of the law, the two of you are no longer joined in holy matrimony. This is the day you've been waiting for, the day of finality after all those days of uncertainty and soul-searching . . . should you, or shouldn't you? The document makes it painfully clear that, whether or not you should have, you *did*.

Congratulations and welcome to the club (more than 650,000 people were divorced in the United States in 1969). You're divorced! So how come you feel like crying?

In the immediate aftermath you find yourself dazed, disoriented. But *why*, you wonder? What's the big difference between being separated from your husband, as you have been, and being divorced? You thought you had adjusted to the breakup of your marriage during the period of separation, adjusted rather *well*, in fact . . . perhaps better than you'd anticipated. You were proud of making a new life for yourself. Now you feel as though you have to start all over again from the beginning.

Know what? You're right. A *separation*, no matter how seemingly final, still carries with it the inherent possibility of *maybe*. *Maybe* you'll get back together again. *Maybe* you'll work things out. But divorce flatly eliminates those possibilities for you.

Your old life is finished. Your new one is about to begin. And make no mistake—new it *is*. New and uncertain. Exploratory. Revelatory. Challenging. How are you going to deal with it? How are you going to make that all-important transition from being married to being divorced? The first six weeks are crucial. They *can* be used productively. We've worked out a week-by-week schedule to launch you into divorcehood. It may be you'll want to switch the order of weeks around a bit. Fine, go ahead. Just don't tackle more than you can cope with in any seven days.

First week: Tell everyone about your divorce. Everyone. Friends, family, co-workers, old schoolmates you haven't seen since your sorority days. *How* do you tell them . . . with tears in your throat? Depends on what you want. If you sound dejected or depressed when you break the news, they'll probably feel sorry for you, but what's so great about that? *You* decided to get divorced because *you* thought it was the right thing to do, the wisest move under the circumstances. Having taken such a bold step, you would be contradicting the wisdom of your own decision by asking for pity at this point. Understanding and compassion, yes. But pity, definitely not. Which doesn't mean sounding as though you've just won the Kentucky Derby (unless that's how you feel).

You probably won't have the time or patience to telephone everyone. Go to a greeting-card store and buy some cards that say things like *Have you heard?* or *I wanted you to be the first to know,* or get one of the astrology cards that illustrates your birth sign on the front. The inside of the card is blank, waiting for your message. Handwritten, of course, it should be simple, direct, yet personal. For example, you would not say the same thing to someone who knew your ex-husband and someone who did not.

Rosemary, who had a very quickie marriage, wrote to one old friend who lived in another city, "I'm sorry that you never met Dick, but it's too late now. Yes, we've just been divorced. If you know any interesting men who are going to be in town, please give them my telephone number." Informative, without the sordid details.

But to a very close friend, who had lived through the minute-by-minute breakup, Rosemary wrote, "I just received the official papers. Thank goodness it's all over with. Do you know of any big parties coming up?"

By informing people about the divorce, you're making a simple, yet socially necessary statement of fact: You are no longer married, no longer separated; you're divorced, and everyone had better get used to it—especially *you*. Outside acknowledgment of your new status will make it easier for you to accept it emotionally, and will also serve another purpose: Many people are reluctant to introduce a woman who is separated to a new man, particularly if the people are friends of both you *and* your husband. Once you're divorced, that hurdle is eliminated, and many of your friends (though not *all*) won't be able to wait to invite you to dinner to introduce you to So-and-So, or they'll ask whether it's all right to give So-and-So your telephone number.

Even if you're not ready to date yet, don't reject any offers; just postpone them. Amy, who had a particularly bruising divorce, told a helpful friend, "Look, I'm still a little shaky. Your cousin sounds divine; can I call you in a month and ask you to introduce me then?" Try to hang on to all the invitations until you're feeling unragged enough to use them. Some girls don't want to meet a new man the day after the final decree because they feel a little squeamish about the idea of dating, almost as though they would be betraying the memory of a marriage. Some *separated* women who have no compunction about dating during the separation turn into timid little buds once the divorce papers touch their hands. They feel a new sense of vulnerability, knowing they can no longer hide behind the protective shield of marriage—even though that marriage is, and has been for some time, nonfunctioning.

Remember that sooner or later you *will* be meeting new men, which *doesn't* necessarily mean having an affair with them (again, unless you feel like it). What it does mean is that you're beginning one of the most important steps to divorce recovery: Getting to know new people, both men and women, whom you didn't know in your old life. It's pretty hard to live in the past if you associate with people you never *knew* then. Written notes to friends about your new status—frank requests that you be kept in mind for eligible men who loom up—are ways of getting to the new people.

This is a particularly good time to drop pitying or patronizing friends, particularly those who use *you* to make *themselves* feel better. Certain women with so-so marriages seem to need to think, "I wouldn't change places with *her* . . . at least *I* have a *husband*."

Watch out for parents, too. Mothers, especially, give moral support on the surface but underneath there's the hint that you should have stuck it out and that you may not find a replacement.

Does this warning mean you're supposed to give up *everybody*? . . . change your job, cut off the home folks? Not necessarily. We'll get to those considerations in a moment. This is only your first week.

Second week: Decide what to do about your living arrangements. Not since the initial split with your husband have you felt so acutely alone. You find that during the day you're all right so long as you keep busy . . . it's the nights that start the memory machine rolling. That's when you plunge into the past and worry unremittingly about the future. Loneliness strikes even if you have children in the house.

If you're a mother, you'll have less flexibility about moving, and it's probably not a good idea to consider any major move during the immediate six-week recovery program. Without children, however, you may find that a roommate can provide the companionship you require. After all, you've been used to living with another person and you just may not be ready yet to go it completely alone. Don't be ashamed if you feel this way. Needing company and admitting it doesn't make you any weaker than the divorcée who prefers to live by herself until her next husband comes along.

If you *don't* feel like sharing your apartment—the one you lived in with *him*—you might move in with another girl. There are two possibilities here. Call a friend and ask whether you can stay with her for a while. A few weeks of camping out may send you scurrying back to your own place. Or, if you suspect a few weeks might not be enough, give up your apartment altogether and look for someone who is anxious to share hers. The classified real-estate section in many newspapers carries listings of roommate-seeking girls. If none of the ads appeals to you, place your own. Many cities have roommate agencies that can help.

Suppose you're just not the roommate type; then decide whether you want to *change* apartments. Some newly minted divorcées find a new apartment an emotional lifesaver . . . fewer remnants of the past to revive painful memories. Other women who have made compulsive changes bitterly regret the move. Figure out which is you. My friend Carla is a regretter. A legal secretary, she made the mistake of asking and taking the advice of nearly everyone in the law office where she works. Move, they all said, including her boss, whose judgment she respected. Even though instinct told her to stay put, she gave up her lovingly decorated apartment to move into a less attractive one at more money. Carla was in it all of three days before realizing she'd brought along all her old memories in the form of furniture, paintings, and dishes. What had Carla gained? Nothing but a moving bill, higher rent, and the realization it would have been more practical to keep her apartment, recover the sofa, paint the bedroom, and throw out her husband's favorite armchair!

Whether you decide to move or not, there seems to be little doubt that a divorcée can be cheered up by changing some of her furnishings. What to change depends upon your finances, as well as the degree to which you're unsettled by certain of your possessions. What unsettles one woman can be comforting to another. Marianne, a four-weeks-old "baby" divorcée, found herself reluctant to get rid of a coffee table that her ex-husband had made one summer out of an old Victorian dining room piece. "Doesn't it make you think of him?" her friends asked.

"Yes, but not in a bad way," Marianne said.

The table, she explained, reminded her of the happy and productive days of her marriage (there usually are some in every marriage!), when she and Joe would relax over drinks and sandwiches and talk about their new business venture, a children's boutique. What Marianne did do—constructively—was completely redecorate her bedroom. Out went the blue bedspread and drapes, candy-striped sheets, hooked rug, even the expensive Art Nouveau prints on the wall. In came a flowered bedspread and drapes, solid pastel sheets, a shaggy rug, and one large original oil painting. "I had to change the bedroom," said Marianne, "because a bedroom's too intimately associated with whomever you were married to."

Throw out or keep; move or stay; redecorate or retain. The right choices will make you feel better.

Third week: Make a change in your appearance. Jane, another baby divorcée (three weeks), woke up one morning feeling so buoyant she went right to the beauty parlor and had most of her long, blonde hair cut off. As soon as she looked at herself after the comb-out, she knew she'd made a mistake. But what had prompted her to do it?

"I suddenly *felt* so different," she told the girls in her office, "I wanted to *look* different."

Nobody could deny that she looked different. Unattractively different. After a few days of trying to get used to the new Jane, she decided to buy a fall and return to the *old* Jane even before her hair grew in again. It was an expensive lesson, and one that a divorcée can learn from. Rule: Don't change your personal style—if it's an effective one—just *because* your life-style has changed.

But what *should* you do when the need to look totally different strikes around this time? Here are several points to consider:

1. Are you changing just for the sake of change or because you honestly believe you will look better as a result?

2. Are you sure the alteration is not some sort of oblique attempt to defy your ex-husband? He loved you in black, so you throw out all your black dresses (in which you look smashing) and buy nothing but geometric prints (in which you look terrible!).

3. If in doubt, why not try a gradual, experimental change in your looks, rather than a drastic or irretrievable one? Instead of permanently dyeing your hair, use a tint that washes out. Try a short curly wig instead of getting a permanent.

But suppose you *like* your hair the way it is or already have found the happiest clothes for you; how are you going to create change? In that case, work on something less major. One divorcée I know got rid of all her safe, sane, white and beige lingerie—and replaced it with bras and slips in the vibrant colors she suddenly craved. Another friend switched from heavy, woodsy perfumes to a lighter scent she instantly felt more at home with. A third threw out six pairs of conservative black pumps and bought sling backs which made her feel sexy. A fourth went wild with false eyelashes, previously denied her because her husband liked "everything about a girl to be natural." A fifth signed up for exercise classes to firm her thighs and wasp her waist. A sixth went on a filet mignon-and-salad diet to get rid of five pounds she'd been meaning to get rid of for five years (instead of feeling deprived, the filet mignon made her feel affluent). Even a small change can be surprisingly invigorating.

4. If you do go ahead and rush into something that you later regret (like hair-cutting), remember there's nothing that can't be undone in time.

Don't brood. You're in a state of flux, and it's only natural that some efforts will be more successful than others. At least you're *trying*, and that's the important thing.

Fourth week: Ask everyone you know to introduce you to a new man, and don't panic on your first date. One friend of mine who's been divorced for several years said, "My first date after the divorce was unbelievable. I won't forget it as long as I live. I was wearing spiky lashes and a marvelous mini. I knew I looked great and yet I felt like an awkward virgin who'd never been in the same room with a man before. I felt . . . foolish. How can I explain it? As though I should have been *beyond* dating. After all those years of marriage, dating seemed beneath me . . . a step backward. I was ashamed people would think I was starting to look for a husband all over again and certainly afraid *this* man would think so. The ridiculous part was that marriage happened to be the last thing on my mind at the moment. All I really wanted to do was enjoy myself for an evening, but I was so uptight worrying about everyone *else's* opinion I had a perfectly miserable time. And, of course, he did, too."

Another divorcée says, "So many women imagine that people see them as objects of pity or desperation once they start dating again after the divorce. Getting over this delusion is part of getting over the divorce itself. It's laughable to me now, but on my first date I acted as though I were wearing a big sign which read: JUST DIVORCED. Instead of being me, I spent the entire evening being boringly defensive. I kept trying to prove I *wasn't* miserable, wasn't sexually frantic, wasn't searching desperately for husband number two . . . wasn't to be pitied.

"But, you see, *he* didn't think I was pitiable and didn't feel sorry for me. In fact, I found out later he admired me for having taken such a gutsy step. Most important, he wasn't *interested* in my divorce; I was the one who kept bringing it up. And finally, I think, he got annoyed, as well he should have, because I was shutting him out. The conversation I had that evening wasn't with him—it was with my own insecurity."

Here are a few *do's* and *don'ts* to keep in mind when you start dating again.

Don't bore every new man with endless details of your marriage and/or divorce, justifying it . . . explaining it. Would *you* want to spend the entire evening listening to him talk about his ex-wife or girl friend?

Don't knock your ex-husband. Men tend to sympathize with each other, even if they won't openly admit it, and possibly *you'll* come out looking like the villain.

Don't assume *he* assumes you're sexual fair game just because you've been married. *Some* men have that attitude, true, but, since there aren't too many virgins around these days *generally,* most men assume *all* women are sexual fair game, unless you indicate otherwise (whether you wish to encourage him is, of course, up to you).

Do appreciate the advantages you have over the girl who's never been married. You're used to the intimacy of living with a man, and this is a very attractive quality to a lot of men, who will find you more warm and "human" than the girl who has always lived alone.

Do remember that men tend to be impressed by women who have been given (even if temporarily) a seal of approval by another man. Having had a husband proves that somebody cared enough about you to ask you to marry him, which is more than any single girl can actually *prove*—no matter how popular she is.

Do treat a new man with the kind of care and consideration that comes naturally to a woman who has been married. As one bachelor put it, "You call for a single girl, she gives you a glass of water and rushes you out to the nearest overpriced restaurant. Divorcées tend to be more thoughtful, more aware of *your* wishes. And a lot of them are great cooks who don't think it's a crime to invite a guy to dinner."

Fifth week: Be prepared for a temporary case of the blues. Just when things were looking up, a sense of dejection and depression sets in. You're baffled by this confusing emotional state, and wonder how it's connected with the divorce. You thought the worst was behind you, but now feel as though you're back where you started, which depresses you all the more.

At the risk of sounding corny—cheer up! The blues are only temporary. Every recuperative period, whether emotional or physical, is prone to such moments. You must make a new life at your *own* pace, and temporary setback is your psyche's way of slowing you down until you're ready for the next step in recovery. Meanwhile, here's what you can do to make this period bearable and even productive:

Stop worrying about it. No matter how bleak you feel, you're going to get over it. If you're fortunate enough to have any vacation days coming, take them now. If you have children, get a good sitter. Then you go someplace new, challenging. Splurge. If you've always vacationed at the beach, try a mountain resort. Or how about that fancy dude ranch your husband kept vetoing because *he* hated horses? Wherever you decide to go, go quickly, with a minimum of preparation. Be luxuriously spontaneous. You can afford to. An attractive woman once told me nothing made her feel sexier than arriving in a new city with only a change of lingerie! Anyway there's nothing that will chase away the *blues* faster than feeling sexy. If you don't believe it, try it.

Suppose you can't possibly vacation now. Then what about your job? Maybe it's time for a change there. Just the prospect of a new job has an uplifting effect. Out comes the old résumé, which will have to be updated. How much more money should you ask for? Should you go to an employment agency, or try it by yourself first? What to wear on interviews? All of these considerations are bound to divert you from the temporary divorcée blues. And who knows? You might even find a great new job you wouldn't have had if this drastic new way of life—single again—hadn't caused some unrest and reappraisal.

You can't get away and have no desire to change jobs either? Now what?! Just as you're asking yourself that question, the telephone rings and it's your dear "friend" Mary Lou. You've put off trying to decide what to do about *her* in recent weeks because you weren't ready yet to face that particular problem. Ever since your divorce, you see, Mary Lou has been telling you what a mistake you made, how unhappy you're going to be, how few men can compare with your ex-husband. Now *you* tell Mary Lou to quit lecturing or stop calling. As soon as you hang up, you feel better! Depression is not yet gone, but one depressing *person* certainly is, and that's headway. One divorcée who had the Fifth-Week Blues rewrote her address book, eliminating the names of people she'd decided to cut out of her life. "It might not sound like much," said Bretta, "but I realized every time I looked up a number in my old book, I'd get depressed just *seeing* some of those people's names. They reminded me of a lot of things I wanted to forget, things associated with my marriage. I felt so good after rewriting the book I ordered a bottle of champagne . . . it was great to get rid of all the deadwood."

While you're reassessing friendships and dumping the blues, consider taking a course or some lessons. You're in the process of breaking old routines, and *need* activities. Don't look for time-wasters; choose something you're really interested in or a subject that might have long-range dividends. Italian lessons for that trip to Rome next year? What about a cooking class to gain confidence for those little dinner parties you're planning? Tennis . . . because you've always wanted to, or just because it's great for your body.

Sixth week: Give a party. Invite everyone you know and ask them to bring one extra person. This is your coming-out party, and as soon as you decide to give it, you will feel a long-last sense of enthusiasm and excitement returning. My friend Valerie said, "I wondered why I hadn't thought of the party idea long before. . . . I guess I was just too busy reshaping my life, trying to give it form. Something told me, though, that the period of transition was over. You know the first thing I did? Bought the slinkiest white-lace pants I could find and a white-lace see-through top. Then I telephoned my old friend Alan.

"'What's the big occasion?' Alan wanted to know.

"'I'm celebrating my divorce.'

"'Good for you,' he said. 'I'll bring along three men you ought to meet.'

"The day of the party, when I was making the guacamole and chilling the Margaritas, I got a telephone call . . . from my ex-husband. He'd looked everywhere for his silly yearbook and couldn't find it . . . had he perhaps left it in the apartment?"

Valerie smiled. "I told him I didn't have it and then, on impulse, invited him to the party. Well, he arrived with a very attractive redhead, and as soon as I laid eyes on her I understood why he wanted the yearbook. It had impressed me once—the prophecy about his being the fullback most likely to succeed. In the Sixth Week aftermath, I realized I was no longer impressed, but the redhead was. To my surprise, I wasn't jealous. Then a man I didn't know walked in and introduced himself as Alan's friend. He'd just joined Alan's firm, and was new in town.

"It was a great party . . . the Jefferson Airplane on the stereo, everybody buzzing and mixing. A couple I was fond of said it was good to see me back in circulation, come for the weekend. My ex-husband told me he had no idea I knew how to make guacamole. Alan's friend said my white lace was intriguing."

Valerie paused and smiled some more. "I guess it was right then I knew I didn't have anything to worry about. Recovery was imminent."

See how easy it is?

VI

LIVING WITH LIBERATION

Think a minute about the hangups you've hoped to iron out (or at least *uncrease* a little!) by reading this book. It's possible that some of the "neurotic" symptoms which beset you are simply *normal* reactions to "second-sex" status. How *can* you keep from feeling persecuted, ignored, and unappreciated when many employers reward *female* competence with a lower salary than a woman's male colleagues earn? Therapists caution "Keep control!" but you may well ask *how*, please, in a society where *men* hold the power over your emotions, career, finances, and other keys to self-esteem.

Such "sexism" *can* explain *many* of life's harassments, and we have Women's Liberation to thank for this plausible supplement to our problem-analyzing artillery. But this insight is only partly comforting without the vital self-awareness kindled by Women's Lib. Most of the writers speaking out in this section want to share their experiences (good and *awful*) in order to say, "This is how being a woman feels to *me*. . . . Do *you* have the same responses? Can we help each other?"

In this mood, then, read on . . . not as a conspirator against an arbitrary enemy, but as a sister to your sex. These revolutionary ideas may mean happier times for you *and* your man!

LIBERATION BAROMETER

Liberation for women hasn't been *easy* to win; once won, it can be even harder to use intelligently. So you have a *right* to some conflicts while you sort out new information and ideas, confront challenging life-styles and career alternatives. As if *that* isn't hard enough, you must also deal tenderly with male responses to these changes. If you do well on even a *few* of these questions, you're getting along *fine!*

1. *Did you play dumb or refuse to argue for fear he'd think that you were being "unfeminine"?*
2. *Are you slackening on the job because of preoccupation with love problems?*
3. *Have you turned down dates with good men just to stay faithful to the one with a retinue of other women?*
4. *Did you defer to the male executives even though you're their peer?*
5. *When discussing Women's Lib with a man/men did you preach . . . or blame men?*

YOUR BAROMETRIC RATING SCALE

4–5 noes   Good for you! You aren't letting that magnetic pull toward the opposite sex turn you against other *women*, or against yourself. Stand ready to make sound choices from among the many—even revolutionary—ones offered here.

3 noes   Congratulations for not turning two deaf ears to constructive feminist messages. Now, on to the rewarding process of continuing self-liberation!

2–0 noes   It's possible you also scored in the average-to-low range on believing-in-you. For *that's* what Women's Liberation is all about—respecting your *female* self. Take a look at *both* sections of this book, and see if your problems aren't related.

1

DON'T MAKE MEN THE ENEMY! Yes, the New Feminists are right: women should be regarded as people, who just *happen* to be the female variety. Of *course* girls are fully human and ought to be treated that way. I also agree with our modern suffragettes that women have the right to equal job opportunity, legal abortions, and child-care centers for their babies. In fact, there isn't a single solid plank in the feminist platform that I couldn't stand on myself!

But I hate, just hate, the way some of these gallant ladies blame women's second-class citizenship on men! Making men into the "enemy" accomplishes nothing positive, and adds tension to the already uneasy truce between the sexes. Besides, blaming the men isn't even logical! None of the men *you* know originated these attitudes, and it's hardly fair to punish the guy living now for a set of assumptions evolved back in caveman days when masculine physical strength *was* terribly relevant to group survival. Nor are men totally responsible for *perpetuating* the myth of female inequality. That women are "inferior" is a cultural idea that exists autonomously; it doesn't seem the exclusive creation of *either* sex. In fact, women, mothers specifically, teach their daughters that it's better to be pretty than smart, and that it's "feminine" to flunk calculus or deliberately lose to a man on the badminton court. And they teach their sons to expect this kind of nonsense from girls!

Men and women are *equally* victimized by our silly notion of "proper" female behavior! How many good men crumble beneath the weight of a marriage in which the wife exacts an impossible tribute to the feminine mystique? The woman who looks to her husband to *define* her as a person puts him under an intolerable strain. He's busy defining *himself*, remember! The wife who neglects her education and leaves her mind undeveloped *bores* her man. The woman who lives only for clothes, makeup, and the sexual jealousy she arouses in other girls is as tedious in bed as out! And what about the poor, overspent husband who manufactures ulcers and nervous breakdowns to provide luxuries for his wife when *she* might be out earning the vital extra cash? Or the castrated, cowed male who has been victimized by the woman (mother or wife) in aggressive revolt against the system's systematic put-down of females!

When Henry Higgins said, "Why can't a woman be more like a man?" he was voicing a legitimate complaint. Women *ought* to cultivate some of the traditionally "masculine" virtues. They should be logical and smart, brave and strong! Many women *do* possess these qualities, and they are not one jot less feminine for having them. No more womanly a creature than Sophia Loren exists, and there's nothing whining or silly or self-indulgent about *her*! (She also is a shrewd businesswoman who makes a formidable amount of money.)

The feminists are wrong to try to *polarize* men and women. A healthy revision of our ideal of womanhood would bring the sexes closer together. As a matter of anthropological fact (see: Margaret Mead, *Male and Female*), societies where men and women are more alike than different, where they do the same jobs and have similar tastes and temperaments, are the same societies where *sex* is the most fun (i.e., Samoans and some other Polynesian Islanders).

Our society still clings to a sick, impossible idea of *both* femininity and masculinity. Women are skittish, brainless, and adorably pretty; men are tough, reticent creatures who never cry or giggle. Naturally, these two stereotypes bore and offend each other; they have so little in common! When we revise our ideal female—so that the way she *is* matters more than how she looks—our ideal male will inevitably go through some changes, too. He'll be free to learn gentleness and to weep when he's moved. And by that time we truly liberated women will be more interested in loving our men than in blaming them!

FEMININE
FEMINISM

Isn't it time for a stereotype-free look at women's liberation? According to many media reports, feminists are male-hating harridans determined to overturn the social tables and relegate men to the dishwashing, diaper-changing detail. Waspish warrior women, castrating Amazons, "uglies" and "nasties" moved by personal failures in sex and love . . . all stereotypes, as old as feminism itself! The suffragettes labored under just-as-derisive labels—"blue noses," "battleaxes," "frustrated spinsters"—similar diversions from the issues. (Amazingly enough, they won the vote *anyway*!)

Now, there *is* some truth to charges that today's women's movement has opened a Pandora's box of feminine resentment. But much of the hostility seems justified, or at least *understandable*—especially to an unwed mother, or competent working woman stuck in a go-nowhere job.

At the same time, how *grossly* unfair to say *all* new feminists think and feel the same way! Women's liberation, I've discovered, admits many viewpoints, including those of staunch sexism-battlers who love their men! To find out how such women define their feminine and feminist identities, I interviewed two of them: Vicki Mayes Sopkin and Carol Gordon. Vicki is a moderate, Carol a radical; but both feel that involvement in women's liberation can only *profit* a girl—that you can work for your rights and *enjoy* life, too . . . maybe enjoy it more than *ever*!

269

Even the most rabid antifeminist would be hard pressed to label new feminist Vicki Mayes Sopkin "ugly" or "man-hating." Married and a mother, this low-keyed movement woman gleams with the beauty and cool of a spun-glass goblet.

"I don't believe in making a frontal assault on men," she says quietly. "I think that's self-defeating." While admitting to "isolation" from the harsher forms of male chauvinism, she insists: "But I can understand antimale feeling. I do think, though, that men will stop oppressing women when they realize it's impractical to keep more than half the population down."

No one has kept her down. Vicki may be slim-stemmed and svelte (hers is the kind of figure that glides effortlessly into size seven pants), but she's hardly fragile. Looking like the early Jean Simmons, she explains disarmingly why she wants to learn about plumbing: "I'd rather know how to fix things than not, that's all. I'm also glad I know how to cook . . . and studied languages—I feel more independent when I'm traveling. I believe in more options for women."

Vicki also maintains that sports can liberate a girl. "Chas (rhymes with "jazz")] and I," she says, referring to her husband Charles, an editor at McCall books, "are absolute fanatics about sports. We're wild about the Mets and the Knicks. But when it comes right down to action, Chas is the one who'd rather watch, and I'm the one who'd rather do.

"I love swimming and walking. In school I was passionate about badminton. I even tried out for hockey, but sort of crumpled towards the end. One good thing about girls' schools: you're encouraged to develop muscle tone through sports. I'm not a health nut or anything, but I think it's important for women to be sturdy."

Perhaps because Vicki felt "sturdy," she was always amused by masculine niceties (designed to make females feel helpless) showered on her by escorts before her four-years-ago marriage. "It never seemed practical to have the man go all the way around to the other side of the car door and open it, when it was so much easier for me to do that myself. And I always thought it was hilarious when men insisted on walking on the outside and then doing this kind of square dance at the intersections."

Although Vicki couldn't leave a car door alone, she never fought chivalry as a whole—the issue didn't strike her as vital. Today she moderates her views on women's liberation with the same discretion, choosing from the movement what she finds relevant to her life.

Last February she joined the New York City chapter of NOW (National Organization for Women), the largest (more than 10,000 strong) American feminist group. Legalistic in orientation, NOW works for equal pay for equal work, abortions on demand, free child care centers, and an end to sex-based job discrimination.

"NOW appealed to me because it's moderate," says Vicki, who has aided the organization with fund-raising, publicity, and stints at the office answering phone calls (which range from requests for information about divorce proceedings and child support to queries about the rights of pregnant working women). "And I liked the members. They are so attractive, so intelligent, so successful. They represent almost all ages, from women in their early twenties to late sixties. A few were even *suffragettes!* I met one woman in her forties who had been working for years with charities before she became involved in something that *directly* affects her and her life. I think that's great!

"We believe that liberation is for men, too. They're imprisoned by the same cultural attitudes that limit women—stereotypes about what's 'masculine' and 'feminine.' Men are told they can never cry or show emotion. And they're made to feel they must shoulder the entire economic responsibility for the family. This isn't good for *either* parent—*or* for children who grow up seeing men and women act only in rigidly defined roles."

Not all of Vicki's friends agree. One of them, also an attractive, affluent married woman, stopped by the apartment before our interview began and said, rather condescendingly, "I'm sorry, I just don't feel oppressed. And if I am oppressed, then I *enjoy* it."

The word "oppressed" echoes ironically in the Sopkins' neo-18th-century living room (where serenity breaks only on the entrance of Nicholas, a rambunctious fellow of sixteen months who enjoys tipping over things). Passionate devotees of the American Dream would be quick to question Vicki's feminism by pointing out that she Has Everything—so what is she perturbed about?

Again Vicki acknowledges her seclusion from the hardships that face less privileged females. Yet women's problems, she says, cross economic lines: "Feminism has something to offer *every* woman. But it's hard to change. Some of us feel threatened by the movement—it *can* suddenly make you think, 'I've wasted so much *time* . . . maybe I've made too many wrong decisions about my life.' Once you get *into* women's liberation, you discover its *vastness*—it raises so *many* personal questions that can unsettle you.

"At first it was very difficult for me to convince my friends that the movement was important to them. And it was Chas who said one night that the problem is twofold—you have to make practical economic reforms, but at the same time you also have to educate people and help them change their attitudes. In this way our movement is really very much like the civil rights struggle.

"I've found that women are drawn to the movement when some very specific trouble happens to them—they can't get an abortion, or the job they want. I think we'd have a much more accurate evaluation of women's attitudes if reporters and researchers would stop asking us, 'What do you think of women's liberation?' and instead ask more specific questions like: 'Do you think working women should do *all* the household tasks?' or, 'Do you think men should have a greater role in raising children?'

"Anyway, I think any woman who just *looks* at her life and her job *has* to recognize the inequality and decide to do something about it. Just feeling discontent isn't enough."

Now thirty-one, Vicki remembers her *own* frustration during ten years at various publishing firms, where she encountered subtle forms of job discrimination. The "prestigious" job titles, she says, merely camouflaged menial work that women employees were channeled into: "I was once called an 'associate editor.' Whenever they *qualify* the word 'editor,' you're in trouble!" At one New York publishing house, Vicki's fluent French caught the attention of male editors, who asked her to report on some French manuscripts. The reward for her extra work?—a thank-you note and (once) a magnum of champagne. "I would have preferred a raise or a promotion," she says, a trace of sarcasm edging her soft voice. "I could buy my *own* champagne."

Eventually she asked for a raise and got one: "It was more the principle than the money. What happened to me is nothing compared to what some women face in the working world. But it's typical of male-dominated publishing. Capable women who have been on the job a long time see raises and promotions go to less competent men. I've never been antiwoman, never felt it was more difficult to work with women than with men. And I was so glad the women at the office felt the same way I did about job discrimination."

Vicki suspects that *all* women are "closet feminists." In that silent sisterhood she even includes actress Ali MacGraw (another woman with the fabled Everything), who was a year ahead of her at Rosemary Hall, an all-female prep school in Connecticut, and at Wellesley College: "Ali always had creative energies to spare. But even *she* had to wait until she was nearly thirty to do something meaningful to her."

Vicki herself emerged from the closet early. A rebel against the sugar-and-spice syndrome, she resisted playing with dolls ("I wouldn't throw a tantrum or anything. I just preferred to read.") Later, another proto-feminist insight surfaced when she sensed "something wrong" at her exclusive Eastern women's college and dropped out after six months of "programmed triviality." (Recent reports suggest that other Wellesley women are beginning to complain about the curriculum.)

"Nobody *read* anything then," Vicki cracks, sounding a bit like a J. D. Salinger heroine. "They just parroted what their teachers told them. Do you know what one of my freshman English assignments was? *Describe what you did on your Thanksgiving vacation!*"

Although some women's colleges do little more than varnish privileged girls for marriage and leisure ("Some of them don't even do *that*"), Vicki nurtured more adventurous plans. After leaving Wellesley, she took courses at several colleges in Manhattan, then at age nineteen spent a year working for *Elle*, the French woman's magazine. Living on her own in Paris began Vicki's *real* education: "So many of the French women I met were into second marriages. The husbands looked more comfortable with marriage—they had fewer demands to meet than the women, who also worked. French working women seemed more aggressive to me than Americans. They put in a lot of hours, but were poorly paid. And they didn't do much to improve their positions or demand promotions. Perhaps they felt lucky to have jobs because most French women weren't really *encouraged* to work. The staff members at *Elle* were different—almost an elite—maybe because a woman is editor of the magazine. Her name is Hélène Gordon-Lazareff, and she made a *tremendous* impression on me. Hélène never had to call up her husband for advice, or any of that sort of nonsense. Once she phoned the Élysée Palace to speak to De Gaulle when there was a rumor that Khrushchev had died. Hélène was a very positive influence, and I now see that she was an important part of my growing-up period."

Back in the States, Vicki tackled the New York publishing business. At one job she met Charles. ("I think many women meet their husbands through work.") The marriage ceremony also elicited nascent feminist feelings: "It wasn't so much losing my last name, because my first name is more important to me. It was the whole idea of signing everything away and knowing that you're going to be on *file* somewhere. Chas was bothered by the ceremony, too."

She fondly describes Chas as "easy-going and *happy* looking. He's got blond curly hair, a great laugh, and a terrific yawn. I married a man I like a whole lot. He agrees with women's liberation on principle, but just doesn't want to get involved in it. He thinks that I should do what I want to do. All he asks is that the house gets *run*. But he helps me. And when it comes to entertaining, he's the one who gets us *organized*."

Her green eyes glow again when she mentions the other male in her life, son Nicholas. "Both Chas and I really *wanted* Nicholas. But he's not my whole existence. I think women make a mistake when they invest everything in children—who are going to leave you in less than twenty years anyway. The feminist demand for free child-care centers is valid and necessary—for the children as well as the mothers. It's so important for children to learn how to relate to other adults and not become overly dependent on their parents. I want Nicholas to be self-sufficient when he grows up."

As it turned out, Nicholas helped catalyze Vicki's participation in the women's movement: "I think it was my pregnancy and my awareness of the need for free child-care centers that got me into the movement. Like a lot of other women at the office, I had to lie about my due date so I could work longer and get paid. At that time my firm didn't provide paid maternity leaves. I was lucky to get hospital insurance. Friends who had children before the firm established that policy assumed all the enormous hospital costs themselves. One minute you're a contributing member of society, paid for what you do; the next, you're unemployed and unpaid just because you're a mother. If I returned to work now and made, say ten thousand dollars a year, I would keep about two thousand after taxes and salaries to professional baby sitters and so on.

"Employers don't like to hire pregnant women. They also seem to think that jobs are a 'luxury' for women, who will eventually marry and stay home. Why should working mothers be expected to stay home and lose pay when their children are sick? Working *fathers* aren't! In Sweden, which has free day-care centers, women receive a six-month paid maternity leave, and they're allowed so many days off with pay when their children are sick. And the fathers often stay home with the kids, too. Why *shouldn't* the responsibility be shared?"

Vicki speaks strongly about a new society and women's participation in it, but she doesn't consider herself a militant. Nor does she attend consciousness-raising sessions (meetings where a group of women discuss their personal feelings and experiences in an effort to share and heighten their understanding of being *female*). But Vicki continues to take part in the women's movement in her own way: she reads books on women's oppression (such as *The Feminine Mystique* by Betty Friedan, NOW's founder; Germaine Greer's *The Female Eunuch*). And with two other mothers, she set up an informal baby-sitting service for the tenants in her apartment building.

NOW, Vicki says, "focuses on economic reforms, but it's also very much concerned about marriage, the family, women's image, the education of children. We don't want to see our children channeled into stereotyped roles—in which the girls always have to play with dolls, the boys with trucks.

"I'm not saying that it's going to be easy for men to change their roles or attitudes, their demands for ego-gratification from women. They must feel terribly insecure, thinking they always have to be *out there* as major provider. And when they aren't worried about the burdens they're stuck with *now*, they're worried about what they stand to lose in the *future*, when women are more liberated.

"Some of us in NOW aren't particularly fond of the name 'women's liberation.' I don't care for it—to me it smacks of guerilla warfare, and I don't think that should be the movement's image. Recently I saw Betty Friedan on a television talk show, and she said she preferred the name 'women's participation.' What she's saying, I think, is that women need to participate in the decision-making processes, political and otherwise, that affect their lives. Women need to be full-fledged, responsible human beings—*people*."

Although Vicki feels uncomfortable in large groups ("Basically I'm shy"), she did join a NOW demonstration with Nicholas this year to support Elizabeth Barrett, a New York working mother and widow, in her effort to deduct child-care expenses from her income tax. Vicki also has marched on other women's lib occasions. She describes her emotions at one march as she saw the celebrating crowds surge through the streets in a spirit of joyful affirmation:

"There were women of all ages, and young men, too, and they would call out to people 'Join us! Join us!' Everyone was so happy and good-natured and full of high spirits and dignified. I'd felt I *had* to go to the march—I didn't want it to be a straggling little group. But when I got to Fifth Avenue and saw the people, it took my breath away. And at Fifty-eighth Street, I turned around and saw people from curb to curb, blocks away. There were thousands. Thousands."

Can a committed feminist find happiness in pretty clothes and cosmetics? Carol Gordon, professional psychologist, divorcee, and mother of a ten-year-old son, resolves what *some* people think is a contradiction in terms. Age thirty-three, 105 pounds, standing five feet three in her size five petites, Carol proves that liberated females can *love* clothes and makeup without becoming fashion-*obsessed*.

"I want to look attractive for me and other people," she says in her airy, uncluttered apartment-cum-office, where light streams through wide windows and a women's liberation poster salutes visitors from the living-room door. "I don't feel I dress just to be attractive to men. I dress for fun. Fashion isn't crucial to my life—it's a luxury, like playacting or wearing dress-up costumes."

Although Carol doesn't color her long brown hair or use face paints, powders, and false lashes, she does enjoy dabbling eyeshadow and liner around her blue-green eyes. "I think it makes me look more interesting," she says. "And I enjoy having different kinds of clothes. I usually buy them at sales and discount stores. I'd rather have an amusing wardrobe than an expensive, elegant one.

"At first I felt uncomfortable wearing a dress and bra to my women's group." (Now she rarely wears a bra, "mainly because I'm practically flat-chested!") "But we talked about our attitudes, the stereotypes about feminists and what they're are supposed to look like." (You *do* know the image, don't you? Seventies-suffragette in Army-surplus drag, fright-wig hair, and proudly-sported acne. Some people trustingly *believe* all feminists look like this!) "We realized that in trying to live up to that picture, we could be oppressive to each other."

Carol's "women's group" is affiliated with Radical Feminists, a loosely knit coalition of New York–New Jersey liberationists who focus on "consciousness-raising" instead of such "reformist" demands as job equality. Unlike NOW, Radical Feminists has no officers and no regular chapter meetings, although members do gather each month in homes and apartments to discuss movement matters.

In recent months the nonorganization sponsored a community "speak-out" on rape, where women described their experiences. A conference followed, attended by movement-activist social workers and psychologists, who presented research reports and mapped strategies to deal with rape and rapists (including a karate demonstration).

Carol, one of the speakers who addressed the conference, says her best self-defense against rape is her psychologist's training. "Once," she said, "I talked a man out of raping me. I haven't learned karate. I'm really a nonviolent person, a pacifist."

Carol also organizes consciousness-raising groups for Radical Feminists. "A lot of people think consciousness-raising is like group therapy, which it isn't," she says. "In group therapy you often attack people, and your analysis concentrates on the differences among individuals. In consciousness-raising, we try to bring out the similarities in women's experience. We're nonhostile. The whole point is to offer each other sympathy, support, and understanding.

"In our groups we discuss specific topics in a very orderly way, going around the room so that each woman gets her chance to speak. It's not a 'rap session,' aimless conversation that can get you nowhere. Consciousness-raising is an educational process to help you evaluate your attitudes clearly. We feel it's the core of the women's movement.

"Reformist measures, such as demands for job equality, assume that change can come about through institutions. But many women aren't interested in careers or job opportunities. You can't impose these things on women until they first change within themselves. Our goal is to help each woman *individually* to change her life.

We practically *forbid* any kind of political theorizing. Consciousness-raising has to be personal, here and now. Why do I feel a man should take care of me? How do I want to raise my children? How do I feel about living in a commune? It's not that we're avoiding society by just looking inside ourselves; through consciousness-raising, you begin to look outward, in a small way. Gradual social change happens from *within*—something like what Charles Reich writes about in *The Greening of America*. At this point, I believe in slow change."

Asked to give an example, Carol smiled and replied, "Well, one woman in my group had dropped out of college and was feeling very disorganized. She enjoyed talking, but her speech was scattered. Through the group she learned how to be a more effective speaker. She returned to school, graduated, and now wants to be an attorney. She'll probably do some very good things for society."

Carol *herself* is responsible for some social good. Besides her private practice as a therapist and her feminist organizing activities, she works part time at a Manhattan clinic that serves low-income residents. In 1970 she joined a group of feminist psychologists in presenting "women's issues" at the annual meeting of the American Association of Humanist Psychologists. Along with other female activists at that meeting, she has since joined the New York Coalition of Feminist Psychologists.

"The women's movement may affect therapy," she says. "Freudian therapy is still dominated by the idea that women are 'naturally' passive, weak, and masochistic, that the goal of the therapist is to help women adjust to these roles. Hardly any research has been done on women and their sexuality. There's been a lot of theorizing, but no really specific results. Male-oriented researchers use terms like 'people' when they make statistical statements about sex. Our group (New York Coalition of Feminist Psychologists) uses research studies *about* women and *by* women, such as New York psychiatrist Phyllis Chesler."

Since Carol's separation and divorce in 1965, she has had several short-term but satisfying relationships with men (including one that lasted a year and a half). Hardly a "man-hater"—but she fearlessly comments on men's culturally imposed limitations:

"There are certain things women can give you that men can't," she says. "Once I thought I was pregnant, and the man said, 'We'll take care of it.' He was logical and tried to comfort me, but couldn't understand why I was practically hysterical. The *women* in my group *could*. That's another good thing about consciousness-raising: because you can go to women for support and sympathy, you stop overloading men. You make fewer demands on them, expect less from them, stop being so dependent on *their* opinions and ideas.

"Now, whenever I can't fix something at the apartment, I try to ask a woman to help me. I don't want to have a man *just* to do things for me that I can't do myself yet—I don't think that's a good basis for relationships. Of course, there is the possibility, and we've discussed this, that women could use men just as sex objects, treating them the way they've treated us. But right now it's easier for women to talk to other women about personal things they'd be embarrassed to discuss with men—child raising or attitudes about sex."

Has Carol's independence ever "turned off" a man? "Some men have been threatened," she acknowledges. "They wanted me to *need* them more, and were bothered because I'm always so busy, involved with work and women's liberation. Others have been fascinated by my activities and energy. They *weren't* threatened. I've seen relationships *improve* because of women's liberation—and I've also seen them fall apart because of the woman's new awareness of her needs—an awareness the man just couldn't deal with."

Lesbianism has been scorchingly debated in the women's movement, but Radical Feminists have expressed their support for lesbians. How does Carol respond to this issue? "I've never had a lesbian experience," she says. "But if the situation was right, I probably would—partly because [she laughs] it coincides with this image I have of myself as a hip woman.

"I also think lesbianism is fine as a temporary solution. I read an article in *Cosmopolitan* that made pretty much the same point: just having a lesbian encounter doesn't mean you're a lesbian. Meanwhile, I think lesbians in the movement will help us gain a freer and more honest attitude about homosexuality."

How did a "nice Jewish girl" who grew up in a dozing middle-class New Jersey suburb acquire such unconventional attitudes? In high school Carol subversively wrote poetry and read widely on the side ("I kept that secret. Girls weren't supposed to be intellectual"), feeling "odd" because she was "achievement-oriented" and liked sports. In her first year of college, at Brandeis University, her fear of expressing her love for math and science subsided. ("Women are encouraged to achieve more in college.") Once she led a seminar on physics, to the astonishment of some of her classmates.

Then at twenty, she transferred to Rutgers University, married her "hometown" sweetheart, a business student, and two years later gave birth to her son Marc. During her first year of graduate school, she and her husband found that they had different values and different notions about life style:

"He wanted to live in the suburbs, I wanted to live in Greenwich Village. It bothered him that I was still in school, not giving him as much attention as he felt he should have. I remember him saying later that the next woman he'd marry would be a dumb blonde who'd stay home all the time. He did marry again. I don't know if she's dumb.

"I'd married very young. At twenty I didn't know of one woman with a career—women married and had children. I was terrified of all the untraditional things I wanted to do, and now think I married instead."

Perhaps it was Carol's mother who dramatized for her that a job could relieve a housewife's boredom and fatigue: "I was thirteen or so when mother got a job. It obviously made her much healthier and happier. But she never thought in terms of a career." Another influence may have been Abraham Maslow, past president of the American Psychological Association and American Association of Humanist Psychologists. At Brandeis, Carol studied under Maslow, inspired by a study he did on self-actualization in women as well as men." Now quoted by feminists, Maslow's research revealed that "self-assertive" females enjoyed a better sex life than their more passive sisters. At that time, says Carol, "though I had read The Second Sex by Simone de Beauvoir, I never thought of myself as a feminist. And I wasn't politically sophisticated at all."

Later on, she persisted in her graduate studies in psychology even while her marriage curdled. "The neighbors thought I was terrible to leave Marc with a baby-sitter or Mother and go to class three days a week. My mother-in-law also disapproved. So did my husband. I felt confused and sometimes ashamed."

After her marriage ended, Carol moved to Manhattan with her son to work toward her doctorate (first at City College and then at New York

University) and realized her dream to live in Greenwich Village. "For the first time I felt clear about what I was doing and was no longer afraid."

Marc attended Greenwich House, a day-care center with fees geared to the incomes of clients, while Carol studied at the university, supported by grants and fellowships. "I think day-care centers have to be staffed by professionals," she says. "Here is another example where attitudes have to change before you set up state-supported services. Women themselves have to be involved in running the centers. Otherwise, day-care centers run by the state could be as bad for children as the New York City public school system, which is very bad. I honestly believe that Marc's school is something of an exception, partly because there's some degree of community control."

Carol's deep involvement in women's liberation began two years ago, when a male patient asked her to work with a group of radical antiwar students in SDS (Students for a Democratic Society). "He showed me a copy of 'The Myth of the Vaginal Orgasm' by feminist Ann Koedt, and said that the women in his group were all reading it. My experience with them later got me into women's liberation."

She feels that the women's movement must follow its own path. "Eventually we may make coalitions, and we've certainly been influenced by the civil rights and human potential movements. But we've come up with our *own* analysis of women's problems and needs—and want to remain independent for now.

"Many women in the movement feel rage. I don't, because I think I've been able to find some solutions for my life. But I understand the feelings—they're valid—and think that the movement must go through this stage. Men will change as more women do. But I don't think they'll change because it's logical. I think they'll change because they'll have no other choice."

Meanwhile, what happens to movement women in this limbo period before the liberation of both sexes? "The payoff," says Carol, "is that women already feel better about *themselves*. And for sympathy and support they have each other."

ON BEING FEMALE

Right on, sisters! Cast down those women's pages with news of midi, maxi, and knee britches. *We're the* front-page news story now, storming magazine offices, marriage-license bureaus, all-male clubs, and Miss America pageants. We're forcing legislators to change fusty laws that made us have unwanted babies and be household coolies for the babies' fathers! We're after *liberation, not* lascivious appraisals from arrogant, exploitive male supremacists. This is our world now. No more kitchen imprisonment or ego-effacing, coffee-fetching jobs for us! We've added the Pill to the vote and become free!

Yes, it's all true. Now that embattled women's-rights-ers have become newsmakers, I read my daily paper with the excitement of a war buff. Those are my *sisters* out there . . . fighting with courage and grit for first-class citizenship. Go get 'em! My sex, right or wrong! Down with the motherhood myth and girls as sex *objects* (instead of sexual *people*)! Up with equal rights . . . to anything and anywhere we want to go!

But wait a moment . . . there seems to be a subsurface *apology* beneath my rage. The old voice isn't entirely steady or free from hysteria as I make my demands. Because—dammit—I'm really *afraid* of that smugly perched man I'm trying to unseat, afraid I still need him to maintain my precarious balance. While the New Woman inside me throws off old confining roles with the abandon of a stripper, I keep hearing in my head that Beatles song . . . "Get back . . . get back . . . get back to where you once belonged"

And so I cradle my head in my shaky but independent hands and try *really* to get back . . . to the childhood that shaped me and find the seeds of my by now fully flowered confusion!

I (like most of my this-generation space sisters) grew up in a male-dominated home. My father was aggressive, self-centered, always and ultimately right. He gave our family the comfortable security of depending on his strength, but only on the condition that we remain *his* creatures, doing as *he* bid! My mother was passive, self-denying, wonderfully nurturing. I could admire and appreciate Mother for her good qualities but certainly didn't want to grow up *like* her. She served *our* needs, it seemed to me, only at the expense of her *own* life and personality.

Among the absolutes, unquestioned in my childhood world, was that Mother would never intrude her intellect into any quarrel with my father. True, she sometimes raised her voice several tones short of real protest but only to complain of "hurt feelings." And I of course followed her lead. Although my father encouraged me to "develop your mind, Carole" (how he bragged about his "brainy" daughter), he and I both knew that my intellect could not (indeed, *should* not) be a match for his or any man's. I was expected, like my mother, to bow to his superior masculine knowledge. Those few times I opposed him in an argument always ended with my apologizing. Apologizing! Because I'd dared to disagree with him and have independent thoughts. I was very young when I learned this first lesson of femininity: any heated disagreement with a man made you *less* a girl, less the darling creature that Daddy (and someday another grown-up man) would love.

When I first began dating, conflicts came in busy droves. I hated having to compete with other girls for boys on the basis of being pretty! On the one hand, I felt degraded by the competition, knowing that a person was more than looks; at the same time, I was heady with triumph every time I won! This conflict made me *ashamed*! What was I but a draggy malcontent who didn't appreciate how lucky she was to be so sought after. But another voice—one all the plump, fluffy, down pillows of femininity couldn't stifle—told me I was *right* to be dissatisfied with this kind of victory. These boys knew *nothing* about me and, worse, didn't *care*. All of me that mattered was that I was pretty and "good company." Being "good company" meant doing just what the teen magazines recommended—suppressing my yawns as I asked "leading questions" about sports and school and cars, which the flattered male would answer at tedious length!

I was beginning, however, by age fifteen to play the game quite success-fully by *girls' rules*—channeling all my competitive energies into activ-ities that were "feminine." Of course, collecting a series of enviable beaus was the best achievement I could hope for; girls' rules were (are) gen-erously studded with restrictions. If I challenged some boy to debate in class, I'd be ostracized by him and his friends. I *could,* however, compete guiltlessly with other girls for a boy's *attention.* And when he asked for a date, I was a success! Score one! The girls that I'd beaten out might hate me, but so what. They are the opposition team!

Hostile to members of my own sex (though *they,* not the boys, were my real peers), how could I help but be drawn toward the danger of self-hatred. To this day, I have less interest in reading a book by a woman than a man, less trust in women doctors than men. This negative view of one's sex (and thus, inevitably, of one's self) goes very deep and is painfully hard to reverse, even as the parade of Women's Lib marches by!

Sex was no pleasure for me in those days. God—I'll never forget those pawing, sweaty interludes in the backseat of some father's car. I would fiercely defend the particular erotic zone declared off limits by the pre-vailing good-girl code. Touching here but not there, on top of clothes but not under—those parts of the body that could or could not be caressed were marked off as precisely as squares on a chessboard. Adolescent sex was, for me, about as spontaneous and emotionally affecting as a math-ematical equation!

Though, in reality, I felt nothing but antagonism for the boys who were forced (by roles *they* had to play) into constantly invading these off-limits body zones, I made a mighty pretense of "loving" them. Coolly, with total detachment, I manufactured emotional responses and en-couraged the boys to do the same. I didn't have the individuality to form an honest relationship, and neither, for that matter, did they! The sex roles we had been brought up to play made healthy relating impossible!

My identity at this time was totally contingent: I *was* whatever boys would declare me to be, tramp if they thought so, precious if they valued me. I *had* to make boys "love" me, even when I didn't give a damn about them. And if this kind of behavior chills your blood, think of your friends who have built *marriages* on this flimsy foundation. You must know girls (*I* do) whose frightened need to be accepted, to belong to someone (translate *be* someone) made them maneuver some man into believing he was madly in love. The implications of "being loved" were such a welcome relief to these ladies (freeing them at last from the burden of having to construct an *independent* identity), they would have married almost *any* man who ambled along!

By age eighteen, planning for my future was another problem-filled area. I'd already rejected becoming a teacher as my mother was trained to be. Where had that professional background taken *her*? Law? That took so long. At eighteen I couldn't afford to take so much time out from the pursuit of my *real* goal—finding a husband! *Consciously,* I fought this narrow view of my future, but *unconsciously* I must have accepted it, because I automatically rejected any career that would take some years of concentrated effort.

When I asked Mother for advice about my "future," she was genuinely puzzled. I was going to a good school, learning important things, reading interesting books, making new friends; what *more* could a girl want! Surely I should be happy that I *was* a girl not having to worry my pretty head about *being* something. And my mother wasn't the *only* one holding this passive view of my identity. All around me, even in college classrooms, there was the implicit understanding among teachers that *real* rewards weren't to be found in any book I was reading or thoughts I was forming. The time a girl spent in academia was diversionary, but the *true* meaning of life would be the gift of some man. Diplomas were nice, but a wedding ring was *reality*!

Recently, a friend of mine went back to her old college to get a transcript of her grades and some advice from the dean before returning to study (ten years after graduation) for a master's degree. The hot pink of rage and shame suffused her face as she told me about her visit. "It turned out I'd had an A-minus average! A-minus! And I didn't even remember! It's a tough school and I had an A-minus average, and it didn't even register!"

It wasn't hard to figure out why my friend had forgotten her good performance in school. Though a good mind and hard work had kept her marks impressively high, her real energy had gone into winning and later marrying her husband. She'd finished school *after* the wedding, put away her diploma, and that was that!

The afternoon my friend returned from school the two of us talked endlessly about how girls today *still* sabotage their intelligence. (Psychologists report that female students consistently perform less well on tests when competing with men than with other women.) The dean had told my friend that although she begs her students to consider how their college programs will fit into a career plan, her advice is almost always unheeded. "I try to convince them that breast-feeding their children and being wife, mother, and hostess of the century may not turn out to be a full enough life for them . . . that they may decide on a job outside the home, only to find the needed preparation has been left undone. I rarely make a serious impression! The girls just think I'm a dikey, frustrated old maid who's jealous of them, who wants to divert them from the vital business of creating a happy home and marriage."

Almost any woman who dares imply that home and husband may be more wasteland than paradise is apt, like the dean, to be called a Lesbian, even though this accusation is based on the now *discredited* Freudian idea of "penis envy." This subject is dealt with comprehensively in chapter four of Kate Millett's *Sexual Politics*, but, briefly, Freud believed that the way in which a girl deals with the supposedly traumatic discovery that she lacks a penis decides the degree of her later stability, sexual and emotional health! If her behavior becomes appropriately (admirably) passive, she has "adjusted" to not having a male organ. *But*, says Freud, the girl who *can't* accept her penisless condition may, out of spite and disappointment, show aggressive "masculine" traits. More sophisticated contemporary analysts are far less certain than Freud about what is inherently masculine and feminine. Yet his old-fashioned, simplistic ideas about penis envy *continue* to condition our view of proper feminine behavior.

Like millions of other women, *I* certainly don't believe a woman is only the sum of her physical parts (give or take a particular appendage), and, intellectually, I thoroughly reject Freud's dictum that "anatomy is destiny." Yet I was raised to believe in a Freudian-influenced pattern of femininity, and the stereotyped mold is difficult to crash out of: showing aggression is bad—the opposite of feminine—and being competitive or ambitious is "castrating" to men. Even *wit* can be unfeminine. Wit has sharp edges, and men have been known to stay clear of witty females because they're out to cut, right?

287

How to stay feminine while still being ambitious and using your intelligence can be a staggering problem; this particular dilemma hit me most forcefully when I had an early, dramatic (and highly paid) success as a TV comedy writer. That first job—which I got simply through marvelous luck—was writing for a major network program. Scared and uncertain, I was nonetheless *optimistic*: surely here in the flashy, creative world of show business, people would be less bound by rigid cultural stereotypes than in traditional environments of home and school. Well, I soon packed up and put away this naïve hope along with other girlish notions! The men I worked with were comedians, singers, writers, producers, but first of all *men*, and they had all the standard hangups when dealing with a "successful" woman. Somehow they couldn't relate to me—unselfconsciously—as a colleague. What I am now sure was outright hostility was disguised as sexual interest (my bottom *stung* from the "loving" barrages of "playful" swats) or masked in innuendo that clearly said, "I know how you got *your* job, baby." My co-workers made a special point of using four-letter words ("dirty" only because they were *intended* to offend) and made ridiculous demands on my time. Their message was unmistakable: "O.K., sweetheart, you want to work like a man—we'll show you what it's like to work like a man."

No more comfortable with my role than *they* were, I know I often made them *more* hostile and self-conscious. If they flirted, I felt put down and came on strong . . . the "neutered" career-bitch, bossy, officious, tough! If they were brusque and businesslike, I felt my femininity wasn't appreciated and played the (thoroughly inappropriate) coquette. I was miserable; so were they. And the anxiety of it all! Here I was on the verge of fulfilling my dearest fantasies, of being a bona fide success, and I was miserable! What good would my career be to me, if I ended up frigid and alone? My social life was a disaster, of course. Push-pulled by conflicting needs, I was *desperately* uncomfortable with men . . . afraid of being "used" because of my connections in TV, yet wanting (sensibly) to use this wonderful job to meet men. Earning more than most of my dates made them *and* me self-conscious . . . should I go easy on their budget in a restaurant, or would that be patronizing? Sexually, I wasn't too stable either! How could I succumb to romantic dependence when I was—and wanted to *stay*—financially independent of men?

This conflict may all seem a little extreme, but I have known many women who get into really top "male" echelons only to feel this kind of concern . . . how to pay for a business lunch without embarrassing the recipient . . . how to be—horrors!—a *boss* over male or partly male staff! And many an executive complains that she must keep her emotions in check, while the *man* in the next office indulges in door-slamming tantrums. Should she cry or show a little pique, male colleagues automatically assume the poor (unstable) thing is having her "period"!

It's time for us to move away from these absurdly polarized definitions of maleness and femaleness. Unlike many of my more militant sisters, I still *believe* in femininity. Whether sex roles are programmed in the genes or wholly a matter of cultural conditioning is, in a sense, irrelevant. I still think it's great to accept the cigarette light, the opened door, or any gesture that doesn't involve denying yourself as a *person*. Some of us even practice reciprocity and light a man's cigar! Later generations of girls may be bred to a whole *new* set of attitudes about female behavior, but I happen to be stuck with *old* ones. I want to be pretty, sweet, and *romantically* dependent on a man. But I want to be smart and independent professionally and competent (extremely!) at what I do. In short, I want to use the old patterns in new ways . . . to be sexy *and* successful!

4

DON'T BE AN UNCLE TOM Fairly thumping his chest with importance, he recounts the Machiavellian way he one-upped the account exec today. You ooh and aah at appropriate moments, then when it seems like your conversational turn, report with shy pride that the Big Boss himself has commended your first sales presentation. Clued-in by the absent way he is fingering his pipe stem and the faraway look in his eyes, you realize that he finds this information less than spellbinding and quickly turn the conversation back to his adventures in the big, bad Man's World. He's off and thumping again. . . .

Or . . . he's home an hour or three later than expected, having had some heavy martini-drinking to do, and your lovely chicken *cocotte* is positively desiccated. You do not chide him for lateness; instead you smile like a lamb at his fanny-patting, burble a little when he calls you his yum-yum, and retire humbly to the kitchen when he disappears importantly behind *The Wall Street Journal*.

Could the self-abnegating heroine of the above vignettes possibly be you? If so, you may be an Uncle Tom. An Uncle Tom (forget the confusion in gender for a minute) is a girl who acts out a man's preconceived idea of her subservient role. Black people use the term to mark the "good Negro" who behaves according to a white racist stereotype. The black Tom pretends to be, or sometimes even believes that he is, dumb, oversexed, and a talented singer, dancer, and pole-vaulter. Because that's the way the whites—who, until recently, had all the power—would have it.

291

Now, the feminists have appropriated the Tom label to describe a girl who "yes massah"s her man. Like the "good Negro," she may do this consciously or unconsciously. Maybe she really *believes* that she's adorably helpless . . . and gets slapstick with delight at the thought of lots of babies to feed and her very own electric range. Or, possibly, she has glimpsed the hypocrisy of the game that's being played but has decided it's the only one in town.

As the feminists explain, a lady Tom accepts *privilege* in place of *responsibility*. Her ability to do important or difficult work is discredited, and her thoughts discounted as "female illogic." At the same time, she enjoys the flattery and "protection" of her man. It's a psychological truism that we grow *into* the roles other people design for us . . . and so the Tom (female version) becomes progressively more inept at so-called masculine activities, like thinking and working, and turns into the incarnation of His Pampered Darling. The man's worship of a woman as sex object "makes up" for her having been cheated and undermined in every other department. Ironically, the Tom girl is herself the system's most ardent defender. She stomps her little foot in rage whenever another woman suggests the female Tom may be underprivileged, insisting that she finds her "femininity" wonderfully, divinely *fulfilling*, and that any woman who doesn't feel the same way is hostile and castrating . . . a Lesbian or worse!

A Tom is a victim, to be sure, but she is also a collaborator. She is actively cooperating with the man who casts her in a subservient role . . . probably because she is a little weak, and more than a little anxious for male approval. She pays heavy dues for her self-betrayal, though. Girls who play the slavey are the very ones who wind up getting stonkered every afternoon in Scarsdale, playing Mah Jong forty hours a week, or developing housewife's ulcer.

It's quite easy, actually, *not* to be a Tom, to eschew trickery, even the unconscious kind, and to hold your man by genuine lovingness and respect. First, of course, you must make yourself into a person he can love and respect right back. He is not going to take any sass from a girl who spends her days munching bon-bons among a gossipy brood of bored (and boring) females. On the other hand, earning a beefy paycheck, or even a master's degree, is *quite* apt to convince him you're a grown-up, worth regarding as such.

Becoming an independent anti-Tom girl means you will have relationships that are free of sticky flatteries and obsequious lies. No, you don't put your man down . . . but you *do* refuse to puff him up! And if his ego is too delicate to take the stresses of an honest relationship, then find another man. You'll deserve one!

5

SO LONG "OO" GIRL... WHO NEEDS YOU?

Farewell, good-bye, good riddance, and drop dead to: The blush. The downcast eyes. The "I can't think of a thing to say, can't you just look at me?" look. The "You're so witty and I'm so dumb, you're so strong and I'm so helpless, you know so much and I never seem to know anything" evening. The "oo" girl.

Who is this "oo" girl? The one who, for every naughty thought and bold opinion, registers only shock as her features click on, in sequence, like a row of timed Christmas-tree lights: her eyes withdraw (is she hurt?), her cheeks flush (is she all right?), her lashes flutter (did we say something wrong?), and her lips struggle, trembling, to say something (yes, that's better, spit it out. What's the matter, dear?). They pucker and she says: "oo." As in: (*oo*) How can we say such a thing? (*oo*) She just doesn't understand. (*oo*) She's not used to hearing words like that. (*oo*) She wouldn't know anything about that. (*oo*) She is not that kind of girl. (*oo*) She wasn't brought up that way.

The "oo" girl is that sexual relic who still makes her appearances as a plantation child, fragile, fluttering, and fainting . . . her pampered pretty little head with all its curls in place resembling a private museum—open by appointment, never touched, and vacant most of the time. Like hoopskirts, it is her sex she invariably chooses to hide behind. Why is she such a hopeless little creature? Because, as she will always tell you, she is *only*

295

a woman. But didn't we dismiss her for the dolt she really was a long time ago? Have we not, after all, in the last twenty-five years really welcomed the New American Woman? Apparently not. For there is still too much worry that a woman who tries a career should remain *feminine* (and who is feminine if not the "oo" girl herself?) and a prevailing feeling that women should not really challenge men . . . that in doing so they somehow betray their sex and lose. But lose what? Their mystique? Their charm? Their allure? Their sexual identity?

Let's go back to the "oo" girl's origins in the 1920s. While many women went about defining themselves in terms of their accomplishments, often despite their sex, the "oo" girl went blithely on claiming only one thing—that she was the true refinement and repository of all things feminine. She was not only a woman but a lady, and women who were not ladies were . . . well, *she* could never allow herself to imagine such things. We fell for such sham for far too long. We may have enjoyed the rebel female more, but we also accepted the myth that she had traded off part of her sexual heritage to work, talk back, become a professsional, make love before marriage, campaign, march, protest, refuse to leave the men to their cigars in the den after dinner, even refuse to leave the cigars to the men. When we began to feel otherwise, that women never really cease being such attractive mysteries, that success and talent almost never detract but almost always enhance them, we still kept half-believing the "oo" girl. Why? Yes, you guessed it, because we might hurt *her* feelings. The "other" woman could, of course, survive.

But who actually feels threatened by the New Woman? *I'm* fascinated by her. Who would really rather trade flashing, bright, sparkling eyes for the sad, wet, hurt ones of the helpless female? That's like passing up Lauren Bacall for Little Miss Muffet. If there is a single, unequivocal declaration I could make about the opposite sex, it is that the women I like the most are the ones I admire the most. And neither should anyone be taken in by the last refuge of the "oo" girl—that other women may be more fun to stray with, but *she* is there for home and a lifetime. Why should any of us want to spend a life with a girl we find empty-headed for an evening? I know I certainly don't. I married a woman who works, cares for our daughter, reads, entertains, wins an argument, and keeps herself looking beautiful. With all those winning qualities going for her, who wants her to say *oo*?

LET'S END THE DOUBLE STANDARD FOR HANGUPS

We won the Sex Revolution and our treaty with men dictated one Single Standard: Girls can make love as freely as men. So the Double Standard died. We said good-bye to "nice" girls and "bad" girls, to virgins and tramps. We said hello to free girls who could jump into bed with a man and *not* have a baby or a nervous breakdown.

Brave words, but the surrender of the double standard was far from unconditional; different rules for men and women still govern a very special area—that of sexual and emotional hangups. And sex revolt or no, what's "sick" for a girl is still considered perfectly O.K. for a man.

Single girls are allowed to make love these days all right, but there are a few tricky clauses: Suppose a girl sleeps with twenty (who's counting?) men during one year. She's definitely likely to be saddled with the Guilt Hangup. She'll worry about being promiscuous. Yet no man *ever* feels hung up because he's slept with "too many" girls.

Another place the single standard fails to catch hold is that many men have been conditioned too long to the role of conqueror and seducer. Ready to cajole and persuade, these men are both alarmed and disappointed by a liberated girl's quick "yes" or by her new, single-standard, actual *pursuit*. For these sexually reactionary males, getting there was apparently *more* than half the fun. Personally, I feel *being* there should be *all* the fun.

Actually, the *male* is as much a victim of his own vestigial double standard as is the female. While women, single standard or *no*, are still rewarded for inadequacy and inexperience in bed ("She's so innocent; I can *train* her"), a man is *punished*. It's even O.K. for her to be slightly *frigid* (presumably she can yet be "awakened" by Supermale), but it is definitely *not* O.K. for a man to be slightly impotent.

The Double Standard for Hangups pits male against female and makes both suffer (probably her more than him).

Take the Jealousy Hangup. A *girl* who seethes with jealous suspicions is a green monster, right? She's sick! But the jealous male? The man who accuses his girl of sleeping out, who frowns every time another man eyes her . . . is he sick? Yes, but the double standard translates his paranoia into supervirility. Girls love him! "Max would kill me if he even knew there was a man at our table in Schrafft's!" It's so flattering (in double-standard society) to be the object of male jealousy.

Possessiveness is another residual in the double-standard group, and men will insult and abandon a girl they feel is "too possessive." "You're mine, all mine" sounds scary on the lips of a girl. But "You're my woman, you belong to me" from a man works magic on his lady love. Uga-Uga, hairy chest, bulging loincloth—he's one helluva man. This bully is allowed to overcompensate for his sick ego by pulling a Tarzan routine. Let's admit it, the average girl feels a primordial thrill around a man who is "insanely possessive." Insane they *both* are. And clinging to a non-single standard.

All totaled, these are the only rights girls receive from the residual Double Standard for Hangups: The right to be slightly frigid. The right to blush happily when accused of infidelity. The right to like the feeling of being captured, dog-tagged, and finally "owned" by a man.

We don't want to say hello to virgins and tramps again—the hangups that went along with *them* were worse. But unless you treasure this sickly Bill of Rights, you must fight to abolish the Double Standard for Hangups.

Fight the good fight. Don't let hangups pass as an acceptable part of sexual identity. We must stop unhealthy mental habits in one sex while condemning them in the other. Then we'll all be able to enjoy the natural (not manufactured) differences between men and women. *Vive les différences!*

AFTERWORD Now that masses of good resolutions are swirling about in your mind, you won't just sit there and wait for them to *seep* into effectiveness, will you? Why not follow this specific plan that *encourages* self-discipline? Here's how you do it with the Weekly-Monthly-Semiannual-Yearly-Good-for-a-Lifetime Coordinated Hangup Barometer: Cut out the barometer on the back of the book jacket. (We've reprinted it on page 301 to show how it works, but the other is prettier.) Pin it or hang it up where you generally fall into your introspective trances, like next to the bed or on your full-length mirror. (Or if you want to keep your campaign *secret,* carry the Barometer in your bag.)

Once a week (more or less, depending on your needs) go over the checklist printed below. (It pulls together *all* the Barometer quizzes scattered through this book.) Set a goal—say, four or more noes in each area, per week. Every time you meet that score, give yourself a star (*) on the appropriate slice of the Barometer. After a few weeks, look over results. Do some sections *bristle* with stars, others stay virginally vacant? You *know* what to do then: Don't self-destruct . . . self-*evaluate.* Good luck!

BAROMETRIC CHECKLIST AND RATINGS

BELIEVE-IN-YOU BAROMETER

1. Did you pass up a good thing for a *safe* thing?
2. At that last party, did you glance away from a man who was watching you, instead of walking over to introduce yourself?
3. Did you worry about your age?
4. After buying something daring, were you too timid to wear/use it?
5. Did you muzzle your lone opinion in a group that disagreed?

Your Barometric Rating Scale

4–5 *noes* What a fine, fortunate girl—you *like* yourself. That's *basic* equipment; read how to keep it in prime condition.

3 *noes* *Sometimes* you feel worthwhile. For insights into those *other* times, take our refresher course.

2–0 *noes* Self-confidence may be the single key to *all* your hangups—and wouldn't that simplify life? *Many* girls have found *all* their troubles fanned out from something as controllable as *state-of-mind*—and a few went on to write the heaps of good advice in the following pages.

AFFAIR BAROMETER

1. Do you often wish it were as lovely as it was in the beginning?
2. Are you afraid he's going to leave you?
3. Do you frequently wonder if his past girls are prettier, smarter, sexier than you, and if you measure up?
4. Are you *still* waiting for him to shed his wife?
5. Do you like him less but *need* him more?

Your Barometric Rating Scale

4–5 *noes* Getting along with men may just come *naturally* to you, you lucky thing! At least, you make it *look* easy! Compare notes with our writers to add a trick or two to your *successful* repertory.

3 noes   If you scored well on *three* questions, why not all? You *have* man-alluring skills—find out how to use them to *full* advantage.

2–0 noes   Perhaps you feel victimized by uncontrollable urges—or an immature *man*. Don't let feelings of insecurity hold you back. You can move on to happier love affairs by reading the wide-ranging advice in this section.

FUN-IN-BED BAROMETER

1. Does your lovemaking follow the same routine every time?
2. Are you scared to let him know your sexual needs?
3. Did you wake up in several different beds this week—and wish you hadn't?
4. Does not having orgasms, or having them the "wrong" way, worry you?
5. If you're troubled by a sexual problem (yours or his), have you looked for help? (asked someone, talked it over, read a book?

Your Barometric Rating Scale

4–5 noes   Even if you "suffer" from a problem or two, your answers indicate that you can work them out because you're willing to accept help and frank information (like the following) without anxiety.

3 noes   Sometimes you're sexually uncertain, but your basic enjoyment of sex can *motivate* you to clarify feelings and improve physical compatibility.

2–0 noes   If this is your *particular* problem area, perhaps you're simply unaware of the facts, don't know whom to ask. Read every chapter carefully . . . underline situations that apply . . . and try the advice given.

EMOTIONAL BAROMETER

1. Have you said or thought "It's all *my* fault" more than once this week?
2. Did you let your temper explode?

3. Did you take more than *two* (desperately needed) aspirins, tranquilizers, or drinks to erase a headache or lift a mood?
4. Are you frequently tired even though you've slept enough, haven't worked overly hard or taken violent exercises?
5. Did you feel *deeply* depressed more than once this week?

Your Barometric Rating Scale

4–5 noes   Sail through *this* section with your customary aplomb, remembering, however, there's no such thing as too *much* understanding of emotional tides—you may learn how to help people you adore.

3 noes   You're skirting an emotional morass. Explore which areas endanger your usual control, and read about what to do *then*.

2–0 noes   If you made a gigantic once-in-a-long-time blooper this particular week, or took this quiz on New Year's Day, you're *entitled* to a sizable share of guilts, mood fluctuations, or exhaustion. Otherwise, emotional management is your own particular Achilles heel.

COPING BAROMETER

1. Were you late more than once? (Count *every* occasion . . . dates, hairdresser and job appointments, self-imposed deadlines.)
2. Did you *create* a crisis by letting obligations pile up until they became unmanageable?
3. Have you spent more than a total of two hours seriously plotting revenge?
4. Did you weep or sulk to manipulate someone into giving you what you wanted?
5. Challenged by a competitor, did you abandon the field instead of redoubling your efforts?

Your Barometric Rating Scale

4–5 noes   *Maintain* your rather formidable copesmanship by gliding through this section—but watch out for unexpected obstacles *others* can blithely strew along your path.

3 noes	You try, and that puts you well ahead of Miss Average. Which occasions seem too much for you? Concentrate on those for a time before tackling anything else.
2–0 noes	The details of life hassle you. Are you too impatient, seeking automatic rewards, expecting others to ease your way? Grow up! Learn how to smooth your *own* daily routine.

LIBERATION BAROMETER

1. Did you play dumb or refuse to argue for fear he'd think that you were being "unfeminine"?
2. Are you slackening on the job because of preoccupation with love problems?
3. Have you turned down dates with good men just to stay faithful to the one with a retinue of other women?
4. Did you defer to the *male* executives even though you're their peer?
5. When discussing Women's Lib with a man/men did you *preach* . . . or *blame* men?

Your Barometric Rating Scale

4–5 noes	Good for you! You aren't letting that magnetic pull toward the opposite sex turn you against other *women*, or against yourself. Stand ready to make sound choices from among the many—even revolutionary—ones offered here.
3 noes	Congratulations for not turning two deaf ears to constructive feminist messages. Now, on to the rewarding process of continuing self-liberation!
2–0 noes	It's possible you also scored in the average-to-low range on believing-in-you. For *that's* what Women's Liberation is all about—respecting your *female* self. Take a look at *both* sections of this book, and see if your problems aren't related.

The text of this book is set in 9½ point Melior, with 2½ points leading. Initials and headings are in larger sizes of Melior Bold. The Melior face is the work of Herman Zapf, noted type designer born in Nürnberg, Germany, in 1918. Zapf has also designed Optima, Palatino, and many other types widely used in contemporary bookmaking.

Part and chapter numbers are Outline Gothic, also used for the book title on the title page.

Book design and covers by Dorris Crandall
Composed by Book Graphics, Inc.
Printed and bound by W. A. Kreuger Co., Inc.